Here *to* Eternity

life beyond the loss of a loved one

DIANNE WILSON

Thorsons
An imprint of HarperCollins*Publishers*

If any copyright holders have not been acknowledged, the author would
be grateful if they could contact her care of the publishers.

Thorsons
An imprint of HarperCollins*Publishers*

First published in Australia in 2006
by HarperCollins*Publishers* Australia Pty Limited
ABN 36 009 913 517
www.harpercollins.com.au

Copyright © Dianne Wilson 2006

The right of Dianne Wilson to be identified as the author of this
work has been asserted by her under the *Copyright Amendment
(Moral Rights) Act 2000.*

HarperCollins*Publishers*
25 Ryde Road, Pymble, Sydney NSW 2073, Australia
31 View Road, Glenfield, Auckland 10, New Zealand
77–85 Fulham Palace Road, London W6 8JB, United Kingdom
2 Bloor Street East, 20th floor, Toronto, Ontario, M4W 1A8, Canada
10 East 53rd Street, New York NY 10022, United States of America

National Library of Australia Cataloguing-in-Publication data:

Wilson, Dianne.
  Here to eternity.
  ISBN 9 78073228 3773.
  ISBN 0 7322 8377 9.
  1. Grief. 2. Death – Psychological aspects. I. Title.
152.4

Image on front cover and spine courtesy of Photolibrary.com
Cover design by Nada Backovic
Internal design by Katy Wright, HarperCollins Design Studio
Typeset in Bembo 11/15.5pt by Kirby Jones
Printed and bound in Australia by Griffin Press on 79gsm Bulky Paperback White

5 4 3 2 1   06 07 08 09

To my precious family,
Jonathan, Rachel, Ben, Beau, Bella, Joshua,
Mum, Dad, Kathy and Sarah,
Thank you for being so brave.
Thank you for living for Eternity.
To Dr Alison,
Thank you for allowing us to hold on to hope.
To Tamara,
Thank you for dignified kindness.
To Julie,
Thank you for serenading with the angels.
To Julia,
Thank you for singing hope.
To Megan and Alison,
Thank you for always being there.
To Jan and Kev,
Thank you for making me grow.
To Sarah,
Thank you for being my Eternity friend.
To Bobbie and Brian,
Thank you for making me strong.
To friends and family,
Thank you for feeding our bodies and our spirits.
To my Heavenly Father,
Thank you for putting Eternity in my heart.

CONTENTS

A Tribute

To our beautiful loved ones
As they go out into Eternity,
a host of angels in Heaven
will be ready to salute them
for a life well-lived.
Well done, good and faithful servants.
We love you so much our hearts ache
but we know that our great loss
is Heaven's great gain.
Farewell, our precious ones.
We miss you and we will always love you.
Enjoy Heaven!

FOREWORD

Loss is a natural and indeed inevitable part of our lives, but the grief experienced as a consequence of loss, and particularly the loss of someone very dear, can seem overwhelming. It is also a time when many seek spiritual answers and comfort.

In *Here to Eternity*, Dianne Wilson offers readers hope for a positive future here on earth as well as for a life ever after. Wisely, she does not try to answer the multitude of 'why' or 'what if' questions that often besiege us in times of grief — sometimes there simply are no answers to these questions.

Instead, Dianne lets us into her world and the world of others grieving, to share in their personal stories of deep sorrow — and, more importantly, their individual journeys towards comfort and healing and a future hope. These stories offer a powerful and compelling format for relating, for learning and for inspiring.

Woven amongst the stories that show bravery and triumph in the midst of deep despair, loneliness and heartache are many practical suggestions for the here and now. These embrace caring for oneself and others who are in pain, finding peace, making those difficult farewells, cherishing special memories, and gaining a clearer perspective on time.

Above all, *Here to Eternity* encourages those who are grieving to journey on to find hope, faith and love again.

Vivienne C Riches
Psychologist
BA, Dip Ed, MA (Hons), PhD, MAPS
Senior Research Fellow and Clinical Psychologist, Royal Rehabilitation Centre, Sydney, and Clinical Senior Lecturer, Centre for Developmental Disability Studies and the University of Sydney

A New Chapter

*The end of life here on earth
is the last chapter of time
and the first chapter of Eternity.*

INTRODUCTION

Here to Eternity

there is indeed a time to live and a time to die

'Those things which to us seem most casual and contingent are,
in the counsel and foreknowledge of God,
punctually determined,
and the very hour of them is fixed,
and can neither be anticipated nor adjourned a moment.'

⤙ MATTHEW HENRY ⤚
ENGLISH CLERGYMAN AND BIBLE COMMENTATOR (1662–1714)

Your great loss is
Heaven's great gain . . .

I WRITE THIS BOOK WITH, I pray, heartfelt understanding, awareness and sensitivity towards the experience life may have brought you or may currently be bringing you through. As a woman, wife, mother, daughter, sister, niece, Aunt and friend who loves many and much, I may not have been through what you are going through, but I do know what it is like to have to walk through love and loss. My life's work is caring for people through whatever life brings. Much of life is filled with happiness, unexpected surprises, joys and wins, yet some is marked by disappointment, pain, loss and regret. I also know from my own life and from helping other people that grieving is as individual as a fingerprint. Births, marriages and deaths are part of life. I have learned that regardless of whether life is up or down or completely upside down, there is always hope. Hold on to hope.

On my way home from a meeting with my publishers about the book that was supposed to be my next, my husband's phone rang with the news that a member of our church had been tragically killed in an industrial accident at work. He was a husband, a father and way too young to die. The roundabout that we had just passed through became a junction of decision for me to write this book.

It was a great idea in theory, but a completely different deal in reality. How on earth was I going to write a book about something that brought me to tears every time I thought about it? Writing about the subject of Eternity has been no small effort. I have questioned, 'Why me?' several times over. Surely there were other people more qualified to unpack the treasure in Eternity. Surely there were other people more eloquent than I. Surely someone else could write this much-needed book to help people see the breadth of what Eternity holds for their lives. And why would someone my age want to write a book about something that even in a lifetime we will never fully understand? All I know is that Eternity burns in my heart and my soul and deep within my spirit.

The word Eternity contains within it more than we could ever comprehend on this side of Eternity. It speaks not only of a place, but also of a perspective and a Person. Having an Eternity perspective gives us the ability to perceive the actual comparative importance of things, especially when it comes to dealing with life's crises. When we can understand what Eternity really is, life becomes more significant and the process of overcoming life's disappointments and sorrows becomes more bearable. It's as though the lights are turned on and we can finally begin to understand that there is a bigger picture from beginning to end, even when we can't see it all yet.

To me, Eternity has many wonderful aspects.

❖ Eternity speaks of a place.
❖ Eternity speaks of a perspective.
❖ Eternity speaks of a Person.
❖ Eternity speaks of a promise.
❖ Eternity speaks of a plan.
❖ Eternity speaks of a precise moment.

My greatest desire is that you will find hope through the pages of this book. Hope to face Eternity, and faith to believe that the best is yet to come. Unlike many of my other books, this is not really a 'how to' book. This is more of a 'how-you-might' book, as the process of overcoming loss is something very unique and personal to everyone who experiences it.

While the world stopped to mourn the loss of countless precious souls in the tragedy of the tsunami that hit the Asian region on Boxing Day 2004, our own family stopped to mourn the loss of a dear family friend, John, who had been such a loving companion to my Grandmother while she lived in a nursing home. We also stopped during that period to come to terms with the pending loss of my Dad's younger brother, Uncle Bruce (my sister Kathy tells his story in Chapter Two). We received a call on Christmas Eve, my Dad's birthday, to let us know that Bruce had been taken to the hospice and that he didn't have long to live.

During that season of intense concern, we had to hold on to hope. Hope that the millions of people who were left without family and homes would somehow come to know true peace and comfort and have hope for the future when all was lost. Hope for John's family; hope that my Uncle would make his final peace before entering into Eternity. Catastrophe is relative. Whether large or small, on a world scale or a dying heart all alone, one thing is absolutely sure: there is a way for everyone to navigate their journey through life with hope and into Eternity.

Another experience that brought the need for this book to the forefront was an encounter I had with a young woman at a department store make-up counter one Saturday afternoon. My youngest daughter Bella and I had gone to town for a girls' day out and I decided it was time for some new make-up. A young woman appeared from behind the counter and offered to apply some fresh colours to my eyes. We got chatting and she asked me what I did for a job and I explained that I was an author. She then proceeded to ask me in detail about each of my books before asking what was next. When I told her about this particular book, she stopped what she was doing, looked at me with her piercingly beautiful green eyes and said, 'When will that one be ready? I want to read that book now.'

I explained that it would take some time to write and that the process of publishing also takes time, so she asked me to write down the name of the book so she could buy it, along with *Mirror, Mirror*, my last book. After we'd finished and I'd bought myself some 'fresh eyes', Bella and I decided to go upstairs to the book section of the department store to buy a copy of *Mirror, Mirror* to take back down to the young woman. I wrote a little something in the front of it, signed it and popped it back in its bag before delivering it into her hands.

When she saw us again, opened the little bag and took out the book, she burst into tears as she read inside the front cover. I felt awful to have made her cry, especially at work. I knew, however, that something deeper was going on inside. Next, a voice piped up from the make-up chair — it was the young woman's mother who had come to visit. She greeted me warmly and told me that her daughter had just told her about us and here we were back again. She couldn't believe it.

The young woman was sobbing and I didn't know what to do or why it was that she was so sad. She went away to hide for a moment while she composed herself, ready for work again. In the meantime, I held her mother's hand and asked, 'Why is she crying?' I sort of knew what kind of answer I was going to receive.

'Her Dad died suddenly on New Year's Eve — just eight weeks ago.'

Everything crystallised. I will never forget the look in that young woman's eyes when she told me she wanted to read about Eternity now and that she couldn't wait until the following year. I will never forget the look in her eyes when I told her how beautiful and precious she is. I will never forget meeting her and her mother that day. I knew that we would always be *Eternity friends*. I walked away from the encounter knowing that this book was for that young woman and many, many other young women and men, and older women and men who, with desperation in their eyes, want to know about Eternity.

Loss can throw us into a world that is unimaginable. Loss not only robs us of a loved one, but can also give us a sense of being robbed of everything that was normal in our lives. Our world is turned upside down and life as we knew it ceases to exist. We may be filled with a heart-wrenching pain that we fear may never go away; we may be confused, overwhelmed and convinced that life can never be good again. We can't even relate to people who say it will get better, because we think that our love was different. This may be our reality, but there is a higher reality. The truth is that there *is* hope and we will be able to go on to live again, to laugh again. Remember, death is not a full stop, but rather a comma in the light of Eternity.

Without an Eternity perspective, loss can become our constant companion, and if we are not careful it can become our focus. Change is often frightening. And being brave about facing it doesn't mean you aren't completely scared of the unknown at the same time. Have confidence that you can learn to adjust to this change in life. Just think of all you've adjusted to so far. You became an adult, which was a big adjustment; perhaps you've had to adjust to becoming a wife or a husband, which is an even bigger adjustment, and a mother and father, which is a huge adjustment, yet you've more than managed to adapt to each change. You were able to adapt because you knew you could be successful, and you'd seen others be successful in doing the same things.

I know that God is faithful. He does not leave us even when we lose a sense of His presence. Deep within we know that when one door closes, another opens. When we walk through any process of disappointment and loss, it will be intensely difficult at that time. But just remember that there is a whole universe to live for when you come through. You may not be able to see it all . . . or even see much of it at all right now. But it will be there, and it holds many wonderful things for you.

All who enter an understanding of Eternity experience many wonders.

❖ faith to believe the best
❖ hope that you can hold on to
❖ love that never ends
❖ comfort in Heaven's embrace
❖ the presence of peace
❖ coming home
❖ memories that never fade
❖ time that changes everything
❖ angels in your midst
❖ farewell until we meet again
❖ your life's purpose remains
❖ Heaven — the final frontier.

In my last book, *Mirror, Mirror,* I included fairytales or parables to help draw a correlation between the life we want and the life we have, to help give people hope that the 'happily ever after life' is attainable. Here, I have included outlines of movies as Eternity allegories at the beginning of each chapter, as so many of us are moved by the 'silver screen' through identifying with other people's stories of dreams and disappointments, life and loss. Movies are something we can all relate to, but most are fictitious, so within these pages there are also some real-life Eternity stories from friends who have graciously opened their hearts and lives to help you hold on to hope.

Everyone has a story and these are real people with real lives who have been through real loss and who have found real hope. These special people are my Eternity friends: people you can identify with from all walks of life who have all experienced loss in many different ways yet have emerged stronger and taller with hope in their hearts, able to help others who walk where they have walked. These friends are Eternity carriers. They carry Eternity in their hearts, on their lives and in their hands — ready to offer its wonders to everyone they meet. Although most of these stories have been written by women, the men in their lives are represented throughout the pages.

I honour them for their courage and I appreciate them putting pen to paper as I know the process of doing so caused many tears to flow again. Many said that the experience of sharing their story brought more healing to their mending hearts.

I pray the 'honour roll' of Eternity stories will bring you much hope.

❖ **Linda's story**
Linda lost both her parents, a nephew and a close friend.

❖ **Kathy's story**
Kathy lost her Uncle to cancer.

❖ **Donna's story**
Donna lost her Dad, who had battled through World War II.

❖ **Alison's story**
Alison lost her husband, who was murdered by terrorists.

❖ **Deborah's story**
Deborah lost her brother to suicide.

❖ **Eden's story**
Eden lost her Grandpa, who was the rock of her family.

❖ **Jeff's story**
Jeff lost his brother to AIDS.

❖ **Val's story**

Val lost her teenage son to leukaemia.

❖ **Pernille's story**

Pernille lost her Mum to cancer after her Dad walked out.

❖ **Marisa's story**

Marisa lost her twenty-one year old son to leukaemia.

❖ **Angela's story**

Angela lost her Dad suddenly and tried to raise him from death.

❖ **Jessika's story**

Jessika lost her Mum suddenly when Jessika was just nineteen.

❖ **Eunice's story**

Eunice lost her son three weeks after his marriage.

❖ **Alex's story**

Alex lost her Dad and no-one in the family talked about it.

❖ **Steve's and Marion's story**

Steve and Marion lost their son to cancer.

❖ **Wilma's story**

Wilma lost her grandson, who drowned on New Year's Eve.

❖ **Julie's story**

Julie lost her close friend to cancer.

❖ **Sue's story**

Sue lost her husband when she was six months pregnant.

❖ **Darlene's story**

Darlene lost her baby at twelve weeks.

❖ **Anna's story**

Anna lost her baby at twenty-six weeks, after four miscarriages.

❖ **Eileen's story**

Eileen lost her baby at twenty-six weeks but carried to full term.

Some whose names don't appear wanted to share their story, but didn't know how. For those who felt they could, I want to thank you immensely, as I know your story came at great personal cost, not just in walking through the process of losing someone you love, but also in having to travel back to a place where you don't live now, in order to tell others about what you've been through so that they too might find the hope you have.

In some chapters I have put one story alongside another as a friend stands shoulder to shoulder with another, to help you understand the breadth of what Eternity holds, because Eternity brings us all hope in our final outcome.

My prayer is that this book will help those who are left here to make the journey of hope and transition to life without their loved ones on earth. My aim is to help you after losing a loved one to move from merely surviving your pain and sorrow to transcending it and coming through to a much brighter tomorrow. I understand that you may not believe this is possible right now, but it's true.

To all who love and have lost, I salute you, fellow Eternity friends. May you always hold on to hope.

Come, enter Eternity with me.

CHAPTER ONE

Eternity

the circle of life

'Space is to place as eternity is to time.'

— JOSEPH JOUBERT —
FRENCH ESSAYIST AND MORALIST (1754–1824)

The Lion King

The Lion King, though a very human kind of story, remains the only Disney film to have absolutely no trace of human existence. The film was also the first Disney animated feature to have a non-villain main character die onscreen.

Simba's father, Mufasa, is the lion king. He rules the kingdom with kindness and wisdom. However, Mufasa's younger brother Scar is jealous of his nephew's position as heir and so plots to usurp the throne. Mufasa teaches Simba about the Circle of Life and that everything is connected in a balance. In a devastating scene, Scar has Mufasa killed and ensures that Simba takes the blame.

Completely shattered, Simba runs away and collapses in the desert. The young cub is saved and befriended by Timon and Pumba. After growing up with the pair, the adult Simba encounters his childhood friend, a formidable lioness named Nala, who has fled Scar's dictatorial rule to seek help. She urges Simba to return to the Pride Lands and retake his rightful throne, but he refuses, still traumatised by the false belief that he caused his father's death. Simba simply couldn't see the future that was his to step into.

After wise old Rafiki shows Simba that Mufasa's spirit still lives on inside him, Mufasa appears to him in a vision and commands him to look inside himself and understand that he is the only rightful king. Simba decides to return home. It was time for Simba to stop running away and to begin to understand an Eternity principle — and that it was now his time to establish the next generation.

When he arrives home, Simba is incensed to find that his once joyful and prosperous kingdom has crumbled into a barren wasteland under Scar's rule. With the support of Nala, who has rallied the lionesses, Simba confronts his Uncle. Scar remains confident, and with his hyenas forces Simba to confess to his responsibility for the death of Mufasa. Then Scar backs Simba to the edge of the cliff as lightning ignites the kingdom. Simba slips and hangs on to the rock as Mufasa did years before. Scar recalls Mufasa's death and — just as he had done to Mufasa — latches into Simba's paws with his claws. As Scar tries to kill Simba, he whispers the awful truth to Simba. That it was he, Scar, who killed Mufasa.

Simba battles with Scar on the summit. Triumphant, Simba shows mercy and tells Scar to run away from the kingdom and never return. Scar remembers those words. They were the exact words that he used to manipulate Simba after Mufasa died. Scar jumps through the flames to finish Simba off, but it is Simba who throws his Uncle over the cliff edge and watches as the hyenas — Scar's former allies — devour the dictator. Simba is finally declared king and leads the Pride Lands back into times of prosperity and glory. Simba and Nala have a baby cub that is presented in a triumphant ceremony mirroring the film's beginning: the circle of life.

Eternity

'To everything there is a season,
and a time to every purpose under Heaven . . .
A time to weep, and a time to laugh;
a time to mourn, and a time to dance . . .
God has made everything beautiful for its own time.
He has planted eternity in the human heart,
but even so, people cannot see the whole scope of God's work
from beginning to end.'

ECCLESIASTES 3:1–11
THE BIBLE

ONE OF MY MOST TREASURED material possessions is my Eternity ring, which sits underneath my engagement and wedding rings. I thought it would be lovely to have an Eternity ring as part of the package — engagement, wedding, Eternity.

I had always wanted a beautiful diamond band just like my Nanny's. It had pretty little diamonds all the way around. I spent many moments sitting with my Nanny as a little girl, twirling her Eternity ring around her finger. It seemed that the older she got the easier it became to twirl.

It was Nanny's last night on this earth with Mum and me sitting by her side as she breathed in and out, creating a rhythm of complete peace. I held my Mum's hand, on which she wore my Nanny's special ring, and I began to twirl it to console myself. I looked into my Mum's eyes, filling with tears as were mine, as she took off the ring and placed it on my finger.

'Thank you,' I said. 'I would love to wear it for a little while.'

Mum smiled and said, 'Yes — you wear it.'

From that evening until now it has never left my finger. I have tried several times to return the ring to my Mum, so that she too could be consoled as I have been, but each time she has insisted that it remain on my finger. I guess it was just something meant to be between my darling Nanny and me.

The significance of the Eternity ring is very closely related to that of the wedding ring — it is a circle of metal that has no beginning and no end. In other words, it is 'eternal'. This symbol of eternal love became a treasure, not just on my finger, but also in my heart. And it was that understanding of both time and Eternity that helped me when Nanny died.

Eternity holds all the time in the world. Each human life is made beautiful in its time. You see, at the moment in time when Nanny's life ended here on earth, her life didn't cease, but it made a journey or transition from life here on earth to life in Eternity. It was at that point that we all had to make a journey — a transition from a life with one we loved to a life without one we loved. Our perspective of Eternity helped us make that transition one of hope rather than of despair.

I pray that you will know that the one you loved has gone to a place of life in Eternity that has been prepared especially for them. Also that you are able to accept the place that has been especially prepared for you, not only in Eternity, but here on earth, where you will know true hope, love, comfort, peace and strength. Eternity with our Creator is time without end, love without end, hope without end for us on this side of Eternity. Life isn't without death, sorrow, pain and grief, but there is life beyond death, comfort for our sorrows, healing to ease our pain and hope for our future.

When your dreams fall apart

❖ Eternity speaks of a place that is a safe haven for anyone who graces its doorstep.

❖ Eternity speaks of a perspective that allows our hearts and minds to know there's always more to what's happening than what we are currently going through.

❖ Eternity speaks of a Person who wants to bring Eternity into our hearts now.

There are seasons in life when we can feel ambushed and in great pain. We all respond differently to hurt and disappointment, but an Eternity perspective brings strength and comfort if we take hold of all that it offers. You weren't born to live in an emotional rut, with loss as your focus forever. You need to allow yourself to process and heal, but the longer we shrug off the reality of Eternity and what it has to offer us here and now, the longer we prolong our own pain. Eternity holds all the hope we spend our lives searching for.

Arthur Stace was considered a loser, a no-hoper. He was an alcoholic and completely illiterate. He lived on the streets of Sydney, regarded by many who saw him as a lost cause. One Sunday night in 1932 he walked into a church in the Sydney suburb of Darlinghurst where he heard the evangelist John G Ridley preaching. In his urgent, commanding voice, John Ridley cried, 'Eternity! Eternity! Oh, that this word could be emblazoned across the streets of Sydney!'

That word, Eternity, was to change Arthur Stace's life forever. From that moment he was filled with a new-found passion to communicate to others the 'Eternity' that had filled his life with so much hope.

Arthur Stace left that church, took some yellow chalk, bent down and wrote one word on the footpath. Although he was illiterate, it was a word he had seen and was able to replicate with beautiful accuracy. And for the next forty years, while Sydney slept, Arthur would take his chalk and write in immaculate copperplate handwriting the word 'Eternity' on footpaths, entrances to railway stations, and anywhere else he thought it would catch people's attention.

As the year 2000 arrived, the word 'Eternity' in Stace's handwriting was lit up for all the world to see — not across the streets of Sydney but across the Sydney Harbour Bridge, and televised around the world. Of all the words that have been spoken during the first two millennia, the one chosen to be featured on the Harbour Bridge at the dawn of the new millennium was Eternity.

Arthur Stace was passionate about Eternity because he understood that there was more to life than what he had experienced here on earth. Find comfort in the thought that regardless of what life has dealt you, regardless of what you have been through or are currently going through, a perspective of Eternity will bring us into a place of great hope. Eternity truly is home to us all.

Eternity is like a magnet between our hearts and the heart of our Creator. It is a powerful force that allows us to trust that there is a reason for our pain and much hope for the future, even when we don't have all the answers.

To me, Eternity has many wonderful aspects.

- ❖ **Eternity speaks of a place.**
  Our home in Heaven
- ❖ **Eternity speaks of a perspective.**
  To take us beyond our 'now' experience
- ❖ **Eternity speaks of a Person.**
  Wanting to bring Eternity to our hearts now
- ❖ **Eternity speaks of a promise.**
  That all things can work together for good
- ❖ **Eternity speaks of a plan.**
  To bring you hope in your final outcome
- ❖ **Eternity speaks of a precise moment.**
  No-one knows when their moment will be.

It is natural to grieve the loss of family members and others we knew, as we adjust to living without their presence and missing them as part of our lives. The loss of a loved one, or even someone we were not close to, can be a terribly painful event. It's very important for us all to understand that the process of grief is a normal yet highly personal response to losing someone we love. It's also helpful to understand what feelings and experiences we can expect to go through in the first year of loss. There are physical, emotional, social and spiritual realities that we will face. There are relational elements too, and this can sometimes be very difficult as each of us feels things differently at different times.

The good news is that while there's life, there's hope, and your future is ahead of you. That means you have the opportunity to explore the many and varied ways of making your life count and filling it with hope, so that you can perhaps help other people. There will be tougher days than others, and certain sights, sounds and smells will remind you strongly that someone you once walked with will walk here no longer. Anniversaries, birthdays, Christmases, New Years and other special occasions will now need to be celebrated with the spirit of your loved one in your heart.

Here are some of the feelings and experiences you may have that are common to those who have lost a loved one. Your heart will ache. Initially you may be overcome with shock and confusion. You may feel guilty. It may all seem like a bad dream. You may find you can only live one moment at a time. You may have to deal with doctors, police and funeral directors at a time in your life when you just want it all to stop. There's no let-up and you're expected to get on with the arrangements. You may have to talk with your loved one's work colleagues, or the phone may be ringing constantly with family and friends sending you their love. This is where *you* become the brave one.

After the official farewell, your heartache may get worse before it gets better. You may feel that the separation from your loved one becomes more painful after parting with the physical body. It's normal for you to be struggling with the unreality of the death every time you face a new situation that would have involved your loved one. At first you will often be faced with the pain that they are not by your side and that you won't see them again this side of Heaven.

Other people are generally attentive and caring initially, but after the first season of loss, they tend to go back to routine and get on with their lives. This can be a very difficult time for anyone who really misses their loved one. Life goes back to normal for everyone else and it can tend to highlight even more that the special one in your heart is gone. Many people find this very hard to live with. You may find yourself fighting against it, crying out and longing to be reunited. That's why it's important to stay focused on your future. That's what your loved one would have wanted, after all.

You may be frightened of losing the memories you so dearly treasure. You may also be afraid of being unable to visualise their face or smell their scent. Be assured, you will never lose those memories while the one you loved remains in your heart. These things just become foggy for a while, but they will become clearer soon. As you hold on to precious memories, you will know that your loved one is close by in your heart.

Each day will bring memories and sometimes subtle reminders of your loss. No more phone calls, no more homecomings. Even though friends and family are getting on with their lives, don't think that they care any less. Most times they will be feeling that the normality of routine is something that will help you, and so they may be encouraging you to get on with your own life. Remember that you shouldn't be punishing yourself by thinking that getting on with your future life is disrespectful to your loved one. It is not.

You may be feeling intensely lonely, even with people around you. That's when you need to ensure that the void you feel is filled with love that will last forever. Love that you shared with the one you've lost, and love from Heaven that is so perfect that nothing can compare with its measure. That kind of love never fails.

You will have felt and may continue to feel exhausted, body, soul and spirit. Your bravery and superhuman energy to get through the initial period of loss may eventually give way to the need for a break and some decent rest. Your loss may have been sudden and the shock of what happened will have taken a toll on you. Or you may have had weeks, months or years of giving out, perhaps keeping a bedside vigil, and that will have taken a toll on you. Whatever the circumstances of your loss, it will take some time for you to regain your strength. There are people who will expect you to be back to business as usual by now, but this may not necessarily be where you are at. If you are having physical problems or if you aren't sleeping, it may even be a good time to visit your doctor so that your health can be assessed.

The good news is that things will not stay this way. As days, weeks and months pass, your heartache will begin to lessen and you may be surprised to feel somewhat normal again. Of course you will experience good days and not so good days, but the good days will begin to outnumber the not so good as you continue to hold on to love and hold on to hope.

There may be times when you find it difficult to believe that your heartache will lift and your journey will take an upward turn. The intense pain and sadness you are feeling will subside, and the spirit of your loved one will remain as you focus on wonderful, happy memories. Try to show children in your world strength, so that when their turn comes they will think back to how you handled loss. I found this idea very helpful to me when I lost my Nanny, who was like a second mother to me. She lived in our home when I was growing up and I only ever knew life with her, so coming to terms with a life without her was extremely painful. Although we all took time to grieve, life needed to go on for our sake and the sake of our children and for others in our world.

If children are a part of the equation, it's vital for you to be thinking about building your future with those left here on earth. The process of grief is not really about those who have gone to a much better place, it's about us and our ability to live without those we love. There comes a time when we need to focus on those we're left to live life with, and to make the most of our future.

Strength and courage reside within you, even if you don't realise it at this time. As you think long and hard and really wrestle to derive sense and purpose from your tragedy and pain, you will discover you are growing and deepening as a human being. Beautiful things can come from what you're going through. Believe the best.

You will discover a new sense of awareness and purpose as you come to terms with what's happened. I pray that you also allow your creativity to be expressed, whether it's in the form of journalling or song-writing or drawing. We all find comfort in expressing ourselves in different ways. Caring for others, finishing something you started long ago, returning to study, developing your spirituality or simply being committed to a life of greater sensitivity — whatever the outlet, be sure to express yourself.

Focus on Eternity, because eternal things matter. The wheel of nature is ever moving. The events of time and conditions of human life, although different from one another, occur simultaneously. We continually pass and re-pass between these events, every day of every year. It's the circle of life.

When my father was diagnosed with cancer of the bladder I found out the very same week that I was pregnant with my daughter Bella. When I told my doctor about my Dad he didn't seem surprised. He said that in his experience one life is often ushered in as another is ushered out. Fortunately, my father received a medical and spiritual miracle and he is alive and well, many years later. At the time, however, it seemed incredibly difficult to comprehend rejoicing over one life at the same time as grieving the possible loss of another.

It's important to read and understand the time and seasons of life. Every change concerning us is ultimately fixed and determined in Eternity. This means that certain things will happen to us in our lifetime, such as having to say goodbye to the ones we love, and we must learn to walk and grow through these significant but incredibly difficult seasons. There is peace to be found in understanding that there are certain things not in our power to change.

To everything there is a season. Everything *under Heaven* is changeable, but in Heaven — Eternity — there is an unchangeable state, and an unchangeable counsel concerning such things. There is a time to be born and there is a time to die. But what about a time to live? With your loved one nestled deep within your heart and soul, your life ahead is what you need to focus on now.

Our time on earth is a period of time in which we have a say, and it is our responsibility to do something remarkable with it. By remarkable I mean not taking family and friends for granted. By remarkable I mean when a family stays together — through tough times and good times, through lack and through plenty. By remarkable I mean when people forgive each other this side of Eternity. By remarkable I mean loyalty that lasts a lifetime. By remarkable I mean making your life count for something more than yourself. By being generous, kind, helpful, proactive and embracing. Make your life count.

We shouldn't take anything or anyone for granted. It's often at the end of a person's life that we learn more about them than when they are with us on earth. It's amazing how often close relatives or friends will talk of how they learned something new about their loved ones at the funeral service when so much is shared.

I am blessed to be part of an incredibly loving family. There is a lot of love in and out of my life. One person who I have highlighted in the pages of this book is my Nanny, because losing her became a pivotal time in my life where I had to face things that caused me to become who I am today. When my precious Grandmother went from here into Eternity it was a life experience for me that closed a thirty-year gulf of fear that existed after losing my Grandfather. My Nanny's story unfolds over the pages of this book to help you also gently close any gulfs and to help you deal with fear and pain that may exist through having to say goodbye to someone you love.

Losing someone you love will always make a mark. It is up to you to ensure that mark counts for something. Please don't allow your mark to become a scar that doesn't heal, however painful or difficult the circumstances of your loss. Allow your loss to leave a mark that empowers you to make a difference in the life you have before you. Be brave; do it for the one you loved and lost, and remember that the mark they have left on your life can help you help others.

Remember, time changes everything.

Every life and every person has the potential to be beautiful in their time. That same time or sense of Eternity has been set deep within our hearts in such a way that we will never properly comprehend what has been planned for us from beginning to end. It is the great unknown over our lives that should cause us to understand that we have a Creator who holds everything and every time in His loving arms.

While the picture is still being drawn, and the house is still being built, and the film is still being developed, we can't see the end; but when the artist, the builder and the developer have completed their work, all is well. There is always a mess in the middle and you may find yourself in the middle right now. Help and hope is on the way. Comfort and peace are yours to be found. Hang in there and pray. Believe in your heart that you will feel like you can breathe again another day.

Believe that you will see the bigness of Eternity and the divine plan for good in your situation, regardless of how you feel right now. Eternity existed before the foundations of the earth were formed. Eternity is a continual line with events or 'time' punctuated at specific intervals. Humanity existed in the heart and mind of our Creator before time began.

To get a glimpse of the fullness of Eternity we need to understand the seen and unseen worlds that coexist. Just as we know there are minerals deep below the earth's surface, there is also the existence of the spiritual world that we can't see with our natural eye.

When we look into the works of nature through a microscope or when we look up into the stars at night, we understand that creation is more detailed, unique and complex than any man-made work of art. Creation holds great mystery. I believe this is to help us remain in wonder and to appreciate that we can't necessarily understand everything that happens in life.

I want to encourage you to pay close attention to the time you have now and ahead, to make it count for Eternity. I believe strongly in creating beautiful memories for my children. I want them to have many wonderful memories in their hearts and minds that will help them get through the tougher seasons of life. An Eternity perspective allows room for all seasons to exist in our life without it causing our life to completely collapse around us. That is why it is so important for us to approach each day with purpose — not taking for granted that we will have the same opportunities tomorrow. Eternity is set. It's our job to make sure our Eternity is secure.

Linda's Story

The first time I had to say goodbye to a loved one was quite some years ago. My twelve-year-old nephew passed away very unexpectedly on the eve of my twenty-first birthday. For me, life was just beginning: I was planning my twenty-first party and enjoying the freedom and responsibility that comes with being a young adult. Then suddenly I was dealing with pain and immense confusion over the loss of one so very young.

Garry was a truly delightful young boy — full of life, spunk and cheek. He was often the one who did the talking for his twin brother, Mark. This only added to the pain and hurt — how was Mark going to cope without his little mate?

My father passed away just over four years ago. He was a lively character, a man who enjoyed his life thoroughly. He didn't spend much time (if any) worrying about the negatives or hardships of life; for him life was one big party. I love him for this and still admire his free spirit and positive attitude.

My mother passed away six months after my father. Even though my parents had divorced more than a decade earlier, there was always a strong bond between them. It was no surprise that my mother, who was ill in the final years of her life, followed my father so soon. My mother was my best friend, the person I wanted to share the highs and lows of my life with. It was incredibly difficult saying goodbye to such an amazing woman.

A dear friend of mine, Lana, passed away very recently at the age of thirty-seven as a result of a tragic car accident. Our friendship dates back to our school days. I am very fortunate to have kept the friendship of my circle of girlfriends from high school. Lana's passing was not part of our plan — we were all looking forward to growing old and grey together. We had recently started brainstorming ideas for a group overseas holiday to celebrate our fortieth birthdays. Even though much of our time together was spent laughing and giggling, Lana was also a person of integrity, wisdom and great joy.

All four passings were different: Lana's and Garry's were completely unexpected; and although my parents' deaths were somewhat expected, the news of each came as a huge shock. All these deaths really rocked me. With each, the initial grief was overwhelming. The pain and hurt just made me want to curl up and hide in my bed, which I did do initially, but you can't stay there forever.

Saying goodbye to a loved one is not an easy thing. There are many events in life — birthdays, engagement, marriage, the birth of children, christenings — that we look forward to, plan for and cherish as significant milestones and achievements in our life. Even though on one level we know that one day we will face death, whether it is our own or that of someone close to us, we are never prepared for it and we certainly don't look forward to it.

I remember that when I was preparing for marriage, I read so many books and magazines on how to plan a wedding and what the correct etiquette is for a perfect wedding. But when I was faced with the loss of a loved one, I realised there aren't any guidelines or rules of etiquette on how to deal with this, only an immense and overwhelming feeling of loss, sadness, hurt, pain and disbelief.

I remember sitting outside in the rain after the viewing on the eve of my mother's funeral. I felt completely hopeless and lost. I had hit a brick wall. I didn't see how I could go on. I didn't want my children to have to go through the pain that I was feeling at the loss of my mother.

But somehow you do go on.

There were a number of things that helped me. My husband didn't fully understand what I was going through, but he was willing to support me in any way I needed. I also have many wonderful friends and family members who were willing to help me, and my children reminded me daily of the joy, hope and beauty of life. I am blessed to be surrounded by so many wonderful people.

But no-one can do it for you. You have to be brave, face the pain and work your way through it.

With the passing of my nephew Garry, I think I put my grief aside so that I could support my brother, my sister-in-law and Garry's brothers and sisters. It was a long time ago, but looking back now I do wonder whether I dealt with his passing or whether I did what I could to just get through that awful time, and buried my feelings. At the time of my nephew's death, a friend wrote in a card to me to 'believe that everything happens for a reason'. I clung to this advice because I couldn't make sense of what was happening. The only hope and comfort I could find was in believing that this is part of God's master plan.

Healing doesn't come overnight, but it does come over time and at different times. Remember those you have lost, feel the pain, work through your thoughts and memories.

Whether I am running on the treadmill at the gym, driving in my car singing along to songs or sitting outside at night under the stars — I do let my mind drift to my memories of them. Sometimes it can be a smell or a song or the most random thing that will remind you of a particular person. Initially the memories bring pain and hurt, and tears start to well in your eyes — this is okay, this is a necessary part of the healing.

I remember being at church exactly one month before the first anniversary of my mother's death. The pastor spoke about the many tables we sit at in our life and how we should learn and grow from these. He used Psalm 23 to illustrate his message. Psalm 23 was a passage that was very dear to my mother and I hadn't read it since her funeral eleven months earlier. Hearing it brought back lots of emotion, but it was also an opportunity to open my heart and heal a little more. I was sitting with my friend Di Wilson, the author of this book. She pointed out a key word in this Psalm: 'through' — 'even though I walk *through* the valley of the shadow of death'. She explained to me that the word 'through' is a very important word in this Psalm and that my mother had walked through the valley of the shadow of death. This really helped me a great deal, and in particular one month later on the anniversary of her passing. Just as your loved one has gone through, you too have to allow yourself to go through the valley, not physically but emotionally. Allow yourself to feel the hurt and go through the pain — you *will* get to the other side.

Often people will encourage you to suppress your feelings. This isn't because they don't care but because they don't know how to cope with your grief. Society sometimes encourages us to ignore our feelings, but it is okay to talk about the special people we hve lost, to remember them and keep them alive in us. Seek out the people in your life that do understand and can support you in what you are going through; often these are the people who have gone through it themselves. If you don't have friends or family who can identify with you there are grief support groups via your local church or local community services.

The healing process is long. Initially it is difficult but it does get easier. As the hurt starts to subside I encourage you to look for the gifts they've left you. One gift might be the influence and impact that their life had on your life. In the case of my parents, not only did they give me the gift of life but they also shaped my life. I love my life and I am proud to be the person I am. I am that person because of the influence and impact my parents had on my life.

My father was quite ill in the final years of his life. He knew the end of his time with us was approaching and the last words he spoke were to my brother Harry — he said that while he was scared to be moving on he was completely happy, satisfied and at peace with his life. He felt privileged to have seen his ten children grow into successful people and was glad he had the opportunity to get to know his twenty grandchildren. He was at peace, even though he was only seventy-one. His peace truly came from knowing that he had lived a blessed life.

Lana's friendship and wisdom was a huge benefit to me when I was dealing with the passing of my parents and the turmoil that came out of the hurt and anger that my siblings and I went through as we redefined our family without our parents. Lana was a beautiful person who lived her life with great dignity. When I talked to Lana about my feelings of loss and my questioning about how to go forward, she said all we should hope for in life is to do the best we can and to live with dignity.

More than anything I want my children to have the same comfort that my father gave me by knowing that he had no regrets and was at peace with his life. I try always to keep my heart soft and open to the many opportunities to heal, whether it's a church service, the joy of watching my children grow or the wisdom that comes from conversations with my friends. Let the young people around you remind you of the beauty of life.

I will always miss Garry, my parents and Lana. I will carry them in my heart forever. I will always remember their laughter, joy and love until we meet again. I will honour them by living the blessed life I have as best I can — a life that is so much richer for having known them. As we all know, 'It is better to have loved and lost than never to have loved at all.' Although there is a cause for grief that they have gone on ahead, there is also rejoicing that they were a part of my life and that I got to share the beauty of their life.

Discovering Eternity

Discover the depth Eternity holds for your own life

Eternity is a subject that many people have varied opinions about. I believe that Eternity is multidimensional.

- ❖ *Believe that Eternity speaks of a place that exists.*
  Heaven
- ❖ *Believe that Eternity speaks of a perspective that will shed light for you.*
  The Big Picture
- ❖ *Believe that Eternity speaks of a Person.*
  The Saviour
- ❖ *Believe that Eternity speaks of a plan.*
  To bring us hope in our final outcome
- ❖ *Believe that you are part of Eternity, the purpose.*
  To rescue humanity
- ❖ *Believe that you'll be ready for Eternity, the precise moment.*
  Your date with destiny
- ❖ *Believe that you will see Eternity, the people.*
  Our beloved awaiting our triumphant arrival
- ❖ *Believe that you will experience Eternity, the promise.*
  Your hopes will not be disappointed.

CHAPTER TWO

Faith

believe the best

*'I shall always be convinced that a watch proves a watchmaker,
and that a universe proves a God.'*

⌐ VOLTAIRE ~

FRENCH WRITER AND PHILOSOPHER (1694–1778)

Bambi

It always comes up when people are comparing their most traumatic movie experiences: the death of Bambi's mother, a recollection that brings a shudder to children and grown-ups alike. That primal separation (which is no less stunning for happening off-screen) is the centrepiece of *Bambi*, Walt Disney's 1942 animated classic.

Bambi covers a year in the life of a young deer. But in a bigger way, it measures the life cycle itself, from birth to adulthood, from childhood's freedom to grown-up responsibility. All of this is rendered in cheeky, early Disney style. The movie doesn't lecture, or make you feel you're being fed something that's meant to be good for you.

The animation is miraculous, showing a lush forest in which nature is a constantly unfolding miracle (even in a spectacular fire, or those dark moments when 'man was in the forest'). There are probably many easier animals to draw than a young deer, and the Disney animators set themselves a challenge with Bambi's wobbly slide across an ice-covered lake on his spindly legs, but the sequence is effortless and charming. If Bambi himself is just a bit timid, as deers mainly are, his rabbit sidekick Thumper and a skunk named Flower more than make up for it, bringing adventure into the movie.

Many of the early Disney features have their share of lyrical moments and universal truths, but *Bambi* is so simple, so pure, it's almost transparent.

The Eternity moment is definitely in the beginning of the movie when Bambi's mother dies. Your heart is just torn and you feel compelled to run and rescue the little baby deer. Everything freezes and Bambi is left with life decisions to make at such a young age. People who have lost a loved one can relate to this. It also addresses people who may never have lost a loved one, who ask the question, 'I wonder if that happened to me, what would I do?'

Bambi is a film that inspires people to keep going and move forward. Even though it is a cartoon movie, very innocent and some may say 'just make-believe', it still portrays life and loss in a great way. Children cry because Bambi has lost his mother, and they see it as a major loss because all they may have and know is their parents.

Bambi was my introduction to Eternity and helped me to understand that when life stops, it really only stands still for a moment on the journey from here to Eternity. Bambi's life went on and so must ours.

Faith

Unlocks hope.

'GOD IS FAITHFUL, NANNY, He is faithful, Nanny . . .' I said over and over again as my cheek lay gently on her cheek with my hand on her heart. I knew no better words to speak over my Nanny's life as she was about to breathe her last breath here before her first in Eternity. God is faithful. That is something I do know. In that room at that time I really didn't know much else. It was surreal. I was exhausted but it didn't seem to matter. I had been up for over twenty-four hours and I had rested on the cold vinyl floor. I had been praying all night and speaking words of faith and love into my Nanny's ear so she knew she was loved by us and by God, her faithful friend.

Nanny learned to be a woman of faith when she lost her husband, my Poppy, when he was just sixty-seven years of age. She lived without her beloved for over thirty years and never remarried. I believe this was because of her deep devotion to family and because he was the only love of her life. I also believe this was because of her relationship with God. Nanny was always so positive, even after she lost her ability to move around after a stroke. She began the day thanking God for so many things and she always said that by the time she finished praying, she had very little to complain about.

When my Nanny suffered a stroke six years before she passed away, she moved from our family home, in which she had lived since well before I was born, into a nursing home. It was brand-new and it was close to us, but it wasn't home. We needed to make it home. Mum and Dad visited Nanny nearly every day of that six-year period: Dad in the morning and Mum each afternoon. Their presence, I believe, made that place home. Eternity's presence made that place home, too. In the loneliest places, God loves to be our friend. That's when our faith in Him takes shape.

Faith transforms a wish into a prayer. The difference between a wish and a prayer is like the difference between wishing your car would drive without petrol in the tank, and asking someone to fill it up for you. Faith allows you to ask for something your heart wishes for and desires, and it is faith that makes way for hope. Gandhi said, 'Prayer is not asking, it is the longing of the soul.'

It was around 4 a.m. on a cold winter's morning when our phone rang. I knew something was wrong. We often used to receive phone calls in the middle of the night when my husband was working on projects in Africa, but that season was over. It was my Dad on the phone telling me that he was at the hospital with my Nanny and that the doctor had asked for family to be called because she didn't think Nanny was going to make it.

Everything inside me wanted to run a million miles, but at the same time everything inside me wanted to run to my Nanny's side. Faith kicked in and I ran to her. I called a close friend and asked if she could quickly come to be with the kids so that Jonathan and I could go to be with Nanny. We left as soon as we could, and as we pulled up to the hospital I found myself literally running towards the emergency room. I was so afraid but I loved her so much that I had to be there.

I found my parents and my sister, all visibly shaken and upset. I found my Nanny. 'Oh, Nanny, you're okay — you're going to be okay,' I said over and over and over again. I too began to sob as I held her hand and watched her breathe as though she were never coming back to us.

My Nanny was dying right before my eyes and it seemed that there was nothing I could do about it except believe she would come through. I got up really close to her face and spoke over the breathing apparatus, saying, 'You'll be okay, Nanny, I'm praying for you. We're here, Nanny, you'll be fine.' These were not just wishful words, they were faith-filled. I honestly believed that she would come through.

The doctor explained that in order to save Nanny's life she would have to give her an enormous dose of antibiotics that could eventually shut down her kidneys. We agreed that we should try to save Nanny's life.

While all this was happening I remembered a scene from the movie *Titanic* that had a profound impact on me. It was when Jack and Rose were in the sea, and Jack, compelling Rose to hang on, told her that she wouldn't die that night, but as an old lady, warm in her bed. That was something I wanted for my Nanny. I didn't want her to die this way. She was so sick and not conscious and I knew that this wasn't going to be her departure. I had faith for her to be an old lady in her bed, going to sleep. And that's exactly what happened.

Faith is the power behind our choice to look beyond what's happened. I have found that people have to learn to let go; it doesn't come easily. Then, when loss arrives, they are ready, softened and open to what happens. They aren't cold, immune or fearful. After a loss, things will never be the same again, but a strong mind isn't enough to get us through. We must be able to feel deeply, to stay warm in our hearts, to have faith to believe for the best to come of what's happened. Faith gives us the ability to trust and accept things even when we don't understand why.

We experience many emotions when we're grieving, including shock, denial, anger and acceptance. Panic can grip us and anger can overwhelm us because every dream about the life we had is now shattered. It takes a while to get up again but gradually hope comes through. However, we won't just become our old selves again. When we go through any significant loss, we will come out of it as a different person and that is where faith makes a difference.

When you have faith you are able to confidently believe in the truth about Eternity. Faith doesn't rest on logical proof or material evidence, it is found hidden deep within the human heart. Your faith will allow you to believe the best when people around you say thoughtless and unkind things. Your faith will allow you to dream about your future in Eternity with your loved ones. Your faith will spur you on to make the rest of your life here on earth count. When you have faith you can be expectant of hope. You can confidently trust in God's ability to help you solve whatever problem lies before you so you can overcome our pain. Having faith will give you a voice, an expression of what you believe, even if you are the only one who believes it.

Faith is not just a way we walk in life. Faith is also a bridge that helps us span the gulf between time and Eternity.

Denial is the only way that some people face the reality of death. Some people simply choose not to believe or have faith. The following two men choose to have no faith.

'I see death as the ultimate end. Like the sleep before REM, when you're unaware of any time passing or any surroundings or anything, only more so. When you die, your mind shuts off like a switch and you never experience anything. It's almost impossible to imagine, which is why religions seek to explain something better. People are scared of oblivion, so they created Heaven.'

—◦ JARED ◦—

'I would relate this question to what I do when I get ready for a major race. While many people pray, I pace around thinking, setting goals in my head, planning my strategy, preparing as hard as I can, and at the end I clear my head and let things come as they will. I think I would do something similar in the face of death. In dealing with it, I just think materialistically. Life doesn't matter, mind is nothing more than electromagnetic impulses, and death is a release from a life of suffering. I don't fear my death for these reasons. I guess in my final moments I would basically drift myself into a sea of stoicism. I guess.'

—◦ JOHN ◦—

I like Abraham Lincoln's view of the truth: 'How many legs does a dog have if you call the tail a leg? Four: calling a tail a leg doesn't make it a leg.' Saying that there is no such thing as eternal life doesn't remove eternal life from the equation. It's still there, simply waiting for us to enter into it one day.

Some of us may have heard the story of the woman who came to the Buddha in great anguish, carrying her dead child, pleading with him to bring the child back to life. The Buddha said, 'Bring me a mustard seed from a household where no-one has ever died and I will fulfil your wish.' The woman's search for such a seed was in vain. Of course she could not find any household in which no-one had ever died, and suddenly she realised the universality of death.

I want to encourage you not to be afraid of God, if that has been your experience. People are sometimes afraid of God because of how poorly 'religion' with all its rules and regulations has portrayed Him. God is loving, compassionate, caring, merciful, generous and kind, and He knows us better than we know ourselves, because He created us.

Faith opens a door to God's world, supports us through our troubles and helps us to know that every pressure and heartache will eventually produce in us patience and the ability to endure.

Faith is the wind beneath our wings. The effects of the wind can be seen: when it's windy outside we can see the grass and trees move. We can also just feel it. This is what faith is like. It requires faith to believe in Eternity, just as it requires faith to believe in wind. Although it's not easy to have faith in something that you can't see or touch, I know that wind is real because of its effects. I also know that God is real, because of His effect on my life and on the lives of many, many other people I know.

A wonderful couple used to visit me when I worked as a travel agent many years ago. They were members of the Salvation Army and were going on holidays back to South Africa to visit family. It was such a great pleasure to organise their travel as they were always so grateful for everything I did. I was shattered when I heard that the gentleman had been killed in the Port Arthur massacre of 1996. I read in the paper that he said to his beloved wife, after having jumped in front of her to save her life, 'Darling, I'm going to be with the Lord.' He was one of thirty-five people randomly killed on that Sunday. His love and faith enabled him to give his own life to save his beloved wife.

Faith makes an ordinary person brave in the face of adversity. Going through tragedy draws us closer to Eternity. Faith allows me to believe that the comfort I can know now is greater than any suffering I may be going through. Faith allows us not to fear when life comes to an end. The fear of death stems from the fear of the unknown.

Even in old age, faith helps us establish our final destiny. Over time, our bodies become increasingly worn out. Joints stiffen and ache. Eyes grow dim. Digestion slows. Sleep becomes difficult. Physical challenges grow larger and larger while options narrow.

Yet if our passing is not the end but the beginning of a new day, then old age is a blessing. Each new ache makes this world less interesting and the next life more appealing. In its own way, pain can make a way for a graceful and ready departure from life here on earth.

It is also true that in times of crisis we not only find out who we are but we also find one another. Natural disasters and times of crisis have a way of bringing us together. September 11 is a prime example of this, as were the Bali bombings and the tsunami of Boxing Day 2004. Hurricanes, fires, earthquakes, riots, illnesses and accidents all have a way of bringing us to our senses. Suddenly we remember our own mortality and that people are more important than things. We remember that we need one another and that, above all, we need faith. Each time we discover Eternity's comfort in our own suffering, our capacity to help others is increased.

The way we pass reflects the way we lived our lives, a noble death putting a good stamp on a good life. As Leonardo Da Vinci once wrote in his notebook, 'Just as a well-spent day brings happy sleep, so a well-spent life brings a happy death.' If we have lived a life of emotional turmoil, of conflict and selfish desire, unconcerned for others, our dying will be full of regrets, troubles and pain. Improving the moral and spiritual quality of life improves its quality for us all. Faith keeps me focused on making sure my life here is well spent before I meet my Maker at the door of Eternity.

I want to leave you with some profound words to ponder by Galileo Galilei: 'All truths are easy to understand once they are discovered; the point is to discover them.' Have faith, seek truth and you'll find hope.

In his book, *Gentle Closings: How to Say Goodbye to Someone You Love*, author Ted Menten writes about 'the white space'.

'Only a few decades ago, people died at home surrounded by their loved ones. Often, in their final moments they saw God, or angels, or some other unworldly guide who came to take them in death. This experience often comforted those who remained behind.

Now, because of technology, we are able to intervene and retrieve someone who is technically dead. In many cases these people report experiences that involve visitations by guides who take them to a clear, white, peaceful space.'[1]

Faith reminds us that we can find hope as we walk over Eternity's rainbow.

Kathy's Story

My Uncle Bruce was born the youngest of eleven, my Dad being number ten in line. Uncle Bruce never married, and neither did my Aunty Norma, who was the eldest sister, so the two — brother and sister — lived together for many decades. They had a very special and close bond. She was eighty-eight and he was just sixty-five when we received the call.

It was Christmas Eve, Dad's birthday. Mum got a call from one of my other Aunties to say that Uncle Bruce had been put into hospital again and this time they felt it would be his last as his condition had worsened. Mum decided not to tell Dad straight away as Dad and Bruce's relationship had been under strain for some time; every time Dad spoke to him, it only seemed to make Bruce angry. Mum eventually told Dad and together they went to visit Bruce in hospital. By this time he had been put into a hospice for the dying. He had been quite agitated when he first arrived and would not cooperate with the nursing staff.

He was quite pleased to see both Dad and Mum. He reminded Mum that he had not ruled out the possibility that there was a God when they had spoken about it four years earlier. That had been when he was first diagnosed with cancer and Mum had asked if she could pray for him. He had not been against that.

I visited him later that week with Dad and we spent a while reminiscing about his favourite music and movies.

He was pleased to see us but was very tired and would drift into and out of sleep. Dad and I decided to leave. We got as far as the lift, but neither of us felt right about leaving without talking to Bruce about Eternity. Dad and I talked and decided that it would be best for me to go back and leave Dad to pray outside as Dad didn't want to upset him. I approached the bed and said, 'Uncle Bruce, I just wanted to come back and have a little chat with you.' I told him I loved him and then started to share with him about the gift of Eternity. He listened to me and said that he had led his life a certain way all these years and it would not be right to change how he felt and that he would not tell me just what I wanted to hear and that he would leave it and wait and see what would happen after he died.

I left that day encouraging him to think about Eternity. It was wonderful that he wasn't upset at all with me and seemed genuinely grateful that I talked about Eternity with him and that I cared.

A few days later my sister Di arrived to take Mum and I to the hospital. When we arrived at the hospice Bruce was wide awake and very pleased to see us. He told jokes and reminded us of things we used to do as children, while Di presented him with a small toy Bambi, which reminded him of Disney's *Bambi*, which he had given to us as little kids on audio tape. We had listened to that story over and over again. *Bambi* has always been really precious to us. Uncle Bruce taught us the wonder of believing as children.

We asked him if he would let us pray for him and he was happy for us to do that and even joined in and said 'Amen!' at the end. I asked if he had thought any more about Eternity yet and he said, 'Yes.' At that moment he invited Jesus into his heart. He added that he had thrown away what he had believed (he grew up as a Communist), as he knew this belief would not help him now. He said over and over again that all that mattered was his family and that politics didn't matter any more.

I also noticed that he was looking intently at something in the room, but I did not ask him until another time what he was looking at. After a lovely visit, with many tears of joy for the genuine peace he had found, and yet sadness that his life was about to come to a close here on earth, we all went home.

I was able to see him again another time with Dad and my daughter Sarah. Once again he was pleased to see us and we chatted about many different things. The rest of the family arrived and were talking to Dad just outside while Sarah and I visited Bruce. We talked with him further about Eternity. This time I asked him what he was looking at, as his gaze was once again fixed on something in the room. I asked what he could see and he said, 'They are here.' When I asked him who he was talking about he replied, 'Give me some names and I will tell you if they are here!' I began to mention names as they popped into my head — asking about his eldest brother Bill, who passed away many years ago. Bruce said, 'He should be here but I can't see him at the moment.' He went on to say that my Nanny was there, his Mum (my Grandma Olive) was there.

On another occasion he did see his brother Bill in the room and many others. He said there were so many in his room, all dressed in white. I knew then he was seeing into Eternity. Bruce had a clear mind when he was seeing and speaking; in fact, he was more lucid than he had been for years. They had stopped giving him morphine, so it wasn't the drugs. For the first time in his life he was experiencing the wonder of Eternity here and now, in his last moments on earth.

Inventor Thomas Edison was bedridden for the last two months of his life with pneumonia. He sank into semi-consciousness, and his second wife, Mina, remained by his side. On his last day, Mina leaned close and asked, 'Are you suffering?', to which he replied, 'No, just waiting.' Edison then looked out of his bedroom window and softly spoke his last words: 'It's very beautiful over there.' He too had seen the other side before he left this earth.

In my heart, I knew Uncle Bruce was not going to be with us much longer. One day I called the hospice and they said it would be any time now that he would leave us. I got on the phone and called Dad and together with Mum they came up from the south coast. I called my sister and she was able to come and pick me straight up. Mum and Dad arrived before us and were trying to call as he only had a short time left and they did not think we would get there in time. Di and I arrived and it was only a matter of another ten minutes. I was able to stroke his head and gently talk to him about going into the arms of Jesus as he breathed his last breath.

So many loving family members gathered around his bed for these last moments. He was still wide-eyed as his last breath was taken. It was almost as if he was trying to tell us something and then he was gone. Many tears flowed as we comforted each other, but I knew where Uncle Bruce had gone: straight into the arms of Jesus in Heaven. He had made his peace.

No more tears, no more pain for my dear Uncle. Just a wonderful Eternity now where he can be the cheeky, creative, charming, caring, comic, classic Bruce he was created to be.

Donna's Story

My Dad's name was Bill, or Billy to his mates. He was a
real 'Aussie battler'. He was a good mate, a hard worker
and liked a beer down at the RSL club.

Anzac Day was always a very meaningful day in our
household. Both my Grandfather and my Pop had served in
World War I, and Dad had served alongside Pop in World
War II. My eldest brother was later to serve in Vietnam. We
were very proud of this heritage and, even as kids,
respected this sombre occasion. On Anzac Day, Dad would
go to the Dawn Service, attend the Anzac March and then
go down to the club for a few beers and a game of two-
up. The rest of the family would watch the march on the
television.

What we didn't understand was that Dad was struggling
internally with some of the repercussions of having fought
in the war. He had begun drinking heavily, gambling, and
not coming home until late. Mum pretty well did all the
hands-on parenting for as long as I can remember. She was,
and still is, a champion. Naturally, the money spent on beer,
smokes and pokies was not coming into the meagre family
finances, and this put more stress on both Mum and Dad.

The drinking became worse and Mum and Dad's
relationship deteriorated. There were a lot of arguments. I
can relate to people who say that they freeze when they
hear the key in the door late at night. We never knew what
kind of mood he would be in. The drinking was changing

Dad. There were two sides to him. The crazy thing is that while Dad was at work or the club our home was happy and everyone got on well. I would have to say that we all loved Dad, he just did dumb stuff sometimes. We didn't go on family holidays and Dad never came to watch me play netball or anything like that. I can't remember Dad ever talking to me much or giving me a hug. He became a loner. Mum was always there though.

I found my teenage years difficult and struggled to feel valued. I began to realise that not all families were the same as mine. My relationship with my father became strained at this point as he struggled to understand an independent teenage daughter. I became angry and hurt and felt that Dad did not care about me. Dad seemed more comfortable with my brothers, perhaps because he found it easier to understand the male way of thinking. My life wasn't very pretty for a while there.

Things began to change for me, and my life began to turn around when I found a real faith in Jesus Christ. I began to learn the power of forgiveness and appreciate that to show grace toward others brings a much happier life. I started to understand that I was far from perfect and that, being very human, I didn't always make the best decisions myself. If I expected others to understand my failings, I would need to extend that courtesy to others. I wanted a healthy relationship with my father, even if it wasn't all that I hoped for. I knew that if I didn't choose to let go of these feelings and embrace the situation from a different standpoint, I would remain in this unhappy place for the rest of my life.

I persevered, and over some time I was able to see my father in a new light, as a man who did the best he could given his own particular challenges in life. I grew to be able to see him as a man who did love me, but just did not know how to express it.

My Dad passed away five years ago now. He had been admitted to hospital with pneumonia and was actually recovering well. He was expecting to come home in two days. We were intending to visit him the next day when we received the call to say that he had had a heart attack and had not survived. At first I was in shock. He was getting better — there must be a mistake! He was in hospital for pneumonia, not heart troubles. How could he have had a heart attack? How come they could not bring him through? He was in a large city hospital after all!

My husband and I rushed to the hospital, almost expecting them to say that it was a mistake and that he was sitting up waiting for my visit. But that didn't happen. He was gone. I must have sat with him for over an hour, thinking about the good things and the not so good. He was gone! Nothing I could do could change that. His life was done, completed. Things were as they were.

I must say there was sadness and disappointment at what could have been. Sometimes we can experience grief long before our loved one departs this earth because their life and your life could have been so different. But eventually I found myself back in that place I had previously discovered, where I could leave Dad's decisions with him and concentrate on embracing my future. I felt that I could lay it down.

While it was difficult to say goodbye, I am grateful that I was able to forgive and see him in a new light while he was still alive. The grieving was 'clean' and not muddied by lots of pain and unresolved issues. Dad and I had never become particularly close, but we had found a respect for each other and had visited regularly. When I think of him now, I don't really think too much about the negative things, but of the new relationship we were beginning to build.

I have been very happily married for many years now, with three beautiful daughters who have known a very different upbringing from mine. Their lives are unfolding wonderfully and they know what it is like to grow up in a secure and loving family. The thing that has made the biggest difference to my life, my faith, is the very thing that I have taught my children to take hold of. I know personally that faith makes a difference, regardless of what life's circumstances bring.

I choose to remember my Dad as the one who taught me how to change a tyre, peel prawns and pour a beer. He taught me to show loyalty to friends and to have a good work ethic, and in his own strange way he taught me to forgive and show grace. For that I am thankful. Eternity has made me thankful.

Childlike Faith

Steps to build faith in your children

I am so grateful to have had an active faith life since early childhood. Encouraging and teaching our children to have faith, to take them through life and into Eternity, is the greatest gift we can give them.

❖ *Have a vision.*

I believe we as parents need to have our sights set on a goal. See your children and family running their race strong until the very end. Many parents put a great deal of time and effort into supporting and encouraging their children in educational, athletic or career pursuits while giving very little attention to encouraging their pursuit of faith in God. I'm not talking about religious rituals, but a personal relationship with God that they can draw faith from.

❖ *Create intentional habits.*

One of the most effective ways to teach children is by example. If they see you walking in your faith instead of just professing it, they will be more inclined to follow your example. Allow your children to see you read, pray and above all be loving towards people, especially those who don't necessarily 'deserve' it.

❖ *Make the most of life's challenges.*

Demonstrate for your children the art of taking the challenges of life and turning them into great opportunities. The challenge might be a financial setback, a health problem or a relationship issue. Responding to these trials by putting your faith into action will go a long way towards teaching your children to respond to their challenges in faith.

❖ *Build confidence.*

Even when we lack confidence ourselves, the best thing we can do is instil confidence in one another. The word *encourage* means to *put courage in* someone. Sometimes we forget that our little people's confidence is quite fragile — especially if they have been through trials that cause them to doubt who they are and what they can do. Build confidence by encouragement and they will in turn learn to become encouragers themselves.

❖ *Be a great example.*

A father teaches his child to play soccer by taking him to the park and kicking a ball around with him. A mother teaches a daughter or son to cook by involving them in the kitchen, not just by handing down old recipes from her mother. Faith is taught the same way, by active expression, watched and learned. If they don't see and hear examples of your successes and failures, they won't know that faith really works, regardless of the immediate outcome.

❖ *Affirm their potential.*

Every child has it! Each child has been given different gifts and abilities. Observe your children's talents and talk to them about how great those gifts will be for them and their family and for Eternity's purpose.

❖ *Pray.*

We should teach our children to pray as a child talks to his or her Dad. Not boring, lengthy prayers that children can't relate to, but heartfelt prayers that will ensure that our children know that God is near and that He is listening and willing to answer their prayers. Mealtime prayers and bedtime prayers are a great way to establish praying in children's lives.

CHAPTER THREE

Hope

hold on to hope

'Hope opens doors where despair closes them. Hope discovers what can be done instead of grumbling about what cannot. Hope draws its power from a deep trust in God and the basic goodness of human nature. Hope "lights the candle" instead of "cursing the darkness". Hope regards problems, small or large, as opportunities. Hope cherishes no illusions, nor does it yield to cynicism. Hope sets big goals and is not frustrated by repeated difficulties or setbacks. Hope pushes ahead when it would be easy to quit. Hope puts up with modest gains, realising that a long journey starts with one step. Hope is a good loser because it has the divine assurance of final victory.'[2]

— FATHER JAMES KELLER —
FOUNDER OF THE CHRISTOPHERS (1900–1977)

Sleepless in Seattle

Sleepless in Seattle has gone down in movie history as a classic love story. But this beautiful story begins with a tragic loss. Sam (Tom Hanks) suddenly lost his wife. The movie shows him about a year later, still lonely, and reluctant to move on. On Christmas Eve night his son, who is worried about him, calls in to a national radio show where psychiatrist Dr Marsha Fieldstone convinces Sam to talk about the great loss of his wife.

While all of this is happening, across America a 'happily' engaged woman, Annie (Meg Ryan), is driving in her car and just happens to come across the radio station Sam is talking on. Though she is engaged, she realises that she is not genuinely happy in that relationship. So, through a chain of events (a letter from Annie to Sam, Sam's son running away to New York), Annie ends up breaking it off with her fiancé on Valentine's Day in New York on the same night that Sam happens to be in New York chasing after his son. The movie ends with Sam, his son and Annie finally meeting on top of the Empire State Building. You can tell by the look in Sam's and Annie's eyes that it is love at first sight.

Now, obviously, the love story in this movie is beautiful and one of the main themes of the movie. But I also believe there is another very important aspect to this movie. The reason the whole love story is so moving is because of the loss of Sam's wife. This brings a dynamic to the story that makes it soar to new heights.

At the beginning of the movie, Sam is absolutely broken. You see him and his son standing alone at his wife's funeral. You hear him saying things like, 'Why? Why did this have to happen?' and 'It's not fair.' And it's not; death is never fair. How dare it take someone away from us and leave us here without the ones we love so much.

The Eternity moment in this movie occurs when we see Sam struggling to let go of his wife so that he can move on and finally begin to live again. I think that anyone who has lost someone that close to them can actually feel what he is feeling in that part of the movie. I found myself wishing right along with Sam that his wife would come back. But it was not possible, and Sam finally let her go. Eternity held another plan.

This movie is a great lesson in moving on after a great loss. It shows us that our life doesn't have to end with a loved one's death. Life goes on as long as we have breath.

Hope

Where there is life there is hope.
Where there is hope there is life.
Hold on to hope and you'll laugh again.

IF I WERE TO PAINT a picture of hope it would look something like my Dad holding my hand, giving me courage to know everything's going to be okay. Maybe you've had to say goodbye to the person whose hand you were most fond of holding and now you need to find another hand to hold. Hold on to hope. Hold hope's hand.

Some experts suggest that the word *hope* may share its origins with the word *hop*, giving it perhaps the meaning of leaping with expectation. When we hope, we not only desire good but we have an expectation or belief that it can and will be obtained. Hope allows us to indulge in impossible dreams and to cherish our desire for good. People will disappoint us, life will disappoint us, but hope never disappoints because hope is founded on the truth that we live in the realm of Eternity.

I'm certain you could do with a word of hope today. We all can, regardless of what we're going through. Knowing that life can pick up again is what helps to keep us going. Hope is one of the three strands that when braided together create a cord of great strength for us in life: faith, hope and love. Hope causes desire to materialise in our heart whether or not we can see it with our eyes. Hope is not a frail or perishable commodity. Hope lives and we must keep it alive in our hearts.

Difficult times are like dark clouds that pass overhead and block the sun. When we look more closely at the edges of every cloud we can see the sun shining there like a silver lining. Hope is like the silver lining under the dark cloud, breaking through to better days ahead. Silver linings give meaning to tragedy. One of the 'silver linings' of World War II was the increase in technology, which has assisted in helping to save human lives. The 'silver lining' of September 11 is a world more aware and more united.

Dark thunderclouds are threatening and frightening and require us to see past them to the hope that lies beyond. It is always possible to get something positive out of a situation, no matter how unpleasant, difficult or even painful it is at the time. In all situations we should hold on to hope. On the day I wrote this, I took the hand of a young woman whose father has been diagnosed with a terminal illness and told her to hold on to hope. With tears welling in her eyes she simply replied, 'Yes. I am.' When faced with a problem as big as that we must hold on to hope.

With faith and hope there is no hopeless situation. Hopelessness is usually defined by pessimism or negative expectancies. Although some people have a natural tendency towards negativity, we can all choose hope, even though for some that choice is harder than for others. Hope brings life; hopelessness brings nothing but further hopelessness. In fact, hopelessness may be an even more important predictor of suicidal intent than depression.[3] When people give up on hope, they give up on faith and they give up on life.

I was in my early twenties when the phone rang one night. It was my Dad telling me that my Uncle, who was also my godfather, had died by taking his own life. I dropped to my knees and cried out to God. The pain wouldn't stop. It was as though the very hopelessness that had caused him to do such a thing had been transferred to all who heard the news. My poor Aunty and my poor cousins. It was unfathomable. I just wish he had known that there's always hope, even when life seems completely hopeless.

This was not my first experience with suicide. As a teenager I used to know a great young guy who was a lovely but somewhat troubled soul. The news of his tragic end came as a shock, but sadly not a complete surprise. He had thrown himself onto a railway line, just wanting the pain in his life to end. I was asked to sing at his funeral and it is one of the most difficult things I have ever had to do. Something happened that caused him to lose all hope.

What can cause us to lose hope? Often, we hope for the wrong things. It's so easy to place our hope where it doesn't belong; in what we can see, taste, touch and feel. Our hope needs to be put in God, who is the only one who knows the final outcome of our lives.

Hope is all about the final outcome.

When things don't work out the way we expect, unrealised hope makes our heart sick. When things don't appear to change, when it seems there's no light at the end of the tunnel, hope still expects the best and looks for what could be.

Here are some practical ways to help you build a sure foundation of hope that will carry you through the difficult times of life.

- Close your eyes and see yourself holding hope's hand.
- Recall the good things that have emerged from life's painful experiences.
- Trust that all things can work together for good in time.
- Pray for a greater awareness of what hope has in store for your future.
- Be grateful for hope, even if you don't feel anything like it right now.

To hope is to wish for something with expectation of its fulfilment. Hope leans towards a future good. There are five aspects of hope that we need to understand.

- ❖ Hope comes from above.
- ❖ Hope looks for that which is good.
- ❖ Hope is about our future.
- ❖ Hope can appear difficult.
- ❖ Hope works in the realm of the impossible.

The relationship between faith and hope is very close. Hope is based on faith, but it is not the same thing. It is the difference between believing that eternal life actually exists and hoping to be part of it. Where faith is certain, hope alone can be uncertain; but when hope is based on faith, it shares in faith's certainty.

Hope keeps you focused on the positive even when you're surrounded by the negative. It puts an excitement into everyday life so you can wake up each morning with new expectations and new hopes. Although there are many definitions of hope, there is a single theme common to all. Hope usually involves an element of uncertainty of an outcome concerning matters of importance to us.

Hanging in the Tate Gallery in London is a painting by a mid-nineteenth century artist of a young woman standing, deep in thought, by the grave of a loved one. The title of the painting is *The Doubt: Can These Dry Bones Live?* This is a question that has been asked by humanity throughout the ages. Is it possible that people live on after they've died? Is there really any hope for them or for us to see them again? On the stone at the foot of the grave near the young woman's feet lies a sprouting chestnut, a symbol of life. This is possibly the artist's veiled answer to the question posed. On the stone is carved a simple but confident Latin inscription: '*Resurgam*' (I shall rise again). That's the hope we can rest in.

Hope emerges. That's one of the best ways to describe it in action. It is so subtle that you might not be aware of its presence.

You begin to notice that your good days start outnumbering the bad, which can have a dual effect. You may feel terribly guilty for feeling good while at the same time you feel encouraged that you can smile again. Walking in hope makes going to work, seeing relatives and facing friends easier. Walking in hope helps you make decisions and handle issues more easily.

You will always miss your loved one or ones. Special family events, such as holidays, birthdays, weddings or anniversaries, or other sights or sounds will trigger the feelings of longing for them to be by your side. It's normal to wish they were still with you, but through it all you will find that you have a future and hope. Eventually the pain will subside and peace will abide. You will learn to accept what you can't change and have faith to make a difference with what you *can* change.

Hope brings meaning to life; through your experience you can have personal, emotional and spiritual growth, and great influence on the lives of other people who have been through similar circumstances. There's no doubt that you will be different now, but make that difference count. Hope to be stronger, wiser, more compassionate, aware, understanding and patient. Our loved ones, having found faith and hope, have entered a beautiful new life without pain and problems and we will be with them — reunited one day. In the meantime, know that they would want and expect us to love and appreciate the life we have with those here by our side and to live it to the full.

Some people have hopeful or optimistic dispositions. They remain hopeful whatever life presents. These kinds of people see life in a positive light no matter how tragic the circumstance. People like this are enviable, providing they are real about what's going on. It definitely takes a special kind of person to acknowledge the truth of their pain but choose to find the light through the darkness. These people command a certain kind of respect, like an inmate in a concentration camp who never doubts they'll one day be free.

I have learned to be a woman of hope. Because fear is something that I have had to work hard to overcome during my life, I value the hope that has emerged. Now when the phone rings I don't automatically presume the worst; even when I hear about something terrible that has happened, a glimmer of hope is always present. Hope is a lifeline. There is a wonderful naiveté about hope. There is a reaching beyond the scope of reason. There is readiness to 'hop' to see the best, even in the heart of our deepest anguish. Mark Twain once said, 'The optimist is a person who travels on nothing from nowhere to happiness.'

Other people have a stronger tendency to be pessimistic or hopeless in their thoughts. Optimists are undoubtedly happier people, who will see a glass half full even when it's nearly empty, while a pessimist will see the water draining out even when the glass is more than half full. Hope is more, and goes deeper, than a mere optimism or disposition of the human mind.

At the core of all the religions of the world is a quest for hope — something that makes sense of the apparent chaos and injustices of life. We long to know why we exist, where we are going, and what makes it all worthwhile. Tragically, so many people are clinging to false hope. Counterfeit or false hope will only ever let us down. The hope I present to you is filled with life.

❖ Miracles do happen.
❖ There is a seed of hope in every desperate situation.
❖ We can experience a life of hope here on earth by looking upwards to our Heavenly Father.
❖ Hoping for the best costs you nothing and gives you wonderful peace.

- ❖ We can look forward to a Heavenly home especially prepared for us.
- ❖ We can look forward to having a brand-new body in Heaven — yippee!
- ❖ We can look forward to eternal rewards for our lives on earth.

Yes, there are reasons to hope. Life will go on. Babies will be born. Life will be more meaningful. You have been reminded of what is precious. Family, friends and faith have returned to a place of high regard. Human beings must have hope to survive, and without Eternity's perspective our problems really can seem overwhelming. But if you view your heartaches through the lens of Eternity, a promise of hope will clearly come into the picture.

Hope is as necessary to the soul as air to the body. When hope vanishes, people can do incredibly destructive things to themelves and others. They abandon families, destroy property, shoot guns in public places, or commit suicide. Our success, intellect and wealth alone aren't enough for our survival. Neither are our looks, a new house or a luxury car. All of them can be lost in a moment. Without hope even relationships with other human beings can't ground your ability to cope with life. Without hope people are more likely to abandon their friends and break promises to their mates and children.

The most telling line in a letter written by a man who took the life of several work colleagues before turning on his own family, killing his wife and two children, then taking his own life, is this: 'I have come to have no hope.' With all hope gone this man was paranoid and thought the world was against him. The final line in his letter declared his intention 'to kill as many of the people that greedily sought my destruction' as he could before dying himself. To use this man's own words, he had been 'dying' for a long time. He had become 'so afraid, so terrified' and had 'come to hate this life'. He had completely lost hope.

I really want to encourage you. No matter what is going on in your life today, hold on to hope. If your present circumstances seem to preclude hope, it could be that they somehow open the way to a deeper and truer hope for you to experience. Perhaps your loss has opened the way for you to have a new kind of hope. True hope looks beyond our own mortality as it is founded on a higher trust. True hope is a deeply spiritual phenomenon because it requires us to lift our eyes to a higher place, above all that is happening around us. This higher place is like the cruising altitude of an aeroplane that has just climbed through turbulent clouds.

I remember clearly when the doctor explained to us that by giving Nanny a large dose of antibiotics to save her life, there was also the risk of it eventually killing her because her kidneys could fail. I had great hope in her life being saved in the emergency ward and I saw the fruit of my faith and hope in her pulling through. But after a few days her kidneys looked as though they were beginning to fail, and the doctors explained that if this happened there was nothing more they could do. I chose not to put my faith in their abilities; rather, I rested my hopes in God for His perfect outcome. And that's when I experienced peace.

There is great danger in relying on or putting hope in people to perform miracles. That's where disappointment, discouragement and despair can enter our hearts and cause us to miss the miraculous divine Eternity plan at our greatest crisis point.

There are four unique promises of true hope.

❖ True hope promises that you and your loved one matter.
❖ True hope enables us to never give up.

⬧ True hope is found above.

⬧ True hope reminds us that Eternity is always with us, lighting our path.

Eternity is hope personified. As Ralph Waldo Emerson once said, 'Aim high; hope for great things.' Where there's life, there's hope. Never give up. Keep walking over Eternity's rainbow.

> 'My hope is in the Name of the Lord,
> Where my help comes from,
> You're my strength, my song.
> My trust is in the Name of the Lord,
> I will sing your praise,
> You are faithful.
> You are faithful.
> You are faithful.'

⤙ DARLENE ZSCHECH ⤚

'MY HOPE'

Alison's Story

In May 1983, my husband Rohan and I, with our two young children, Sonja, aged two, and Nathan, aged three months, left Australia to return to Rohan's homeland of Sri Lanka. It was a big move for us as a young family, but we knew that God was calling us back to a people that needed to hear about His wonderful love.

Our first three-year term was very challenging, with the worst riots in the history of Sri Lanka taking place just two months after our arrival. I suffered culture shock and depression in the first year just adjusting to my new home and a totally different lifestyle. It was tough as a young mother, missing family and friends who loved and supported our little family. But by the end of the first three-year term, my heart had totally gone out to the people of Sri Lanka. I had adjusted, and more than that, I had fallen in love with this beautiful tear-shaped island and its people.

Before our return to Australia for a six-month break, we began some pioneering work up in the hill country of Sri Lanka in a place called Nuwara Eliya. We had recently visited this town for a holiday and we loved it. When we were asked to start a church there, we immediately felt very excited about it and began the work just three months before we went back to Australia. Every weekend we would travel for five hours to Nuwara Eliya, visit families and hold services on Sunday, and return Sunday night.

We made the decision to move our family to Nuwara
Eliya the week before we left the island for Australia. It was
a big move but we knew we were meant to be there. I felt
so good about our life in Sri Lanka. I had a wonderful
husband, two beautiful children and a mission that I just
loved with all my heart. It was easy for me, at this stage of
my life, to share how everything was wonderful and that I
would give my life for the people of Sri Lanka. I was
willing to grow old and die in Sri Lanka. That is how
strong my love was for this nation.

Little did I know what was in store for me and how
God was going to use my declaration of love for the people
of Sri Lanka. My life was to change drastically but my love
for people in Sri Lanka would remain strong and firm
through it all, even my love for those who literally
destroyed my family.

We returned to Sri Lanka in May 1987 after six months
in Australia. Rohan and I had just celebrated our seventh
wedding anniversary, which was an important milestone for
us. Life was very happy for us. Rohan was in the prime of
his life and loving what he was doing. He was a man of
great hope. We felt like we had it all together and that
more than anything God was working through our lives,
and we were just loving what we were doing. We worked
with everyone from the poorest labourers in the tea estates
to the wealthy English-speaking people of the town. Life
was great and every moment precious.

In September, we were invited to visit the north of Sri
Lanka, a place called Jaffna. I decided not to travel at this
time, as we felt the ten- or twelve-hour trip would be too
much for the kids, and we also knew that it was dangerous.
The civil war between the Tamil rebels and the government

had been going on for many years, and in the months leading up to Rohan's trip the Indian army had come into the area. The area was quite hostile, but during the time Rohan went there was a peace treaty between both parties. Rohan was excited about the trip since he would be able to visit three of the students he had taught.

So on 4 September he kissed us all fondly goodbye and left for his long journey with another young man from Nuwara Eliya. There was no mobile phone to keep track of him but we just waited to hear from him the next day when he arrived safely, which he did.

On 7 September, after a church meeting, Rohan and others were stopping to pick up one of his ex-students when the van that Rohan was driving was met with a spray of machine-gun fire from a group of terrorists waiting in ambush for his vehicle. Rohan was killed instantly and four others died soon after, with just a few survivors.

I learned of Rohan's death the next day from my sister-in-law, Debbie, who was a friend indeed during many sad days trying to cope with my grief and loss. I immediately questioned God: 'Why did you take Rohan in the prime of his life? Life was so good and we were doing so much for you — why?' All I know is at that very moment, a peace that I cannot explain came into my life. I simply trusted God for the future of my children and me.

The funeral was held in Colombo, with a packed church and many outside as well. The next few days seemed like a blur, and even today I can't remember a lot of how I felt or what was happening. All I knew was that, at the age of twenty-six, I was a widow and a young mother of two fatherless children aged just four and six.

I felt my life was over. My heart broke for my loss of a

loving husband and a best friend. But even more than that my heart ached for my children, because they lost a father who absolutely adored them. He was like the pied piper when it came to children. He loved and helped so many. Because he lived in hope, he gave his life in hope.

After one week in Colombo, the children and I headed back to our home in Nuwara Eliya before leaving for Australia.

My heart was aching for something else as well — for the people I had fallen in love with in our church in Nuwara Eliya. How could I say goodbye to them? They were devastated at the loss of their pastor and friend, and now I would also be leaving them. I felt like I was letting them down, giving up.

As we arrived at the home we were about to leave in Nuwara Eliya, the first things I was given as I walked in the door were three letters with cards. I immediately recognised Rohan's handwriting and excused myself. Falling on my bed and crying intensely, I made myself read the cards. Rohan had sent a card to each of his children and to me, telling us how much he loved us and missed us. Telling his children to always follow Jesus and to look after their mother. It was as if he had been saying goodbye and telling them what to do. These letters had been sent the morning of the day Rohan died. Many more tears flowed down my cheeks.

I spent most of the next two days in my room feeling quite devastated and lost. I opened my heart up to God and, in very simple words, just cried out my sadness to Him. I told God how my heart ached for my kids and for the people He gave me to love. I felt so restless inside, so unhappy and bewildered in what I was doing. Then God reminded me of my own testimony of hope and how much

I had come to love the people in Sri Lanka and how I would give my life for them — even to the point that I wanted to spend the rest of my life in Sri Lanka.

Now my husband had been murdered — martyred, paying the ultimate price for his faith. The question remained: what was I going to do with my life from here onwards? I wanted to return to Australia but felt compelled to return to Sri Lanka, because that's where my heart was.

I made a very simple decision to remain in Sri Lanka and continue the pioneer work we had started and to see it established. I was now a single mother of two young children, but I knew that God would supply all my needs and that He would also give me the ability to conquer fear and doubt about my situation. I knew that with God by my side, I could do anything.

Both the Sri Lankan and Australia World Missions were thrilled about my decision to remain in Nuwara Eliya. I continued Rohan's dream, helping his brother Michael and Michael's wife Debbie, who officially took over the work.

Many would say that I was crazy to make the decision to remain in Sri Lanka and some even said I was wrong to do that to my children. But I must say that God has never, ever let my children or me down. Through those early years after Rohan died, our sorrow was turned into great joy and victory.

Although my daughter Sonja and son Nathan had lost their father, many men including Uncles and close friends became role models. At school, teachers reported that they were very stable children who were very caring and a blessing to their school community.

Even though I was busy with my kids and mission, inside I was feeling very lonely and empty. I felt like I had been chopped in half. I think this is what death does because marriage brings two people together as one, and when one dies you feel like part of you is missing. So when people told me time would heal, I couldn't understand. But it is true! Time does heal, and if you can look to the future, concentrating on the positive things in life, then healing will come even though it feels like it never will.

Today, time continues to heal. I am now happily remarried to a wonderful man, Narel Atkinson, who is Sri Lankan. He loves me and truly is my best friend, whom I share all my life with. I appreciate him so much and never want to take our love for granted.

We have three wonderful children, Rebecca, Joshua and Jacob, who are such a delight and blessing from God. I am so grateful for God's faithfulness and hope in all things, even in death.

I did leave Sri Lanka for some years after marrying Narel and during our children's early years, but eventually returned. Now Narel and I are in the process of setting up a recovery centre for abused children, street kids and orphaned children just out of Colombo. We know that this centre is going to be a refuge for many hurting children where they will find love, acceptance and healing.

Sonja is a pre-school teacher and is married to a Sri Lankan man, Kalinga, and they are youth pastors in Sri Lanka. Nathan has just completed his apprenticeship as a carpenter/builder and has a lovely girlfriend. He lives in Australia but is planning to return to work in Sri Lanka.

I am very proud of Sonja and Nathan, not only for what they have achieved but also for standing up for what they believe. God truly has been a Father to them. They love their little sister and two little brothers. They have a lot of love and respect for their stepfather too, which is wonderful.

I am so glad that I didn't give up and go back to Australia when Rohan died but chose to stay where I knew I was meant to be. I learned never ever to give up. Life is too precious. There is hope for the future no matter what may come our way. When the tsunami of Boxing Day 2004 ravaged the shores of Sri Lanka, it brought home once again how precious life is, whether one or 100,000 are lost. I pray that my life will always be a source of hope to those who have lost their own loved ones.

Deborah's Story

'For sudden the worst turns the best to the brave ...'

—◦ ROBERT BROWNING ◦—
'PROSPICE'

On 27 May at about 3 a.m. our phone rang. It was my Dad from South Africa saying that my brother had taken poison. This poison has no smell, taste or colour; he used it to control hungry dogs and wild animals that killed the sheep on our family farm where he was working. I could tell from my Dad's voice that this was very serious.

I felt so far removed, being in Australia. I wanted to be with all of them. We kept talking by phone throughout the night.

It seems that late in the afternoon my brother Braham had spoken with a man who had just purchased the top part of the farm from him to develop for export grapes. Perhaps it was after this meeting that Braham took the poison. He arrived home not long after the meeting and while having a bath told his wife, Hilda, that he had taken poison and that he wanted her just to lie down with him on the bed and hold on to him. It was then that he began to show signs of becoming unconscious. His wife and her brother quickly grabbed him out of the bath and wrapped him in a blanket to put him in the car.

He asked again — if could just stay home! They rushed by car to the nearest hospital, an hour away. On the way there his wife tried to make him vomit a few times in the back of the car. My Mum and Dad met them and escorted them to the hospital, where the staff first pumped his stomach. He sat up once and said to his wife, 'I'm sorry, Hilda, I'm sorry, doctor.' Knowing Braham, he would have also said sorry to God. He went up to intensive care where his heart stopped a few times; they put him on full life-support trying desperately, over and over again, to rescue him.

He died about eleven hours later. The staff allowed my parents and Hilda to stay with Braham for a long time. It was then that my Dad, starting with Braham's hair and head, looked at every healthy part of his body right down to his feet as he had to farewell his beautiful son, who was only forty-three years old. His smile and face were always soft and caring but now all life was gone. My Dad has commented a number of times on how good it was for him to linger with Braham.

My younger brother Jako, who lives in Australia, flew back to South Africa with me for the funeral. Before leaving I could not tell our two children, aged fifteen and seventeen, what had really happened. We simply said that Braham's heart had stopped.

The pain was excruciating. At that time someone came to me and suggested that I had not been able to tell my children because of the shame that goes with suicide, but it had nothing to do with shame — all I felt was intense pain. How could my beautiful, beautiful brother have died in such a horrific way?

When we arrived we went to view his body. He looked so beautiful. I knew I had to cut a piece of Braham's hair for all the family — that would be the only thing we had that was part of him. I was so careful not to cut gaps but to leave him looking right.

I found it so hard, being with the others, to cry. Looking back now, I think it would have been good to have been there with him alone.

I told my Mum I would hate a black hearse. 'Can we go and see what else they have?' I asked. My Mum was so great through all of this. At the end it was a silver hearse. I would have loved a white one. I always say to Michael, my husband, that I would like a white plain coffin and a white hearse with a big pink bow right around when I die. I want this life I lived to be celebrated well!

Going to the funeral I felt such a sense of hopelessness. Amazingly, everyone that spoke at the funeral carried such hope and talked with boldness about Braham's life and how he had loved God. Walking out of there felt so good. We all knew that it was okay.

It seems, looking back now, that there were so many things in Braham's life adding trauma upon trauma. There was the constant fight with hungry dogs, jackals and wild cats (the African kind) killing sheep, not to mention people stealing sheep — loading them up by the truckload. Braham loved his animals so much.

There were incredible years of drought. Once, around thirty-seven farmers worked in that area, but at the end only about five were left, and now my brother is gone too.

Braham began seeing a counsellor about two months before he passed away. I found out later that he was suffering with anxiety attacks.

Returning to Australia after the funeral, I went straight back into a full life with lots of responsibility. I thought there was something wrong with me. I bought a book on grief, and reading it I realised what I was going through was very normal. The tea towel in the kitchen and my top sheet at night took a lot of tears.

We had been back in Australia about two weeks when a very good and respected friend rang and, meaning well, said to Michael, 'Tell them they can live above that, it does not need to affect them.' As Michael shared this with me I felt I should 'shape up and be fine', even though I was dying with pain on the inside. I felt confused many times — knowing I could not talk about it, I needed to be fine.

I remember after the Bali bombing thinking how much we've got to be thankful for — many families never got to see the bodies of their loved ones.

Almost two years after Braham died, our daughter left home to start business college in another city. I felt I was grieving for her leaving home. It was then, as I talked with my very special friend Margaret, that it came out that the grieving process in my life never went further. So Yentl's leaving for college, on top of Braham's loss, was too much to cope with.

I knew I had to go back to South Africa for the two-year anniversary of my brother Braham's death. I had to look at the grief process in my own life and make sure I was working this through properly.

Braham's ashes were still in a little box in my parents' home. We opened it up and took some of the ashes to a very tall mountain on the farm; on the way we picked wild flowers for our little gravesite. It was a beautiful sunny day up there and there was one lone tree — we all felt that this was the perfect place for the ashes, under this tree. The whole day was such a day of healing and release. My Mum made a hole, while my seventy-seven year old Dad sat there watching us. We collected rocks to place on the top. I took a beautiful shrub to plant there. We took photos. Everything was just right. We were all free to express ourselves and do whatever we felt we needed to do. My husband Michael was truly amazing through all of this. I took a little of the ashes and walked away where I could be by myself and made my own little gravesite.

Michael was like a son to my parents. He helped to have a stone engraved and to place the remainder of the ashes at the central church in my parents' city where the family can visit. Our committal service there that day with Michael and myself, my parents, Hilda (Braham's wife), and their two children, Pieter and Eliz Marie, was beautiful. We talked about the food Braham loved. How he could eat a huge meal and then have a large pack of chips after. Pieter shared how his Dad had taught him to drive and to shoot.

While I was still in South Africa I was desperate to do everything I could to work through this. I even went back to the hospital and up to intensive care, to the bed where he died. I took a photo of the empty bed in the corner. I also brought back one of his favourite work jumpers and a polo shirt. It will be special to wear them.

I realise that this is all a process. Healing takes time. I have magnificent memories of a brother who was only one year older than me. He valued people for who they were. His warm presence brought great acceptance to others. He was known for his upright character and integrity. The richness of his life has made *me* feel rich. I have learned from his life that hard work is good but playtime is essential. He had such grace and such a wonderful ability to hear whatever I had to say. I miss him greatly and always will.

I trust that as I live this awesome life, I will deal with every situation well and move on. Here I am today, holding on to hope and feeling great.

Hold on to Hope

How to cope after a loved one has committed suicide

Coping with a loved one's suicide is difficult, but there are things you can do to help you through the process.

- ❖ Allow yourself to go through your feelings about the death. Normal feelings include shock, anger, denial, depression and anxiety.
- ❖ Let go of any self-blame you may have. You can't take responsibility for what someone else does.
- ❖ Get help through your doctor, a good counselling service and at your local church. Don't try to walk this path alone.
- ❖ Look after yourself. Give yourself plenty of time and space. Walk and pray. Listen to soothing music and inspirational words. Light a beautiful-smelling candle to help you relax.
- ❖ Take any pressure off yourself to 'move on' quickly. You will be sorrowful for some time. Rushing won't take away the pain.
- ❖ Purchase a journal to express how you feel and write about all the good times — add in photographs and cards.
- ❖ If you are having trouble sleeping or if you are experiencing ongoing anxiety, talk to your doctor.
- ❖ Support groups are extremely helpful for this type of grief, especially when your family and friends are also facing loss themselves. There is nothing like being with others who understand how you feel.

❖ Understand that there will be good days and not-so-good days, especially initially — but allow yourself time and space and the days will all get brighter for you in the future.

CHAPTER FOUR

Love

love never ends

'I hold it true, whate'er befall;
I feel it, when I sorrow most,
'Tis better to have loved and lost
Than never to have loved at all.'

～ ALFRED, LORD TENNYSON ～
'IN MEMORIAM', 27

Titanic

The *Titanic* was called 'unsinkable', the 'ship of dreams'. It was a dream come true to many aboard, including Jack Dawson (Leonardo DiCaprio). A working-class young man who lived each day by chance and didn't have a cent to his name, he won his ticket on the *Titanic* through a lucky hand in poker. He went on board not knowing that he was going to experience much more than just a boat ride to America.

There was a girl on the *Titanic* by the name of Rose (Kate Winslet). She grew up in high society and was engaged to a very wealthy businessman. Though she would always have every luxury she would ever need or want, she felt as though she was trapped in a prison, not able to live her own life or even dream her own dreams. She finally got to such a point of desperation that she decided to take her own life. But that's where these two opposite worlds collide. Jack saves her from ending her life, marking the beginning of a great friendship and a great love.

Even in the midst of the tragic story of the *Titanic*, they fight for each other's lives until the end. And though Jack does not survive the sinking of the great ship, his memory and love live on forever in Rose. Even as an old woman (nearly a hundred years old!), as she tells this story her love for him seems even stronger than when he was actually with her. She never lets go of the life and love that she gained from him.

The Eternity moment in this movie is when, knowing he would die, Jack spoke life into Rose so she could keep on living. The power of his selfless love rescued her. Though Jack did not live, his selfless love lived on in Rose. This love is so important to have in every relationship in our lives. When someone we love so dearly passes into Eternity, their love, a part of them, still lives on in us. It sounds backwards, but their death can actually propel us into a fuller life.

When Jack dies, Rose is left, half frozen, clinging to a piece of wood in the ocean. There is a moment when she considers whether to save her life or to die and join Jack in Eternity sooner rather than later. But then she remembers he has told her never to let go, and that she's going to die an old woman, warm in her bed. And that pushes her to get help and save herself. She ends up living the life that they were going to live together. She takes the higher road after his death and their tragic experience.

Though there seemed to be no hope, she saw a glimmer of hope and grabbed on to it with everything she had. She lived her life to the absolute fullest and, in the end, was reunited with Jack in Eternity. Love is one of the only things, if not the only thing, in this life that is eternal.

Love

*'Love does not delight in evil
but rejoices with the truth.
It always protects, always trusts,
always hopes, always perseveres.
Love never fails.'*

1 CORINTHIANS 13:6–8
THE BIBLE

My friend Linda sent me an email about love and what it means to some people — in this case, children. A group of psychologists in the United States asked a group of children aged between four and eight, 'What does love mean?' The answers they received were broader and deeper than anyone could have imagined.

'When my Grandmother got arthritis, she couldn't bend over and paint her toenails any more. So my Grandfather does it for her all the time, even when his hands got arthritis too. That's love.'

— REBECCA (AGED 8) —

'Love is what makes you smile when you're tired.'

— TERRI (AGED 4) —

'Love is like a little old woman and a little old man who are still friends even after they know each other so well.'

— TOMMY (AGED 6) —

'Love is when Mummy gives Daddy the best piece of chicken.'

— ELAINE (AGED 5) —

'When you love somebody, your eyelashes go up and down and little stars come out of you.' [What an imagination!]

— KAREN (AGED 7) —

'You really shouldn't say "I love you" unless you mean it. But if you mean it, you should say it a lot. People forget.'

—◦ JESSICA (AGED 8) ◦—

The purpose for the questioning was to find the most caring child. The winner was a four-year-old whose next-door neighbour was an elderly gentleman who had recently lost his wife. Upon seeing the man cry, the little boy went into the old gentleman's yard, climbed onto his lap, and just sat there. When his mother asked what he had said to the neighbour, the little boy said, 'Nothing, I just helped him cry.'

It really hurts when we have to say goodbye to someone when we simply don't want to. There are some who find it harder than others to say goodbye. I for one am a sop when it comes to things such as airport farewells, and I really do not like to say goodbye. I much prefer to say 'see you soon'. Goodbye is so final. It's closure. It's the end of something. It tends to go against the grain for some of us.

I can remember as a little girl growing up, every time we lost a beloved family pet — usually a cat because my mother collected any stray that needed a little tender loving care — hearing my mother say, 'We aren't going to have any more pets. It's too hard to say goodbye.' A little later after the initial pain had passed I would hear her say, 'Having that precious animal was worth it — even if we had to say goodbye.'

It's that tension that seems so cruel and it's that tension that keeps some people from wanting to get involved; from wanting to get in too deep, just in case they get hurt or have to one day say goodbye.

I remember shedding a tear on my wedding day as I said 'I do' to my husband, when I thought of the day I would have to say goodbye. I started to miss him ahead of time. Ridiculous maybe, but nevertheless my reality.

What is love and why is it such a powerful force? Our memory holds on to both positive and negative emotions long after the events of life have happened. Some memories are set in concrete and other memories are set in jelly — they tend to move around a bit. When we face the loss of someone we love we often hold on to the good, and the negative dissipates quickly. That's love and that's what it should be like while we still have that person here on earth. Love is often more forgiving in loss than it is in life.

I want to challenge and encourage you to love with Eternity in mind. Love is forgiving. Forgive now while you can let the person know that they are forgiven and loved by you. It's sad when the nicest things said of a person are said about them once they have gone and not actually *to* them while they are living.

When we understand what love really is it will help us understand why our heart aches so much to say goodbye to the ones we love. Love has many meanings in English. Each of its meanings reflects the many and varied feelings that accompany it. It can mean an intense feeling of affection, an emotion or an emotional state. In everyday use, it usually refers to interpersonal love. Love is the cohesive power of attraction throughout the ages. Love lives in the heart. It is a quality of our soul.

Love was the impelling motive for creation. It is the creative, attractive force on the earth. Love is magnetic, powerful; it creates understanding and is radiant. It is the unifying agent of universal design and it cannot be limited to one person because it flows constantly from and to and through everything. Love solders relationships. The power of love melts away all distinctions and makes us individuals of soul and spirit, not just body. Love embraces the entire being. We don't fall in love intellectually. Instead, we receive a total image of the person and we respond according to the impression that they have left with us. For example, things that are left with us may be their body (image and appearance), mind (what they said or didn't say), and soul (how we felt when we were in their presence).

Deep, tender affection, romantic attraction, a sense of oneness, intense desire or emotional attachment — we call it all love, and love to us is to feel or express any of these. The ancient Greeks had four different words we translate as 'love'. It is important to understand the difference between the words.

Eros love

* romantic love
* passionate love
* affectionate love.

Phileo love

* relational love
* the love of our family
* the love of our friends.

Storge love

* instinctive, automatic love
* protecting and nurturing love
* love for the sake of loving.

Agape love

* the unconditional love of God for people
* the love of people for God
* the unselfish love of people for others.

Human love is very powerful, but we need to understand that human love isn't perfect, is conditional and will at some stage fail. That's when we need to draw on a love that is greater than our relational, human love. That's why we need to draw on the highest form of love, which is unconditional. Humans have a natural inbuilt capacity to love and a desire to be loved. Love is not only a feeling, it is also an active expression of our will. It is a matter not only of the heart but also of the mind. In life we can choose what we want to love, when we want to love, and how we are going to express our love. We stand or fall in love.

Our most common understanding of love is that it is an emotion. Love is a stirring of one's heart. Love melts the soul and softens the heart. Love can bring delight and fulfilment to the soul as much as pain and sadness can. Love, however, is more than just an emotion. When you truly love it changes your life. Love transforms people's ideas of happiness, fulfilment and meaning.

Love endures throughout Eternity. Love comes from within the soul, and always implies 'another', the object of one's love. It requires us to focus our attention on the other person, to the extent of sacrificing one's self so that the other might benefit from our love.

French philosopher Descartes stated, 'I think, therefore I am' (*Cogito, ergo sum*). However, I believe a deeper revelation of our existence is found in the Latin words *Amo, ergo sum*, meaning 'I love, therefore I am'. But without God, love would not exist. Because God not only loves, He is love, therefore we exist and therefore we love. Love and only love lasts forever.

The pursuit and expression of genuine love should be the goal for our life. Loving should come naturally, but sometimes, because of pain and hurt, love ceases to operate in our lives. Sometimes we are afraid of love and we are afraid to love. Best not go there! Best just remain an island where no-one can come close, where we don't inflict pain, where we don't get hurt. But that's not the way we have been designed to live.

Love has a definite character — it is full of extravagant patience and hope. It is with that character of love that I want my life to be branded. I gave my husband Jonathan a fantastic book called *Lovemarks: The Future Beyond Brands* by Kevin Roberts, the CEO of Saatchi and Saatchi.[4] In this book Kevin Roberts talks about a future in marketing, beyond brands. The concept is that people are looking for more than just a good product with an identifiable trademark and an appealing brand; they are looking for a connection with the product itself. That connection is created by a feeling for or identification with a product that can't necessarily be defined but goes beyond a rational decision based on price, predictability or practicality. People buy the product for emotional reasons. 'I like it, I prefer it, I feel good about it.' The connection is created, a loyalty is generated and that product, trademark, brand becomes a lovemark to them. I can think of several for me: Disney anything; Qantas (my favourite airline); Vegemite; Levis.

My husband Jonathan was inspired by the book and talked about a principle he felt the book highlighted because people are looking for connection in life. People are looking for something that will touch their lives, and the experiences that touch our lives, both good and bad, leave an impression on us that can either be a mark or a scar. Marks can bring connection and identification with people who have faced similar experiences; scars will cause pain and disconnection. We can live marked for life or scarred for life. It's our choice but it makes a world of difference to the way we live, love and relate to people in our world. Personally, I choose to live *marked for life*.

When we walk through life marked by love, we become so different that we are unrecognisable from what we were. The following are examples of things that can mark our lives for good, at times when they could be scarred by pain.

Personal responsibility

In a world that is marked by people shifting blame and responsibility, we need to take personal responsibility for the life we now have.

❖ We need to face our pain and look for ways of dealing with it positively.
❖ We need to stop hiding away, and look life in the face again.
❖ We need to stop blaming others or even God for what has happened, and let it go.

A renewed mind

The greatest curse and the greatest blessing can come to us through the way we think. Our mind is the gateway to our heart; as a famous proverb says, 'For as a man thinks in his heart, so he is' (Proverbs 23:7). Our mind is the battleground of our soul. It is important to realise that we have a role to play in the renewing of our mind.

❖ Allow your belief system to be challenged; previous experience versus the truth.
❖ Read positive, inspiring stories of hope that will lift your spirit.
❖ Capture and lock away thoughts that will only keep you trapped in grief and sorrow. Don't go there!

Focus on others

Sometimes, even in the midst of grief, we need to think of others so that we can become a better person through the experience of loss. When many people are hurting at the same time about the same thing, someone at sometime must give way for there to be a breakthrough.

- Focusing on another person's pain will help alleviate your own pain.
- Empathy allows you to know there are others worse off than you.
- Loving others will cause them to hurt less. Love will ease the pain.

As a little girl, I only knew love and happiness. I didn't know loss and pain until my Grandfather passed away. Up until that point I had experienced nothing in my life to cause me to grieve. Grief was something that I wasn't familiar with and something that as a seven-year-old I was very afraid of.

I thought I had done something to cause my poppy to go away. I thought that it was because I wasn't nice to my sister or because I hadn't tidied my toys. I didn't understand that not having him around any more wasn't a direct result of something I had done. Inside of me, I wanted — I needed — it to be my fault, so that I could at least try to fix it. If it was me that caused him to go away, then maybe it could be me that could cause him to come back again.

My little mind was so confused and so full of pain. It was hard — no, impossible — to reconcile what had happened.

I have vague recollections of my Mum, Dad and Nan going off to the hospital to visit Poppy and leaving us with my Aunty and Uncle, but I didn't understand what was really going on and I simply believed that everything would be okay because everything was always okay.

So what about Poppy? Why couldn't he just come home? Why was he being held away from me, from us? I couldn't understand, so I started to write. I wrote love letters to my Poppy and to Jesus, my friend, and I stuck them up all around the house. I couldn't sit on Poppy's strong knee any more and tell him how much I loved him, but I had to express myself. I simply couldn't hold it in. I thought I was going to die, but I didn't really understand what that meant either. I knew what it was to lose someone I loved, but the reality of death still didn't sink in. I was just too young to understand. I didn't know that I didn't need to be afraid.

Where God's love is absent, fear will prevail. God's love drives out all fear. The fear within human beings comes from a lack of trust that we develop over time. When you lose someone the one thing you crave is a sense of security and comfort. Fear wants to consume us at our greatest point of need. When we give way to fear we are likely to give up hope and slip into despair.

Children are no exception; at a time of loss, there seems to be much to fear.

❖ Adults around them are upset, sad and angry, and conversing with others in tones that reveal emotional distress.
❖ They know something is wrong but do not know what it is or cannot understand the reason.
❖ Changes occur in their family life.
❖ Daily routines may change as family members take care of arrangements.

To help children deal with this or any other tragedy, it is important to recognise that they may react differently than adults. Young children have a hard time identifying and verbalising their feelings. Children perceive events egocentrically and tend to blame themselves for events around them. Therefore it is important that adults carefully observe children during stressful events and recognise signs of distress. Signs to look for in young children include:

- ❖ changes in eating and sleeping habits
- ❖ fear of separation and refusal to let the parent or caregiver depart
- ❖ refusal or reluctance to go to school
- ❖ frequent crying spells
- ❖ rebellious or aggressive behaviours
- ❖ regressive behaviour such as thumb-sucking and bed-wetting
- ❖ nightmares
- ❖ avoidance of interactions with other children.

With older children, look for:

- ❖ signs of depression and hopelessness
- ❖ anger and acting out
- ❖ social withdrawal. [5]

Talking with children and allowing them to talk is essential. One way that adults can help children cope with tragedy, fear and grief is to maintain structure and routine. It is important for children to have a sense of security and predictability in their lives. As far as possible, continue with familiar routines for sleeping, eating, playtime and other regularly scheduled activities.

I had absolutely no concept before the news of Poppy's passing that such a thing could happen. My parents thought it wise to protect us from the concept of death until we had to face it. I understand and appreciate their choices. They chose this way because they thought it best, because we were too young to understand, and because they themselves were not secure about Eternity. That security was yet to come.

I didn't realise how affected I was by my first loss experience until I said goodbye to my Nanny and saw her into Eternity. I finally had closure on something that had remained uncertain. I was thirty-five years old when I said goodbye to Nanny. This experience became a defining moment in my life and something was 'broken off' me that had kept me afraid for many years. Even though I have believed in God and Heaven ever since I can remember, there was an element of mystery about what actually happens at that moment when the one you love passes from here to Eternity.

Love is made complete in Eternity. Faith and hope are necessary for living here on earth and to pave the way for us to enter Eternity, but when we arrive in Heaven we don't take faith and hope with us. We don't need faith and hope in Heaven. Love is all that remains. The more we express our love sacrificially and selflessly, the more we are preparing to love in Eternity.

The full meaning of human love is found when we take part in our Creator's love. When we accept His love for us and recognise His love for others, our love capacity is strengthened and through that we become better givers of love. We also become better givers of love when we understand the characteristics of God's eternal love and try to live out those characteristics. Eternal love is unconditional and since God loves us so much, He encourages us also to love one another. God's love is then the model and the incentive for our love. The key that opens the gates of Heaven is love.

May the warmth of unconditional love fill your heart and take you one step further over Eternity's rainbow.

Love

'"Which is the greatest of all the commandments?"
Jesus replied, "Love the Lord your God
with all your heart, mind and strength,
and love your neighbour as yourself."'

– MARK 12:28 –
THE BIBLE

Eden's Story

I am the daughter of a pastor and the granddaughter of a pastor. Being raised in a family that is completely devoted to loving and helping people is something I am grateful for. My Eternity story is about the very first time I experienced loss in my life and it is a reflection of what ministry is really about. Knowing about and believing in Eternity doesn't take away the pain of having to say goodbye to someone you love. It just gives you the ability to hold on to precious memories and to be committed to making good memories for others in your own lifetime.

I once heard a quote in a movie about how everything we do has an echo in Eternity, and it never left me. Hearing it made me realise that I'm not here by mere chance, but I have a purpose in this world. Watching my Grandpa for sixteen years reaffirmed this belief in my heart. His life changed thousands of lives and made us realise that life is a gift and what you do with it should echo in Eternity.

At a young age my Grandpa took sick with rheumatic fever and at the age of fifteen his heart was so enlarged that the doctors had given him up to die. But my Grandpa had a wonderful Grandma who took him to a gospel meeting. His condition was so poor that they didn't know if he would make the trip. He was carried into the meeting on a stretcher and God miraculously healed him.

As great as this miracle was, he always felt that the greatest thing that happened to him was the day he dedicated his life to God. Together with my Grandma, he devoted his life to helping all kinds of people. Hospitals, prisons, streets, nursing homes, schools, colleges — anywhere where there were people, my Grandpa was there making friends and helping make people's lives better. His faith caused him to be without fear. He would go into places to share love and hope where others refused to go.

He loved to pray for the sick and saw many wonderful answers to prayer and many miracles. My Grandpa was a phenomenal man! I can't remember one day when he wasn't smiling. He was full of such joy and peace that everyone loved to be around him. I loved to be around him. His passion and purpose could get anyone excited. He never took a moment of his life for granted. He lived each day like it was his last. And his words were always encouraging and uplifting.

On Friday, 8 March 2002, after a church service, my family all drove off in separate cars towards the restaurant where we were going to have a late-night snack. I saw Grandpa in his car as we drove by. He looked like he was having a little rest. We got to the restaurant and my Dad got a call and he and my Mum went to the hospital. We waited at home for hours, then my Mum and Dad got back from the hospital and we heard the news. Grandpa was gone.

How could he be gone? Grandpa was so full of life that I couldn't imagine what mine would be like now without him. Before this I had never experienced the unbearable pain that death could bring. I wanted to see him again and hold him and tell him how much I loved him. I wanted him to walk through the door and say, 'Just joking!'

We didn't get to say goodbye to my Grandpa, so we really made sure that we said farewell to him at his

memorial service. This service was forever memorable! Two
thousand people came to celebrate the life of my Grandpa.
He had touched and changed so many people's lives
forever.

Losing him was a very hard year for me, as I felt very
lost and hurt at times. Yet while I was missing him so
much, I experienced a peace that never left my heart. I will
always miss him, but because I believe in Eternity I know
that my Grandpa is there and I will see him again one day.

I visit his gravesite often. It's a place where I can go to
just think and reflect on a life that challenges me to live as
fully as I can. My Grandpa's life inspires me to live for
helping people and to continue the legacy he left in my
heart for others. I am truly blessed to have been a part of
his life — a life well spent, a life that echoes in Eternity.

Jeff's Story

Losing a loved one to an AIDS-related illness is one of the hardest experiences one can go through. It isn't something that has a quick end to it; the grief that is attached to it, and the understanding of the loss that is to come, start years before, at the point of detection. In many cases the grief and pain start once you experience a loss, but if someone is dying of an AIDS-related illness you live it with them every day, as the person slowly wastes away from a vibrant, active individual to a bedridden skeleton, and there is nothing you can do. It may take many years to get to this point and this makes it harder as it is dragged out over time.

I remember my brother telling me that he was HIV-positive, and how he laughed it off. He tried to deal with the news he had just received the best way he could. His very words were that it was 'very trendy', but this was his way of dealing with tragedy. Over time I saw that the underlying reality was starting to come out in the way he thought of life in general, not only his life.

One day we were sitting in the lounge room and I could feel his sense of despair as he looked around, as though he was just thinking that everything he had worked for was for nothing. Then he just sat and stared. Yet still in the silence of the room he turned to me and smiled. It was as though he was trying to say that it was all right without uttering a word. He was endeavouring to find peace and accept the inevitable. If there was ever a time I loved my brother the most it was now. As youngsters we fought like cat and dog, but here we were now standing united together in the midst of tribulation, in a bond of love.

He believed in living life to the full as long as he could; there was nothing going to stop him from taking hold of every opportunity. Soon after his diagnosis he planned an overseas trip with his partner and off they went: travelling around Europe, racing down the autobahns of Germany, making up for lost time. Knowing very well that whatever he saw or did on his travels would be for the last time.

Dealing with an upcoming loss, I had to focus on the fact that I had been blessed. This person had been put in my life for a reason and I should be thankful. For I found that no matter how real grief is, it could become an inward focus and so powerfully consuming if I allowed it to be.

I remember being at the hospice and walking onto the balcony and crying, saying to the nurse how unfair it was. She agreed with what I had said, as I felt so helpless in the whole situation. There were others in the hospice in the same circumstances. They were mums and dads, sisters and brothers visiting their loved ones. There seemed to be a bond of understanding and support between the visitors as we were all there for the same reason, yet no words were spoken, we just had a smile for each other. It could be called a kindred spirit, yet not all were Christians as I was.

As I changed my focus from myself, I turned it to God for His strength and understanding, for His comfort and grace in my time of need. However, more important was the need for my brother to know about and receive the gift of Eternity in Heaven. As I drew closer to God I found that the peace and strength I needed was there and that the sadness I had faced for so long was changing to a hope that the time would come for my beloved brother to step into Eternity in Heaven with his Heavenly Father, who accepted and loved him more than words can express.

Throughout all of my brother's illness his partner had been a tower of strength, taking him to many hospital visits, maintaining the home, being everything that was required and in the end being faithfully beside him till his last breath. In this time of feeling unable to be as great a help as I desired, I found my role was to love, pray and believe. Time has passed, and although I don't find myself dwelling on what happened every moment of every day, it is definitely something that has made a mark on my life. It is something that I knew one day I would need to talk about to help others going through the same situation. I decided to write a book entitled *Homosexual to Husband*[6] where I describe my brother's last days:

> *'Soon my brother was seriously ill and confined to hospital. I was praying every day that he would be reconciled to the Father and healed. He was a man whose company I hadn't enjoyed until later in life, and now he was facing death. I didn't want to lose him, because I had learned to love him. I remember sitting in the hospice room in a corner while the family was standing beside the bed. The words of an old hymn were ringing in my head: "Be bold, be strong, for the Lord thy God is with thee."*
>
> *It got louder and louder until I responded — a bit slowly, but I was only a new Christian. I simply said, "If it was you, Lord, take these people out of the room." To my surprise everyone walked out. I asked for the words to say, and they were so simple. I held my brother's hand and told him how*

much I loved him and how much Jesus loved him. 'When you have had enough and you want to close your eyes for the last time, ask Jesus to take you home.' Simple words — nothing fancy.

After this the family returned to the room. There was an incredible peace and a sense of the Lord in the room. My brother responded by looking at me with drug-glazed eyes, unable to speak. I remembered a good friend telling me, "Where there is spirit there is life", and that God can bypass the mind and speak into the heart . . .'

My brother slipped into a coma and died three days later. I believe God honoured my prayers for my bro's salvation.

I found that the peace that had entered the room was so comforting, sadness dissipated and there was no need even to see him any more. He had been born again and my role was finished. The grief that had encompassed me had turned to joy. At the funeral I had an inner peace; I missed my brother but was not consumed with the loss. I miss him even now as I write, but the love we shared in the last few years sustains me and blesses me. I have found myself talking to him and shedding a tear when there is something new in my life, being unable to share it with him as I used to do. I feel so loved, but I do miss that there is no-one any more to call me 'little brother'.

My bro can never be replaced. He was unique and he was mine. I thank God for His comfort then and now. He gives me strength when I am weak. I carry my bro's memory with me always and can still laugh at the times we used to take out vintage cars and have them break down every time. I can see him driving down the road in my Dad's MG with a huge Christmas tree hanging out of it. I can see his hurt when he couldn't understand how God could let our mother die at only forty years of age. However, it was his love and finally his Eternity that is the greatest memory of all. God has healed the disappointment of the years that we used to fight and left the happy memories. And of course, love.

Love in Action

How we can put our love into action

❖ *Who is my neighbour?*
Two thousand years after the parable of the Good Samaritan was first told, some are still asking the question, 'Who is my neighbour?' perhaps hoping that it won't be someone *really* in need.

❖ *The challenge*
This parable was given to challenge the 'religious' leaders of the day. Today, the parable compels us to challenge our own faith. Do we really care about people in need?

❖ *The scene then*
There were four main characters in the parable: the victim, the priest, the Levite and the Samaritan. The only thing we know for certain about the victim is that he was in great need. He had been beaten and was wounded, bleeding and possibly dying. We don't know why he was beaten; that was irrelevant.

❖ *The scene now*
Today, as many as 46 million people are infected with the AIDS virus. In southern Africa, one in five adults is infected. There is so much suffering of so many kinds in our world. Jesus, in the parable of the good Samaritan, encourages us to look to the needs of the suffering and those cast out by society.

❖ *Love, not judgment*

In truth, we are bound to respond to all those beaten and left by the side of the road by this devastating virus. We don't need to judge, we just need to love.

❖ *Our response*

The parable of the Good Samaritan ends with a powerful challenge. When Jesus asked the expert in the law which of the three men had been a neighbour to the man lying on the side of the road, he could only answer, 'The one who had mercy on him.' Jesus then looked at this man and concluded what is perhaps the most powerful moral teaching in all of history with a command of just four words. 'Go and do likewise.'

CHAPTER FIVE

Comfort

heaven's embrace

'If you look for truth, you may find comfort in the end;
if you look for comfort, you will not get either comfort or truth;
only soft soap and wishful thinking to begin,
and in the end, despair.'

— C.S. LEWIS —
MERE CHRISTIANITY

Ghost

Ghost is a love story, a supernatural tale and a murder-mystery thriller with a little comedy mixed in, all blended together to make a powerful and emotionally evocative movie.

The story opens with a young couple, Molly Jensen and Sam Wheat (Demi Moore and Patrick Swayze). Tragedy befalls the happy couple when Sam is murdered during a night robbery by a thug, Willie Lopez (Rick Aviles), who was supposedly after money.

Sam's presence, however, lives on. His spirit hangs around their dream apartment at first, wishing to comfort his grieving love, but unable to do so. When his murderer comes back into the apartment, Sam follows Willie back to his place on the rundown side of town. Sam decides to seek help to find out more about why his presence is still on earth after his death.

When he finds out who is really behind his murder, and why he was killed, Sam resolves not only to protect Molly, but also to get some justice, with the help of would-be medium Oda Mae Brown (Whoopi Goldberg).

There are two Eternity moments in this movie. One is in the beginning when Sam is murdered and Molly is left by herself in the new apartment. The second is at the end, when Molly finally believes and she sees Sam for the last time. Sam says farewell, till they meet again in Heaven, and they kiss and he walks into the 'light'.

Heaven is portrayed as something up in the sky. Before his soul could get to Heaven, Sam had to take care of business on earth. In the movie the logic goes that before you can arrive in Heaven there must be a finish to your earth life so nothing is holding you back.

Although this movie is 'make-believe', we feel deeply emotional about Sam's death and return because it portrays the cry of the human heart to put right the wrongs in this life and to be reunited with our loved ones in Eternity.

Comfort

'The Lord is my shepherd, I shall not lack.
He makes me lie down in green pastures,
He leads me beside quiet waters,
He restores my soul.
He guides me in paths of righteousness for His name's sake.
Even though I walk through the valley of the shadow of death,
I will fear no evil, for You are with me;
Your rod and Your staff, they comfort me.
You prepare a table before me in the presence of my enemies.
You anoint my head with oil; my cup overflows.
Surely goodness and love will follow me all the days of my life,
and I will dwell in the house of the Lord forever.'

— PSALM 23 —
THE BIBLE

MY KIDS LOVE ME TO sit on the side of their beds, or even hop into their beds at night for a cuddle before they go to sleep. It brings them comfort when I am close to them; I don't even have to say anything. Comfort comes through physical, emotional and spiritual embrace. Being there ... a foot touching ... no words needed — just being there. Comfort is a deep sense of ease and security that brings peace. Comfort is not just a feeling — it is a vital element of life.

Comfort is a state of being relaxed. Comfort is also reflected in the feeling of freedom from worry or disappointment. It is also, in one form, consolation, which is the relief of affliction or the ease of bereavement. When we receive comfort, we receive emotional strength. Comfort also comes from reading words that feed the soul.

The words of Psalm 23 are well known and loved by many. This beautiful psalm, beginning with 'The Lord is my shepherd', has served over and over to bring great comfort to my own family in our greatest time of need. They are more than poetic, they are life-giving, if you really believe what they say. This psalm presents a vivid image of a shepherd guarding his sheep as they walk through a dark valley and the presence of the shepherd and the touch of his staff being a source of comfort to the sheep. The individual passing from time into Eternity walks through a similar valley and they need the presence, touch, comfort and words of loved ones around this time, as they embark on their journey.

Mountaineer Joe Simpson fell into a crevasse and was left for dead when his friend cut a rope that was holding them together, in order to save one life rather than lose two. In his book *Touching the Void*, Joe talked about the thing he feared most, which was to die alone. Family and friends who are providing comfort to a loved one are themselves also walking through this valley, and need comfort too — words of encouragement, the presence of family and friends, counsel and support. This is also a time when the greatest comfort of all for the person walking through the valley from this world to the next is their own personal faith.

The other picture that is clear in this psalm is of the valley, which is like a corridor between two spacious places or plains. For the person leaving this world, it is the spacious plain that they have lived in, in time, leading into a spacious place in Eternity. For the family and friends who stay, it is that valley or corridor between a world with the one they love to a world without the one they love. This is an important and necessary valley for everyone involved to walk through. A corridor is a place we walk through, not live in. Sadly, many people spend too long in that corridor. With the comfort of family, friends and faith, however, that journey can be deeply significant and meaningful and can bring great hope for the future.

One of the amazingly positive things that happens in corridors is that you meet people: people you don't normally meet; people you haven't seen for a long time. Often discussions are had, forgiveness given and relationships restored as people stand in the corridors of hospitals realising what is really important. It can be a powerful place of connecting, regrouping and families helping each other to walk through this valley united and together. Corridors can actually become places of comfort.

One of our greatest sources of comfort is people, whether family and friends or complete strangers. And when we choose to look up for comfort, our cry is heard and a plan for our comfort is put in motion. Eternity speaks to the hearts of those willing to listen and it assigns us the role of bringing comfort to others. God's method of comfort is humanity. I saw an interview once on *Enough Rope* with Andrew Denton where three priests were interviewed on faith. Denton asked one of the priests why God would let forty teenagers die of a drug overdose if he really cares about us. The priest answered, 'God completely cares but it was us who were sleeping while those kids were killing themselves. It's our responsibility to make a difference. God has called us to do something.' We can bring comfort to others.

All of us, at some point in our lives, have experienced loss or change. It is one thing that unites us as human beings. Loss is the great human equaliser and grief is the natural response to any loss or change in our lives. Just take a moment and acknowledge losses and changes you may have experienced.

Grief is a spiral of feelings and reactions. It is not a line with a beginning and an end. It can be a roller-coaster ride of unexpected memory triggers. At the Centre for Living with Dying, these triggers are described as being like landmines because they are sudden and unexpected.

There are three types of landmines:

◈ sensory triggers
◈ memory triggers
◈ time triggers.

Trauma research shows us that stress and trauma are taken in through the senses, so even when our mind is keeping a distance, we are still imprinting in our brain all of the details of the illness, the trauma, the pain. This occurs in both witnessed trauma and imagined trauma. Trauma and grief know no time. It doesn't seem to matter how long ago the grief happened, sometimes, when we hit a landmine, it feels like it happened moments ago. Current grief can stir up grief that we have experienced in the past. So not only do we need to deal with present losses, but we may have to deal with the past as well.

Comfort is something that needs to touch every element of who we are for it to take full effect. We are taught at school that we have five senses:

◈ sight
◈ hearing
◈ touch
◈ smell
◈ taste.

Our senses respond to information that is received through various triggers or signals. Ensuring that each of these five senses receives comfort is an important part of the healing process.

◈ **Sight or visual therapy**
When we have had to say goodbye to someone we love and when we know we will never see them again, in order for our sight to be comforted we need to ensure that we lock into the positive memories of our loved one or ones, and that we remember them at their very best. Having pictures framed and in places of prominence will help with the process. Initially you may find it difficult to look at photographs, but over time, these pictures will help you bring your loved one home in your heart.

An article of clothing, jewellery or even a blanket is something that may help to bring you comfort as you look with eyes that remember the good times. Sometimes it's too difficult to see the room where your loved one once slept — the bed, the wardrobe, the drawers. That moment of seeing those surroundings for the first time after your loss is very personal and can bring comfort to some and trauma to others. Some people simply cannot face seeing life as it once was, so they close the door and never go through it again. Others seem to be able to work away at sorting through everything in order to start life again. Some even keep a memorial place — exactly as it was left, out of respect for the memory of their beloved. Neither is right or wrong, just different.

When it comes to receiving comfort, you need to be able to face your surroundings in a way that brings you hope and not further pain. Take your time to decide what you want to do with the way your home will need to be in the future, but remember that your loved one will always remain in the eyes of your heart and soul, even if their belongings are packed away.

Your 'vision' at this point is important. That is, what you see not just with your eyes, but with your heart. You may need to take on some 'visual therapy' to help you regain the strength of your vision if you feel that you can't see past today. Visual therapy is where we tap into 'imagineering'. We get to see in our imagination how we want things to be. We can turn nightmares into dreams through changing the way we see things.

Perhaps a simple walk in a beautiful garden will be something that can help your vision. Looking at the beauty of nature can help reduce stress and anxiety, and when you are more relaxed, you will feel comforted. Tranquil environments contribute to comfort and help to disperse unhelpful thoughts. They allow for time to pass at a pace you can manage. Creation is there to help bring us comfort, as nature is part of our healing process. See the arms of your Heavenly Father holding you close.

❖ Sound or music therapy

Comfort can come through the sound of tears. It is very difficult to receive comfort if we are unable to mourn. Something that has helped me tremendously is to recall conversations and words of encouragement that were spoken by my loved ones. These words echo in my mind and heart even though I haven't heard them audibly for many years now. Sound is something that brings us comfort. We can hear in our spirit and we can hear with our hearts as well as our ears.

We need to fill our hearts with the sound of hope. My favourite method is through music and through listening to inspirational messages from men and women who speak words of hope into my life. You can choose what to listen to when you are grieving the loss of a loved one. You can listen to people around you who have no hope, or you can find some Eternity friends who are going to speak words of life to you and not words that will make you feel worse about what you're going through. Open your ears to songs of hope, words of inspiration and friends who will encourage you.

I have found music to be a key to my healing process. You can simply turn the radio on or put on a CD, or you can take part in some music therapy to help ease the pain and to bring comfort into your world. Music therapy is the use of music and music-related activities to promote emotional and mental growth. It is an established technique that addresses a range of physical and psychological conditions. Music can make the difference between isolation and interaction.

Music is an incredibly powerful form of expression. Certain songs can trigger specific memories in one's mind. There is no doubt that there is a strong connection between music and our feelings. Not all of us like to just start pouring our hearts out. Through music, however, we can feel safe to unlock our feelings at our own pace, in our own time and in our own space.

✤ Touch or massage therapy

I miss the touch that only my precious Nanny could give. She stroked my back, my arm, my hair, every day. I miss her touch. I miss the comfort of her touch.

Perhaps you have lost the one who brought you physical touch and you can't imagine anyone being able to comfort you in that way again. Physical touch is vitally important to our wellbeing so it's something that you'll need to seek out through the hugs of family and friends.

Sometimes grief can cause us to turn to the wrong places for comfort; this will only cause more heartache in the long run. You will need to be touched and embraced, but be careful not to fall into someone's arms just for that purpose.

You may even find comfort through massage therapy. A friend of mine is a massage therapist. Heather is not married and she says that massage therapy is vital to her wellbeing, as it is her only regular form of human touch. Heather has many stories about the comfort that massage brings.

'One story that comes to mind is of a man in his late forties. He and his wife and kids had been clients of our massage clinic for about two years when he was suddenly diagnosed with lung cancer and given around six months to live. It was particularly

shocking because he had always been such a healthy, strong, outspoken and successful businessman.

The first place they came upon hearing of the diagnosis was to our clinic, where I taught his wife some very basic massage strokes. Every night until he passed away she would give him a massage. It had become a powerful tool to convey to her husband how much she loved him and wanted to make him comfortable. He told me in that time how they had grown so much closer because of this massage time and how it was one of the only things that helped him calm his anxiety and control his pain.'

This story demonstrates the power of positive touch in unlocking emotions and how it can help people to connect with the ones they love.

Just as a mechanic has many different tools, there are dozens of different types of massage therapy and complementary therapies that promote overall wellbeing. Many varieties of massage have been around for centuries and are rooted in traditional beliefs. Many modern styles of massage use techniques aimed at addressing very specific ailments or conditions. Discover the amazing variety of massage therapy styles and techniques. You're almost certain to find one that suits you perfectly.

❖ Smell or scent therapy

A baked dinner, Youth Dew perfume by Estee Lauder, Thirroul Beach, hot scones. All smells that remind me of my Nanny.

Nanny loved the perfume of fresh lilies so I ensured that she had an unending supply of them while she was in hospital. These flowers became so precious — the scent, however, is something that I find really difficult now. Baked dinner and hot scones are scents of comfort, but the scent of lilies makes me remember her in hospital.

Of the five senses, the one most likely to trigger our memories is the sense of smell. When a smell links to an important event in our lives it can engender waves of emotions or reactions that take us back in time. For example, if you smell hot cross buns, you might think about Easter. Unfortunately, some of our negative experiences may also be associated with a fragrance, and when you smell that scent again, you may become agitated, unhappy, or frightened.

Fill your home and life with scents that bring you comfort and hope. Whenever you face a scent that causes you to feel despair, do what you can to relate it to now and not the past. The smell of your family home may be something that you will need to become used to again, or the scent of your husband's car. Create a new memory relating to the scent in order to gain comfort.

To find out more about scents that will help bring you comfort, speak to an aromatherapy expert. Certain aromatherapy oils are wonderful to help alleviate stress, such as bergamot, chamomile, geranium and lavender. Although these aromas may be good for you, their scent may make you feel uneasy, so test-drive some for yourself. Speak to an expert; smell each of the essential oils and pay attention to how you react to the fragrance. Some you are going to like, others you won't. When you find the two or three that you like, you can start making a blend that will be just right for you.

❖ Bath — add drops of the essential oils into the bath as directed. Sit back and enjoy!

❖ Massage — add drops of the essential oils as directed to lotion or plain oil (such as canola, sweet almond or vegetable). Gently massage.

❖ Room spray — add drops of the essential oils as directed into a bottle of water with a spray attachment. Spray your room with fragrance.

❖ Candles — buy some lovely candles with a scent that you know will bring you comfort, and enjoy them as the fragrance and light fill the air.

❖ **Taste or food therapy**

Certain foods will cause you to remember your loved one. Food is often a family affair. We do so much around food that it would be impossible to separate people from mealtime memories. Finding comfort in food is something that Nigella Lawson has become famous for. Hot chocolate with marshmallows, hot chips with chicken salt, Mum's favourite dish, Dad's barbecue. Lots of foods can make us feel great, providing we eat them sensibly and not to fill up an empty space in our hearts.

Some people lose their appetite completely when faced with loss. This may be short term or long term. It is difficult to eat when you are in shock, but fortunately appetites soon return. When loss of appetite continues a long time after the shock has subsided, medical advice should be sought. A good friend of mine is struggling at the moment to get her Mum to eat, as her Dad passed away a few years ago and her Mum became uninterested in food and in life in general. We need to encourage our loved ones here to keep on living and making sure that they look after themselves, including eating healthily, whenever we can.

On the other hand, when we feel lonely and helpless we can be drawn to something that feels satisfying, and food can be used as the 'comforter' to fill the void. The difficulty is that overeating — like other common responses to loss, such as drug and alcohol abuse or sexual promiscuity — quickly becomes a problem in its own right.

We eat for comfort because it can set off many basic emotions that will in turn shut down unhelpful feelings that we may have, such as stress, disappointment or sadness.

Eating may make you feel better in the short term. Some foods, such as chocolate, affect the chemicals in the brain that regulate your mood. For that reason, you often feel better straight after you have eaten chocolate, but these effects usually don't last for very long. Eating in response to emotions, particularly if you are not hungry, is known as 'comfort eating'.

Eating your favourite food when something upsets you is okay, and everybody is likely to do this from time to time. Comfort eating may be a problem if you are regularly feeling sad, angry, hopeless, bored or lonely and are using food to cope with these ongoing feelings.

There are several differences between emotional hunger and physical hunger:

- ❖ Emotional hunger comes on suddenly; physical hunger occurs gradually.
- ❖ When you are eating to fill a void that isn't related to an empty stomach, you may crave a specific food, such as pizza or ice cream, and only that food will meet your need. When you eat because you are actually hungry, you're open to options.

❖ Emotional hunger feels like it needs to be satisfied instantly with the food you crave; physical hunger can wait.

❖ If you're eating to satisfy an emotional need, you're more likely to keep eating even when you are full. When you're eating because you're hungry, you're more likely to stop when you are full.

❖ Emotional eating can leave behind feelings of guilt; eating when you are physically hungry does not.

The first thing to do is recognise that your eating may be a substitute for love and affection. If that is the case you need to see that you are hurting yourself with this habit and know that it is within your power to stop overeating. That's where faith can help you do what you know you must. It won't be easy, as you may need to develop new, healthy coping mechanisms to replace the harmful one you've adopted. Perhaps the best way to begin is to seek out a good counsellor or to join a support group.

Many grieving people don't want to face their pain — they just want to stop hurting. But ultimately, the only way to feel better is to confront your feelings and to come to terms with your loss. Along with grief counselling, keeping a journal about your feelings may give you comfort, so you no longer feel compelled to overeat.

If you are using food to cope with your feelings it may be something you have been doing for a long time. This may mean that it will take time to start using other methods to manage stress or your concerns. It is a good idea to try to eat healthy foods most of the time rather than those that are high in fat and sugar.

As well as the five senses already mentioned, there are three different types of processing that we mainly use: *visual, auditory* and *kinesthetic*. People with a strong visual sense can usually picture things in their minds, such as a house they lived in as a child. When they close their eyes, they may see the kitchen, the back yard, the living room, the bedroom and other houses in their street. They often remember what people look like so they recognise them when they see them again.

People who cannot 'see' things when they close their eyes probably have a stronger auditory or kinesthetic sense. People with a strong auditory sense can often recall conversations word for word. They may hear the voices in their heads. They may have trouble turning the voices off, especially at night when they try to sleep. For those who toss in bed rehashing conversations, it may be a good idea to listen to classical or relaxation music. When the mind starts to respond to the music, it turns off the conversations.

People with a strong kinesthetic sense process information by *doing*. They engage themselves in their environment. After a trip to the beach, they may remember the feeling of wet sand between their toes and of gentle waves rolling over them as they sat by the seashore. They may remember the sights and sounds of the ocean's waves. They may also remember the emotions they felt during the experience.

Kinesthetic people fall asleep at night because they are exhausted from immersing themselves in life's experiences, as opposed to needing to turn off pictures or conversations in the mind.

We can find out what our predominant sense is by thinking about how to spell the word *elephant*. People who see the whole word spelled out probably have a strong visual sense and have good spelling skills because spelling requires visual memory. People who sound out the word before spelling it probably have a strong auditory sense. By contrast, people with a strong kinesthetic sense picture the elephant in their minds rather than seeing the spelling of the word or hearing it sounded out.

Though one sense is usually predominant when we process information, we use the other senses as well. We will go from auditory to kinesthetic or visual to auditory in a sequence of events, but our predominant sense is usually the first sense we use.

When we know the way someone is 'wired', it helps us recognise the most helpful methods of comfort for them, using one or a combination of the five senses to reach them.

It's also important to realise during this time that children require different forms of comfort from adults. Children need three basic things to help comfort them while they are grieving:

❖ Honesty — brief but clear explanations and answers to their questions. If you don't know the answer to a child's question, be honest about that and explore with the child what they think. What children do not learn about from adults, they will manufacture in their own minds. Truth will be a friend to them at this time.

❖ Choice — children should have a certain level of choice when it comes to their level of participation in arrangements, at the hospital, in the home, etc. Again, talking with them will enable them to feel involved.

❖ Safety — children will need to know that they will be taken care of and that their feelings and wishes will be taken into consideration.

We all require different needs to be met in order to reach a level of comfort that relieves us from pain. However, in grief and trauma, we are more alike than we are different in our responses most times. What we don't need is people with their tool belts out trying to fix our pain. What we do need is lots of cups of tea, as much time and space as is required not to ache any more, and friends and family who won't give up on us. That is what we find most comforting.

Facing the truth is part of the healing process, and truth is often confronting before it is comforting to us. But it is that truth — the revelation of what is real — that will bring us freedom from pain in the long run.

We will never find true comfort if we lean only on ourselves, friends or family members. We need to draw comfort from the only accurate source of truth. That's when we will experience truly abiding comfort. As human beings we have limited knowledge, but our Creator knows exactly what's gone on and what's going to happen next — only He knows the beginning and the end.

Many search for comfort in all the wrong places. Most of us can relate to having an area of our lives where we tend to go to excess, or even feel out of control at times, searching for comfort. Common excesses in our society are food, alcohol, cigarettes, spending, working, or less tangible forms such as people-pleasing, rescuing others or thinking too much. No matter what form it takes, these excesses take us outside ourselves, a welcome diversion from the stress and distress we feel within. If we don't have the skills to soothe and comfort ourselves from within, it only makes sense that we will reach outside for something to meet that need. Unfortunately, these external solutions to our distress often wreak havoc on our health and happiness. The evidence is hard to miss in the high rates of obesity, addiction, credit-card debt, chronic disease and strained relationships. We need to draw strength from a higher source.

We can gain great comfort in knowing that God is our Creator. People who have drawn comfort from this are able to offer comfort to others in turn. For example, I know a woman who within two years lost her husband, her father, and her two sons. At the funeral of the last one to die, she graciously went around welcoming those who came to pay their respects. She offered comfort to others, when you would think she would be the one needing it. On the other hand, some people are devastated by personal hardships and they find no peace or consolation, and are certainly in no position to help others.

Many people seek comfort in all the wrong ways.

- ❖ trying to minimise and devalue their loss
- ❖ thinking that things will just get better
- ❖ thinking that they can't be helped
- ❖ trying to forget
- ❖ trying to fill the void with food, drugs, sex or alcohol
- ❖ complaining.

True comfort only comes from the God of all comfort. God comforts us when we need it most. He does not desert us in our time of need. He will never leave us nor forsake us. He will also never allow us to go through anything that is beyond our ability to cope. Even when we walk through the valley of the shadow of death, He is very present to comfort us. Indeed, the greater the affliction, the greater the comfort!

The ultimate purpose of true comfort is that we are then able to comfort others. The comfort God provides is not just for our private consumption. Our comfort is designed to be shared.

Val's Story

Have you been praying for years, asking God for something specific? I was one of those people. For a number of years, I tried to fall pregnant and continually prayed for a child. Over the years, I kept praying. Oh, how I yearned for children. When I finally fell pregnant with my first son, we knew he was a miracle. Jeremy Daniel Steele was born on 18 August 1982. We were so grateful to God for His gift to us, our precious son, for whom we had waited so long! This was a real answer to prayer. Our families and friends rejoiced with us.

When Jeremy was three and a half, I was pregnant again. Life was good. Jeremy was a delight, bringing great joy to those who knew him. He was a bright young boy who loved stories and playing board games. Whatever the game, Jeremy was determined to win — a trait that followed him through life.

A few weeks before Jeremy's fourth birthday, we were at Koala Park when a wombat attacked Jeremy. Immediately an unusual bruise came up on his leg, which caused us to visit the doctor the following day. Jeremy was sent for blood tests and that afternoon we were called to the doctor's surgery, where we were greeted with the news that Jeremy had leukaemia. Immediately, we were sent to the Royal Alexandra Hospital for Children, then at Camperdown (in Sydney).

At that moment, our lives changed forever. Before leaving home for the hospital we called our pastor to pray with us and we contacted family and friends. Surely this was a mistake? We had prayed so long for a child ... this couldn't be happening to us. What words did the doctor say — Oncology Ward? What did oncology mean? We soon learned the meaning of that word as we saw children battling various types of cancer and leukaemia. That evening, we walked into the unfamiliar, yet soon to be all too familiar, surroundings of the hospital. After many tests, the diagnosis was confirmed: acute lymphoblastic leukaemia, the most common form of childhood leukaemia. Thus started our eleven and a half year battle with leukaemia, which saw Jeremy as the longest surviving child on chemotherapy at the kids' hospital, having had 345 hospital admissions during that time. It was a battle in which leukaemia indelibly marked all of our lives.

Jeremy easily adapted to hospital routine and responded well to treatment. As a little boy, Jeremy mirrored in play what was happening to him in real life. He often pretended he was a doctor treating Benson Bear, Harry the Dog, or any adult willing to be his patient. Through the years Jeremy coped well with chemotherapy and was rarely ill through side effects to the drugs. When asked how he was, he always responded, 'I'm fine.' God was certainly looking after him.

Early on I learned that I had to watch out for children with measles or chicken pox, as both seemingly simple childhood diseases could kill Jeremy. We made many frantic dashes to the hospital for an injection to boost his immunity after a chicken-pox contact. There were also the midnight trips to hospital if necessary. Two packed bags were always ready for us. Each day I prayed for God's strength to see me through that day. They were long years.

Jeremy loved life and lived it to the full. He loved school, achieving outstanding results even though he was absent at least one day a week. Although Jeremy didn't want it to be so, his long-term treatment made him unable to keep up with other kids in physical activities. However, God provided unique experiences that caused Jeremy to develop his creative gifts. Through waving to everyone from a hot air balloon in a Camp Quality television commercial, announcing on Radio Lollipop (the hospital's radio station) and appearing in a hospital scene from *Babe: Pig in the City*, Jeremy realised that he could achieve success through drama, magic and puppetry.

Over the years, Jeremy's encounter with leukaemia had driven me to God, often with questions. I spoke to people, trying to understand the battle we were waging for Jeremy's life and how this battle was affecting me. I knew God was there and He loved me, but sometimes I needed Him here in the daily scheme of things — in my pain as a Mum, seeing my eldest son dying, my marriage suffering and my second son Nathan feeling rejected. Deep down, regardless of the storm around me and regardless of how crushed I felt, I knew God was right by my side, walking with me.

I saw how God had provided me with good friends to support and love me, to provide practical assistance and comfort, to cry with me and to pray for me. There was one special friend, Narelle, with whom I could share my thoughts and feelings. Many times she would just listen when I needed to talk. My friends became a practical reminder of God's love for me.

Throughout Jeremy's years on treatment, I had handed him over to the Lord on a number of occasions. After ten years, I surrendered him yet again. Surrendering wasn't easy. It was painful and I was fearful. I didn't want our son to die. This was the miracle baby God had given to us. I accepted God knew best and I trusted Him with Jeremy's life. I also realised that I needed to be emotionally honest, especially in my relationship with God. I had to start feeling and allowing tears to fall.

When Jeremy relapsed for the third time, we realised that the battle had become intense. We had seen many children die over the years, although seventy per cent of kids with leukaemia survive. We prayed, our friends prayed, many Christian schools prayed. A few months later my husband and I were faced with a decision of whether to give Jeremy further heavy treatment to prolong his life, knowing that it would eventually kill him, or place Jeremy on palliative care. We felt that Jeremy should have quality of life, so we opted for palliative care.

In the midst of this, there was Jeremy at his Year 9 high-school camp, telling his story to staff and students, encouraging them to believe that God has a plan for their lives. In those last months he was a junior leader on a holiday camp. It didn't matter that he had a platelet transfusion at camp. He was there to tell the primary-aged kids about Eternity and to perform magic tricks to illustrate the truth of what he was saying.

On 5 March 1998, Jeremy was hospitalised for the last time. Although his body became weaker, his mind was still active and alive. Using one of the beautiful hospital team as a scribe, he finished writing his last story, which was included in a collection of hospital stories published shortly after his death. In the last week, an endless stream of visitors came to say goodbye. Patients with their parents, hospital secretaries, volunteers, cleaners, friends from school and church, pathology technicians, doctors, nurses, hospital teachers, chaplains, occupational therapists, teachers from school, Camp Quality companions. The list goes on ...

Jeremy died on Friday, 13 March 1998. He was a young man whose enthusiasm for life was infectious. He lived life magnificently, boldly and courageously. His creativity and friendship touched many, many people.

Through those fifteen and a half years, God was with me. He has never abandoned me once. He provided strength for every day. I've come to understand Him more, and our relationship has deepened. I still have unanswered questions but I know God can be trusted and He is in control.

When Jeremy was a little boy being tucked into bed at night, after we prayed with him and turned out the light, he would call out, 'See you in the morning!' That statement spoken by Jeremy is so true. I will be reunited with Jeremy one glorious morning. I will see him again as I am ushered into Eternity. My questions will fade into insignificance as my precious son, Jeremy 'The Magnificent', whole and brimming with health, welcomes me into my Heavenly Father's presence with the words, 'Hi, Mum, I'm fine.'

Pernille's Story

It was 6 a.m. on a sunny Thursday morning. I was asleep on the couch in the living room where her hospital bed was set up. The sound of her heavy breathing woke me up and I listened without moving. It was slow and unusually long. I quickly got up and, as I took her hand, I realised that she was about to leave this world. Suddenly, every breath became very special, as the pause grew longer in between. I tried to breathe with her, as if that would help her to do it properly. Her skinny body was looking so fragile and unreal. It was not really my Mum lying there, but a poor shadow of the woman who had walked with me all through life. But her presence was still with me and it was just the two of us there. I had no sense of how long I was standing there, just waiting for another breath to appear. Tears were silently streaming down my face as another short and too brief breath finally came and then no more.

I ran to the bathroom and knelt with raised hands towards God, thanking him for taking care of her and keeping her until I would join her in Heaven one day. Joy inexpressibly filled my whole being, in the middle of the most tragic event of my life. I knew God was there and my Mum was with him, safe and free.

Three months earlier we had celebrated her fiftieth birthday with an open house for friends, neighbours and family to drop by. She was too tired to have thirty people for dinner and people were aware that she had just been diagnosed for the second time with cancer. This time it had spread throughout her body, and she was feeling very tired, although still up and going as always.

It was a beautiful day, when everyone in his or her own special way celebrated her birthday and at the same time knew that it would be the last to celebrate. But we didn't talk about that fact. Everybody was having a good time, chatting and celebrating her day. I think I struggled with celebrating at that time. Looking back, it was the best day we gave her. But the reality of her leaving in a short time was shouting so loudly at me that I felt everything was so false and it was just such a superficial day. I had tried a couple of days earlier to be sentimental with her and talk about all the travels we had done together, looking through our many photo albums that displayed some of the most joyous times we've had. I guess I needed to face reality in a very real way with her, but I realised later that the pain and fear of dying made it too hard for her to actually appreciate the past at that time.

I grew up as an only child and my Dad left us when I was two years old. I continued through my life to see him and develop a great relationship with him. I always felt that Mum and Dad were meant for each other, but for some reason that I was never let in on, they couldn't make a marriage work. A couple of weeks before my Mum died, my Dad came by to visit. When he saw her he was shattered. I left them to talk by themselves, but couldn't help hearing how they expressed mutual care for each other. I heard my father say the words I'll never forget: 'I still love you, Hanne,' to which she replied, 'I love you too, Johan.'

That became a very special day for me, almost like a landmark in history. I so believe in the importance of reconciliation and the uniting of people. It's crucial that it takes place, at least before they leave planet earth. Unforgiveness is really the greatest disease on earth, because it eats away at your inner life and freedom. Whatever had divided my father and mother from living a life together was forgiven and forgotten that day. It was the last time they talked and it ended in love. My Dad was a different person after that conversation.

The weeks and months after her death were an unreal and very hard time for me. As a family we stood very close together, and my father, Aunts and Uncle, cousins and friends were 100 per cent there, for which I'll always be grateful. Grief became a natural part of our daily life, yet surprised us when we least expected it. We all grieved in our own way.

I was torn between finding myself smiling when thinking of her and what she meant to me, and then finding myself in complete anguish and crying until I had no tears left in my body. The strange thing about crying was that it didn't seem to relieve the pain. The pain was there continually until it would be swallowed up for a moment of joy, thinking of her love and her presence again. I spent countless hours just sitting and staring emptily into Eternity — realising gradually she was out there but not here with me any more.

I don't know how people go through grief without going a little insane. It's a time where nothing makes sense and 'tomorrow' doesn't really matter. In my case, the knowledge of God's presence relieved the unbearable emptiness. I grieved fully knowing I was not alone and that a stronger hand was carrying me.

I remember the funeral, the preparation of her favourite flowers, the people arriving (some I hadn't seen for years), and how I felt such a compassion and a need to reach out and care for everyone else present. I went around and hugged everyone as they arrived, although people started crying when they saw me. There was a greater strength working in me beyond my self. My Mum had always been the most important person in my life, and a source of indescribable strength, mainly because of her selfless love towards me.

It was not a fair death. She died far too young and with too much life still to be discovered. But a thing that I have spared myself from asking is 'Why?' Instead, I was proud in a way to represent her that day of the funeral, as to some extent I still do today. People saw something of her that lived on in me, and that was, and is, an amazing privilege. As I have grown older I see that I look like her, talk like her, and make decisions as she would have done, and that makes her alive to me in a very special way.

Comfort

How to comfort someone who has lost a loved one

Offering comfort to someone who is going through the process of grief and loss is something we need to do intentionally yet sensitively.

- ❖ Please don't say things such as:
  'It was God's will.'
  'I know how you feel.'
  'Let me tell you about someone who's been through worse …'
  'At least they didn't suffer long.'
  'How blessed you are to have other children to live for now.'
  'Well, it's been twelve months now …'
  'It's time to move on.'
  These clichés give more pain than comfort, yet they're some of the most common things people say to a person who's lost a loved one.
- ❖ Searching for something meaningful to say often leads us to blurt out things we don't really mean, so please take your time to think before you speak.
- ❖ If in doubt about what to say, don't feel pressured to say anything at all and just offer lots of hugs and cups of tea.
- ❖ Please don't attempt to minimise the loss by referring to the positive aspects, such as how quickly the person died, their age, or how little they suffered, as this really doesn't help or bring comfort.

- There's no need to carry on as if nothing ever happened, thinking that by mentioning the dead person you'll bring back sad memories. Nobody ever forgets the person who died. Ask the grieving person how they are doing through it all and simply be prepared to listen.
- When you do talk, be as natural as you can. Use the name of the person who passed away. This will help the person you are comforting to know that you also value their loved one, as you mention them by name.

The Weaver's Prayer

'My life is but a weaving between my Lord and me
I cannot see the colours He worketh steadily.
Oft times He weaveth sorrow and I in foolish pride
Forget He sees the upper and I the underside.
Not till the looms are silent and the shuttles cease to fly
Shall God unroll the canvas and explain the reason why.
The dark threads are as needful in the Weaver's skilful hands
As the threads of gold and silver in the pattern He has planned.'

—∽ AUTHOR UNKNOWN ∽—

CHAPTER SIX

Peace

the presence of peace

'I am leaving you with a gift: peace of mind and heart.
And the peace I give isn't like the peace the world gives.
So don't be troubled or afraid.'

⤍ JESUS ⤎
JOHN 14:27, THE BIBLE

The Elephant Man

This movie had a profound impact on me as a young woman; for days I would weep every time I thought of it. It opens with Frederick Treves (played by Anthony Hopkins) showing an incredulous group of doctors a truly astonishing and horrible sight — John Merrick, a man so deformed that he is condemned to a life as a freak in a circus sideshow.

After a detailed examination of his appalling affliction, Treves sends the Elephant Man back to the circus. But his 'owner' beats him up during a drunken rage and Treves takes him to the London Hospital, although the chairman of the hospital committee warns him that incurables were not to be admitted. Nonetheless, he allows him to stay until a proper home can be found for him.

At home one night, Treves wonders: What is in the Elephant Man's mind? As he and the other doctors are talking outside Merrick's room, they hear him beginning to recite Psalm 23, having been taught the first few lines. But the Elephant Man goes on to complete it, to the amazement of the doctors. Having established that the Elephant Man is intelligent, the doctors allow him to stay. His precious mother had given him an understanding of Eternity.

From the window of his new rooms, Merrick can see the top of St Phillips Cathedral and he begins to make a model of it out of cardboard.

One day the Elephant Man produces a small framed portrait of a beautiful woman — his mother — to show Treves's wife. He recalls how kind and good she was, and says that his pitiful condition was due to the fact that she was knocked down by an elephant when she was four months pregnant. His love for her is so strong that the doctor's wife is moved to tears.

The night porter decides to show the Elephant Man to those from the pub willing to pay the price. The drunken crowd break into the Elephant Man's room and humiliate him shamelessly. When they finally disperse, his old boss grabs him and drags him away — back to the sideshow. He treats him so badly that the others in the circus take pity on the Elephant Man. He gets away, collapsing as the police arrive. They take him back to the compassionate doctor at the hospital

It is obvious that the Elephant Man doesn't have long to live. An invitation to the theatre does wonders for his spirits as he sits in the Royal Box with Princess Alexandra and his friends from the hospital. At the end, the performance is dedicated to him and he receives a standing ovation. Later, back in his room, Merrick thanks Treves for his wonderful evening at the theatre. He adds the finishing touches to his much-loved model of St Philip's Cathedral before signing his name at the base of the spire. He is very tired and in considerable pain. He gazes at his mother's picture before falling asleep.

On Friday, 11 April 1890, Joseph Carey Merrick died from asphyxiation. After a life of torment, he was finally able to rest in peace.

Peace

No more sickness, no more pain, no more tears.
Peace.
All we want is peace.

THERE IS NOTHING MORE WONDERFUL than having a calmness deep within. The more turbulent the weather, the more we appreciate the calm. I have learned to be a good flyer, although for many years fear gripped me every time I got on board a plane. I don't even know why, but I do know that fear is not always rational.

One time the flight I was on was so turbulent coming in to land that many people on board started to call out, 'He's not going to land it — we're not going to make it.' I was so frightened by that experience that when I got off the plane (which landed bumpily but safely) and into the arrivals lounge I went and sat in a corner to compose myself. The only problem was that I was in transit and had to get back on another plane in an hour's time. I had a choice to either stay put and allow fear to control my next move, or I had to get some peace into my heart. Getting peace requires action. You have to want it and fight for it. I got on board the next flight and really prayed; amazingly, the weather was calm and so was I. Peace will enable you to go where you would otherwise be unable to go. That is why having inner peace is so important.

Perfect peace is not subject to circumstances. I once read a story about a submarine that was being tested and had to remain submerged for many days. When it returned to port, someone asked the captain, 'How did the terrible storm last night affect you?' The officer looked at him in surprise and exclaimed, 'Storm? We didn't even know there was a storm!' The sub had been so far beneath the surface that it had reached the area known to sailors as 'the cushion of the sea'. Although violent storms might stir the ocean above into huge waves, the waters deep below are never stirred. And so it is when you are at peace.

It is possible to have perfect peace. *Perfect* in this context means complete, with no parts missing. We can have peace about our family, about our finances and about our health. When we trust God, He gives us a peace that transcends natural understanding; it is literally able to bypass the cares of our mind.

Peace is not the absence of war, it is the tangible presence of peace in our hearts. When I think of what peace feels like, it brings to mind seven key things.

- ❖ freedom from fear
- ❖ freedom from anxiety
- ❖ harmony
- ❖ understanding
- ❖ reconciliation
- ❖ rest
- ❖ sleep.

Peace is a state of being where we can find comfort and rest. It is a place where we can see and understand. Peace helps us balance the needs of our body, soul and spirit. It also allows loss to enrich our soul and soften our hearts. Peace is total wellbeing, prosperity and security. *Shalom*, the Hebrew word for peace, which is used as a traditional Jewish greeting or farewell, holds a wide range of meanings, including wholeness, health, security, wellbeing and salvation, and can apply to an equally wide range of contexts.

- ❖ the state of an individual person
- ❖ the relationship between two people
- ❖ the relationship between two nations
- ❖ the relationship between God and mankind.

Peace is an inner triumph. It's not something that a person or a material object can give to you. To embrace peace in all life situations, you need to develop the skills to become like the person in the eye of the hurricane — calm and still — peaceful inside even when your world may be upside down on the outside. Some people believe that if they could just go somewhere else, do something else, then they would know peace. Peace is not vocational or geographical. Peace resides in our hearts and we can take it wherever we go.

In speaking with many people who have lost loved ones, either suddenly and unexpectedly or slowly over a long period of time, it seems that those who have longer to accept their situation also have more time to work at developing peace strategies. Those who have to deal with sudden and unexpected loss don't have that same time. Their peace must come afterwards and this journey isn't always easy. We find peace when we stop trying to figure everything out, when we stop blaming ourselves or others, and when we stop thinking we can change the past.

I have lived my life giving my cares to God and I know that's why I am able to live in peace, even when my life is, at times, anything but peaceful. The end result of resting in God is that we will experience deep and lasting peace. Unlike peace that we try to create on our own through our environment, through external or even internal methods, this peace is confident assurance in any circumstance. With inner peace, we have no need to fear the present or the future. If your life is full of stress, it can still be filled with peace.

Even though sleep does not come easily during a crisis, we can sleep peacefully, even during a storm, when we have peace in our hearts. We just need to cry out to God, who is faithful, to hear and answer our prayer. It is easier to sleep well when we have full assurance that someone is in control of our circumstances. If you are lying awake at night worrying about things you can't change, pour out your heart to God, and thank him that He is in control. Then sleep will come.

At the heart of peace is harmony. To be at peace with someone, whether it's a family member, a neighbour, a friend or oneself, is to be in a harmonious relationship with them. Anxiety is the opposite of peace. Fear is a natural emotion that needs to be faced so that it doesn't get the best of you. Here are some ways to help you overcome anxiety and bring peace and harmony to your life.

◈ Tell yourself you have no need to be afraid.

◈ Think about good things and don't allow your mind to imagine anything awful that hasn't even happened.

◈ Speak up when you feel afraid. Let your family and friends know that you need them.

◈ It costs you more energy to fear than to have faith. Fear presumes the worse scenario while faith presumes the best.

◈ Ask a friend if what you fear is rational or not. Talking will help shed some light on the darkness.

◈ Don't attach your heart to anything that doesn't matter in the light of Eternity.

◈ Use the opportunity to grow the courage that resides within you.

◈ Fear itself is often more damaging than the very thing we fear.

◈ Hire a funny movie and watch it with friends. Laugh out loud!

Peace is something to be pursued and involves work on our part, especially when it comes to being a peacemaker.

'The wisdom that comes from Heaven . . .
is also peace-loving, gentle at all times, and willing to yield to others.
It is full of mercy and good deeds. It shows no partiality and is
always sincere. Commit yourself to the good deeds that are the
mark of a true peacemaker.'

—ᴏ JAMES 3:17–18 ᴏ—
THE BIBLE

We can find rest in peace now. Sometimes we can throw ourselves
into projects in order to avoid the pain we are feeling. The lack of
rest, however, will eventually take its toll. Rest is important to
maintaining a balanced life. We live in an action-oriented world!
There always seems to be something to do and no time to rest. It is
right and needful for us to take a break. Going and going until you
fall down is not wise, and if you try to fill your life with more activity
to try to mask pain, the pain will still be there at the end of the night,
when you're too exhausted to deal with it. Rest and you'll find
handling life much easier. To develop and maintain inner peace we
need to learn how to rest, physically, emotionally and spiritually.

Physical rest

❖ *Eat well.*

Health-care practitioners will tell you that you have to
provide your physical body with high-quality fuel if you
want it to run properly. Eat a healthy, chemical-free diet high
in vital nutrients. Take the herbal and vitamin supplements
that will support you in your good health.

❖ *Sleep well.*

Get the appropriate amount of uninterrupted sleep you need
to engage your REM patterns. REM sleep is your nervous

system's way of healing and refuelling your body. If you're feeling overly tired during this period, don't feel guilty for having an afternoon sleep or at least time to sit down and unwind during the day. You could try to develop and practise a regular pre-sleep routine so that you can teach your body and mind that it's time to relax and prepare for sleep. If you do this you'll fall asleep more easily. Also, avoid worrying or working in your bedroom.

❖ *Exercise.*
Exercise helps you live a longer and healthier life. The body needs to maintain action and movement. If you are looking to increase your physical energy levels, then you may need to increase the amount of exercise you are doing, because we reap energy from sowing energy. You may not like doing exercise, but you will enjoy the benefits that exercise can bring to your life.

❖ *Keep working.*
Believe it or not, it's beneficial for you to maintain as much of your normal routine as possible when you are going through a time of trial and sorrow. This may seem impossible but it is a key to your healing. When we get back into the things that are familiar and safe to us, these activities bring with them security that builds a bridge from the past that we know to the future we will be walking into.

❖ *Laugh.*
There is much research available showing that laughter and fun help to keep people healthy, as well as help to heal sick bodies. We need to look for the humorous side of every

situation and try to keep laughing. At the core of life's most serious moments lies the seed of a brighter season to come. Usher in brightness through laughter and try not to take yourself too seriously.

❖ *Socialise.*
There are times that require space and then there are times that require space-invading. You do need to find the balance for yourself, but put a time limit on how long you will say no to family and friends who want you back in their worlds. It is not good for us to spend too much time on our own, even if that's what we feel like right now. We weren't designed to be islands set apart from the rest of the world. We have been designed for relationships, and the sooner we connect with those we love and trust, the sooner we will start feeling normal again.

Emotional rest

❖ *Stay focused.*
Feelings of regret or worry about a past event, or worry and anxiety about a future event, are not only a waste of your precious life time, they also add stress to the soul. Stay present and focused on the gifts this moment is offering you and look towards your future with a great sense of newfound hope. Finding something positive to focus on will help bring you peace.

❖ *Stimulate your mind.*
Allow your mind to expand, grow, learn, experience, decipher and explore. Read more books. Consider the possibility of returning to study to get the qualification you may have always dreamt about. While there is life there is

hope, and while there is hope, your mind can be renewed, refreshed and charged with all sorts of positive possibilities. Instead of wishing, make decisions that will give you peace of mind.

❖ *Meditate on God's promises.*
Not only is meditation simple, it has also been known to reduce your heart rate, reduce your stress levels and increase feelings of peace, serenity and joy. Read at least one promise from God every day and then sit quietly and meditate on what that means for you; now and for your future. Not only will you feel better for it, but your life will be transformed. (See the end of the chapter for ten verses on peace.)

❖ *Think positively.*
What you allow to enter your mind you will end up believing in your heart. That is why it is vitally important to screen and process your thoughts so that unhelpful thinking can't take hold in your mind or in your heart. Whatever is good, whatever is lovely, whatever is hopeful and helpful — think on these things. Think thoughts of peace.

❖ *Face your emotions.*
It is only a matter of time before buried emotions come to the surface. If you don't deal with them as you go and allow yourself room to express how you feel, then these emotions are likely to surface when you least want them to. We choose — process now or process later — but in the end the process of dealing with our feelings is part of life and healing. Face your feelings, express them in a helpful way. Whatever you do, don't try to suffocate them.

Spiritual rest

❖ *Make peace with God.*
We are able to make peace with God through the
acknowledgement of our need for Him in our life and also
our need for forgiveness. Peace comes instantly when we ask
God to fill the void that only He can.

❖ *Keep short accounts.*
Once we make peace with God, we need to make peace with
people. Life is too short to carry around hurts that only weigh
down our spirits. Once we have asked for and received
forgiveness ourselves, in order to enjoy peace, we need to
forgive others for what they have done wrong. Whether they
are alive or not, forgiveness releases us from pain.

❖ *Talk to God.*
The best way to pray is to talk to God. Have a conversation
just like you would with your best friend. A good
conversation involves speaking and listening; these are the
two key elements of a fulfilled prayer life. Sometimes we
spend more time talking and asking, but we also need to
allow time to hear from God in our spirit and to allow time
to know that our prayers will be answered, even if the
outcomes we hope for aren't seen immediately.

❖ *Read words of life.*
There are so many words that pull us down, but reading
words that lift us up is essential if we want to experience
peace. My Bible is my favourite book in the entire world. It
contains every answer to life and every promise of hope for
my future. It feeds my soul, enlarges my world and keeps my
spirit alive. It also gives me peace.

The practice of peace is a way of life. Once we understand the wonderful gift of peace made available to us, we also need to understand our responsibility to walk a life of peace, because peace is active. Keeping peace of mind is not just something that happens when everything is going well. It is something that we can draw from a combination of many sources, that can sustain us even when things are not going well. Even through tragedy.

Peace will remain with us when we forgive easily, accept others readily, and live with a clear conscience. Know where you can turn for support, for a shoulder to cry on, and for other forms of help when you need it. Know your friends and never allow pride to stop you from requesting help when you need it.

You can also bring peace into your surroundings by keeping your home in order. When you are tidy and organised, you feel at peace in your home. You don't have to become a 'neat freak' or obsessed with what you don't have, but taking care of what you do have is important. I have the letters P E A C E sitting on top of the mantelpiece in my living room. They remind me of the importance of peace in my surroundings.

We often think of surroundings as what we are aware of visually, but the other senses may be involved too. We may need music, or silence. We may choose to enjoy the scent of burning candles, or a cake baking, coffee brewing, or well-polished furniture. Wouldn't it be wonderful to have a home that reflects the peace we long for in our hearts!

When we have incomplete tasks, unfinished goals and overdue bills, peace of mind can diminish. Make a plan to chip away at your unfinished business. Create a routine. Enlist a friend or family member to help you if necessary, but make it a priority. Just knowing that you are making some progress will enhance your peace of mind. Reaching closure on these things will do so even more.

When your peace of mind is challenged, you need to realise that you do in fact have choices. If you feel you do not, look again, and see that what you have previously dismissed as lack of choice is actually a choice that certain alternatives are unacceptable, or perhaps there are options you have not seen. Reconsider your options. Your will is a powerful tool in maintaining a lifestyle of peace.

All living beings have the same basic wish to be at peace and to avoid anxiety, but very few people understand the real causes of peace and anxiety. We generally believe that external conditions such as food and shelter, relationships and material possessions are the real causes of happiness and peace, and as a result we devote nearly all our time and energy to acquiring these. Superficially it seems that these things can make us happy, but if we look more deeply we shall see that they also have the potential to bring us a lot of anxiety, suffering and problems. This shows that the solution to our problems, and to those of society as a whole, does not lie in knowledge or control of the external world.

Peace and anxiety are internal states of being, and so their main causes cannot be found externally. The real source of happiness is inner peace. When our mind is peaceful we can experience happiness regardless of external conditions; but if it is anxious, disturbed or troubled in any way, we shall never be happy, no matter how good our external conditions may be.

God gives power to those who are tired and worn out; he offers strength to the weak. When we rest in and wait on God we will find new strength. We will run again and not grow weary. We will walk in peace and not be faint.

Marisa's Story

Allan was gorgeous. Allan was somebody who always knew what he wanted out of life, he had his life so planned — and he was a clown! He was somebody who would stop anything to go and do what he wanted, it wouldn't matter what it was. If he wanted to do it, he just went and did it.

He had heaps of friends, he always attracted people. He always had so many people around him. When Allan died, it was then I discovered more of who he really was. The guy from the funeral place asked, 'Who was your son? For a young person, there were just so many people at his funeral.'

There were between four and five hundred at the service. When we came out, I saw people waiting and they were all friends. They had been listening on the speakers set up for the ceremony. It was amazing.

The way Allan walked through leukaemia was incredible. He said so many times, 'Mum, don't worry, God is in charge. I will pass this test with an A.' And even now he is gone, I know that he passed with an 'A' because he got the best gift — he got God, he got Eternity.

My husband would not talk at all during this time. He thought — 'If I don't talk about it, it won't happen.' He didn't even want to let close family know — he told no-one. I hear him say to others now, 'Why couldn't I save my son?' He has prayed for other people who were sick, and they were healed, but his own son died. I think he is

all right now, but I don't go there much. I know he
questioned God; I don't think he does that any more, but
he didn't talk about Allan until we went to counselling.

Allan had been searching for God since he was a small
boy, but at the end he found Him. In the last weeks a
friend came and prayed for him; Allan accepted the gift of
Eternity and he became so peaceful. It was from that day
that I lived with him at the hospital because he didn't want
to be on his own. I used to wake up about 6 a.m. and I
would see Allan sitting reading his Bible, and my husband
used to come from work and they would chat about
Eternity. For me, that was beautiful.

He was allowed to go home every afternoon for an
hour or so. One afternoon Allan told me he wanted to
confess his sins to me. I told him, 'No, no!', but he wanted
to tell me everything that he had done — you know, stupid
things that kids do. And I would say, 'Allan, you don't need
to tell me', and he would say, 'Yeah, but I need to tell you.'
That day, I knew he really had Eternity in his heart.

I miss him. It's getting better, but there are still some
days like Christmas, because the last day that he was home
was Christmas Eve. On Christmas Day we took him back
to the hospital and he said, 'If I am not able to walk again,
there is no way I am coming home, I'm not coming back
until I am well again.' He died on 12 January. I didn't
question God when it happened to my son. For me, he got
the best healing of all because he had Jesus in his heart and
a life of Eternity in Heaven.

God chooses whoever He wants for His kingdom and
Allan was so amazing that He needed to have him with
Him. I still have things to do here and it is true that one
day we will all be together. He is gone because he was an

awesome kid — he was great. He had such a good life —
he had done so many things. We travelled overseas with the
kids three times, and he went and did everything he wanted
to do on his own as a teenager. Even though it was a short
life, it was a happy life.

He had parents who loved each other, he had brothers
who loved him; they would fight as kids, but that is
normal, it was nothing serious. He had beautiful friends
and you could see that everyone loved him. No regrets
whatsoever.

Most of the time Allan handled his illness well. There
were times when he was in hospital and people would
come and ask him questions — doctors and nurses, they
would ask the same thing ten times. They would ask how
he was feeling and what needed changing, and it was hard,
because as a seventeen-year-old who has just been told you
have leukaemia, it is like you are going to die tomorrow.
He would get a little bit emotional but would remain calm.

Allan was very protective of me. When I would go to
cuddle him, when he would start to get emotional about
his illness and this and that, I would just hug him and he
would straighten himself up and go, 'I'm fine, Mum.'
I should have let him cry. You say, 'If only I could have
done this differently.' Although there are not many things
that I would have done differently.

I was given a book about leukaemia and what to
expect. It was really good. At the hospital, stuff would
happen that we might have panicked about had we not
known what to expect. It was as if the book came to life. It
was really helpful — you need to be informed. Some
people don't want to know — but you need to, it helps so
much.

Allan had a transplant relapse, and then he had a different treatment where he was tested with platelets from the donor (my other son, Ian). My husband and I were not keen on him having the treatment because out of the twenty-two people that they had tried in the UK and America, none of them had survived. So we were asking what the point was in going through it all. Why? But he wanted to do it.

The day that he was to get the treatment done, I went with him to the hospital and we were talking, and that is the only time that I saw Allan really upset about this thing. He asked for his brother, Pablo, who had already left, but he kept saying, 'Where is Pablo, where is Pablo?' He had this urgency to talk to people. I said that Pablo had gone but I could call him to come back and he said, 'No, that's fine, that's fine.' I wanted to talk to him, and he said, 'Come on, Mum, I want to pray for you.' He prayed for me; I laid on his bed and he put his hand on my head and he prayed for strength, then he said, 'Why don't you pray for me?' I have difficulty praying out loud, I'm somebody who thinks too much about what I am saying, instead of relaxing, so I really feel more comfortable doing it quietly. I said, 'But I don't know how to pray as beautifully as you did,' and he said, 'It's okay, Mum, you just pray.' And I prayed and when I'd finished he said, 'See, that was really nice, Mum. That was beautiful, thank you.'

Some people might think that he was hanging on to Jesus because it was all he could do, or that we hung on because we'd lost a son. That isn't true. It brought us closer to God, but God was always there. For Allan, he had such a love for God, and in the last few weeks of his life he concentrated on Eternity with Him.

What happened hasn't changed what I think about Eternity. I always believed and knew. It just assured me more that what I believe is true — it is real. No matter what, make sure you have your foundation. It probably caused me to go closer to God, to build more upon what I already knew. We could not have gone through what we went through if we had not had God. He held everything together.

Allan's life was never in vain; God was always at work and Allan touched a lot of people. I've grown a lot since Allan died — in my walk with God. I don't worry any more. I used to worry a lot, but now I just think, 'What is the point of worrying about it?' I just give it to God to sort out, He is in control. Nothing is too big or small for Him. Maybe not right now, but it will come. He has my son there in Eternity. Things will happen now and I call to Allan — I know it is God we call on, but it is as if Allan is there with God, helping Him. He is like one of the angels. I have great peace in my life knowing there is a God and He has my precious son with Him in Eternity.

Angela's Story

I had the best childhood, and, like most children, I had a 'hero' who I thought could do anything. My hero stood 188 centimetres tall, with dark hair, dark eyes and brown skin. To me, he seemed perfect. He could fix a car and answer all my homework questions, and always seemed to know more about everything than anyone else. If I was in trouble, he could fix it; if there was a need, he would meet it. My 'hero' — my Dad — was a man of few words, and when he spoke you listened. He had the best sense of humour. He was also patient, having learned to live in a house with women!

When we would talk about Eternity, he would get tears in his eyes. You could tell this is where his heart was. He really knew God and lived his faith before everyone. Not just as a church attendee, but also as a man in a relationship with His creator. How can someone be so strong and brave, yet so tender? I love that.

For thirty-four years I knew this man, and I'm so grateful for all of them. I am going to share this loss of a hero, and how I walked through that first year. I was living in Australia with my husband and kids, and one day, in the early hours of the morning, I received a phone call from my sister Julie in the United States to let me know our Dad had had a stroke. We were told it wasn't severe, and he should be okay. I was stunned and half asleep.

My husband and I had moved over to Australia in 1998 and this had been a big decision because of my closeness with family. I just assumed that my parents would live to a very old age and had made a 'deal' with God. So, when this call came, I never thought my father wouldn't make it. I was a little scared because I was so far away, but felt confident that he would be all right.

The next day we called back and forth, and everything was still on track. We were busy running errands and doing all the last-minute organising and preparations for the trip home, when I received a call to say that my Dad had had another stroke, and that I needed to get home as quickly as possible. I think it was at this point that I started to spiral into a strange slow-motion frantic place. I am not normally a person who is likely to lose her cool when a problem occurs. I am usually pretty level-headed and controlled. But I was feeling things I have never felt before. It felt out of body ... a very strange sensation. I quickly called my husband, Tom, and told him in a squeaky, teary voice what had just happened, and that we had to rearrange flights. He is an incredible negotiator and worked it out, and for that I am eternally grateful, because in around thirty hours my father would die.

By that afternoon I was on a flight heading back to the United States. When I arrived, I drove almost two hours to the hospital where my whole family were gathered. I was so thankful to find out that he was alive and vitals were maintaining. I was told by my mother that he didn't look great, so not to worry when I saw him. I went in to his room in intensive care and there lay my hero. My very strong, no-problem-too-hard, no-mountain-too-high hero. He actually didn't look as bad as I had imagined. He just looked a little under the weather. I went and stood next to him and rubbed his dark, wavy, receding hair. I was so thankful to be there; I can't find words to describe how happy I was to be with him, and my family.

I whispered in his ear: 'Hi, Dad, it's me, Angela ... I flew all the way to see you ... you are going to be all right, hang on, Dad. I love you.' He couldn't talk or do much of anything, but his right leg would jolt around when we would talk to him. I knew he was still in there and I knew he was aware that I was there. I held his hand and just stayed with him for a while. Before I left the room I said, 'Dad, we are going to go, so you can rest and use your energy to get better. We will come in the morning and we expect you to be stronger. We are praying for you, Dad I love you.'

No-one expected the phone call that came the next morning to let us know that my Dad had taken a turn for the worse in the night and that his blood pressure had plummeted. They told us to get in as soon as possible. When we arrived at the hospital, I looked in and noticed they had moved him and someone else was in his bed. I waited with my mother as they told her that it didn't look good, and that we needed to be prepared for him to die in just a few short hours.

I remember this very well, because life stopped at that moment. The pause button was pushed for all of us. When she had finished speaking I asked where Dad was and she pointed to the room I had peeked in earlier, and I said, 'I don't think that is him.' We went in and it was him, but he wasn't there. I knew he had left his body. The machine still had his body working, but I knew he wasn't there any more.

By this time all our friends and family had arrived. My brother-in-law spoke up and said, 'Why don't we each come and hold Dave's hand and tell him goodbye in our own way?' What do you say when a hero dies? You have to say goodbye but you don't want to. I just wanted him to know how much he has always meant to me and how much I love him. I knew that after I said what I wanted it would be over and done with and that I would be at peace.

I walked over and held his big, warm hand that has been a source of strength for me all my life and I just broke. 'Dad, I'm sorry I wasn't here earlier. You have always been the best father, you have been my hero — the reason I could obey God and trust Him with my life. I don't want you to go. I love you so much.' I think after that I just melted down. I walked out the door and into my brother-in-law's arms, and sobbed. After everyone had time with him, we wanted to give Mum time alone with Dad, and then the machines would stop and his body would function on its own.

It was under fifteen minutes before his faint heart stopped beating. At this point I went and called my husband Tom, to let him know Dad was gone. We went back to my parents' house along with about twenty-five others. It is actually nice not to be on your own in these times. A strange thing happens when someone you love dies. This slow-motion shock comes over you. You lose all sense of hunger and need for natural things in that first few days. Thoughtful people brought food and flowers over. Friends sent flowers and a card that just shared their sorrow for my loss — such a wonderfully kind gesture and one that won't be forgotten.

I woke up the next morning with a real sense of sadness. I knew I needed a good cry, to get ready to be strong for my Mum. They had been married nearly fifty years and they had a great relationship. I knew this would be very hard for her. That day my mother came into my room with wild eyes and said, 'I know what we are going to do . . . we are going to raise your father from the dead.'

I believe with my whole heart, as did my Dad and my Mum, that it is possible, but at that moment I wasn't sure how to respond. I'd never been involved in anything like this, and neither had my mother. To make a very long story short, we did go to the funeral home and we did pray for my father. We did not make a big scene, and we did not shout and scream, but we did pray. I felt like it made God smile: 'Look at those kids giving it a go.' This was something we laughed about the rest of the day. (Not because it is funny, but because it was not a normal day.) I told my sisters they owed me big-time because they weren't there! I learned to find humour in this situation.

I love that my Mum's faith grew stronger every moment and that she was as committed as ever to praying for sick people. What happened to my Dad wasn't going to stop her believing in miracles for other people. That's how my Mum and Dad have always lived and how my Mum will continue to live.

That night my sister and I went and bought a huge bouquet of flowers — the most gorgeous bouquet of flowers I'd ever seen. We put it in her room with a note written by us girls, and we signed it from Dad. The note thanked Mum for forty-eight and a half years together and told her how much he loved her. Their marriage has been a great source of strength for all of us over the years and we wanted to honour that as well as his life.

We planned the funeral together, which was a wonderful time of bonding with my family. Looking through old family photos brought some good laughs but was intensely sad. It is so important to be with one another during times of loss and pain. We are stronger together than alone. Later we drove into town where my sister and niece met us for some pampering. It took our minds off all the things we needed to get done, and all the emotions that each of us was drenched in.

I stayed with my family for a total of two weeks, and didn't want to leave. My mother and I went on walks almost every morning and were able to spend quality time together. Looking back, I'm so grateful for the memories of this time. I was able to just stop for a season and reflect on every feeling.

There have been a few outbreaks of tears, a lot of looking through photos and many conversations over coffee with friends in the months since the death of my father. Another one of the ways that I have worked through this loss has been staying in touch with my mother consistently. Helping someone else through the pain gives your pain purpose. She has been very courageous. I am so proud of the choices she has made throughout this season of her life.

Every now and again my heart aches for my Dad. The ache helps me remember his life, and I never will forget this wonderful man that lived sixty-seven years and had an impact on so many. He was wise, trustworthy, humorous, soft-hearted, generous, and a most wonderful husband and father, loved and admired by all who knew him. He left behind an amazing wife, my Mum, who is grateful for the years they had together, and now, with peace in her heart, will finish her life strong and brave, ready for new chapters to be written.

Peace

'I will lie down and sleep in peace, for you alone, O Lord,
make me dwell in safety.

–ᴑ PSALM 4:8 ᴑ–

THE BIBLE

'The Lord gives strength to his people;
the Lord blesses his people with peace.'

–ᴑ PSALM 29:11 ᴑ–

THE BIBLE

'When you lie down, you will not be afraid;
when you lie down, your sleep will be sweet.'

–ᴑ PROVERBS 3:24 ᴑ–

THE BIBLE

'He will swallow up death forever.
The Sovereign Lord will wipe away the tears from all faces;
he will remove the disgrace of his people from all the earth ...'

–ᴑ ISAIAH 25:8 ᴑ–

THE BIBLE

'Peace I leave with you; my peace I give you. I do not give to you as the
world gives. Do not let your hearts be troubled and do not be afraid.'

–ᴑ JOHN 14:27 ᴑ–

THE BIBLE

'I have told you these things, so that in me you may have peace. In this world you will have trouble. But take heart! I have overcome the world.'

⁓ JOHN 16:33 ⁓

THE BIBLE

'Therefore, since we have been justified through faith, we have peace with God through our Lord Jesus Christ ...'

⁓ ROMANS 5:1 ⁓

THE BIBLE

'May the God of hope fill you with all joy and peace as you trust in him, so that you may overflow with hope by the power of the Holy Spirit.'

⁓ ROMANS 15:13 ⁓

THE BIBLE

'And the peace of God, which transcends all understanding, will guard your hearts and your minds in Christ Jesus.'

⁓ PHILIPPIANS 4:7 ⁓

THE BIBLE

'He will wipe every tear from their eyes. There will be no more death or mourning or crying or pain, for the old order of things has passed away.'

⁓ REVELATION 21:4 ⁓

THE BIBLE

CHAPTER SEVEN

Home

coming home

*'Warmth, completeness, vulnerability, transparency, security, intimacy,
my family, memories of good times and bad, safety, unity, love.
I get teary when I think about it as I wholly value
the home that I have come from.'*

— A FRIEND —

The Wizard of Oz

Dorothy is a little girl who lives on a Kansas farm with her Uncle Henry and Auntie Em, and her little dog Toto. One day Dorothy and Toto are caught up in a tornado and then thrown down in a grassy field in the country of the Munchkins. Their landing kills the Wicked Witch of the East, who had established a reign of terror over the Munchkins.

The Good Witch of the North comes with the Munchkins to greet Dorothy. In order to return to Kansas, the Good Witch of the North says that Dorothy should go to the City of Emeralds and ask the Wizard of Oz to help her. The Good Witch of the North kisses Dorothy on the forehead, stating that no-one will harm a person who has been kissed by her. On her way down the Yellow Brick Road, Dorothy meets some remarkable characters: she liberates the Scarecrow from the pole he's hanging on, restores the mobility of the Tin Man, and encourages the Cowardly Lion to journey with her and Toto to the Emerald City. The Scarecrow wants to get a brain, the Tin Man a heart, and the Cowardly Lion courage; and they're convinced by Dorothy that the Wizard can help them too.

When they arrive at the Emerald City, the Wizard of Oz agrees to help each of them, but his help is conditional. When they next meet the Wizard, he tries to put off Dorothy and her friends again. Oz tries to persuade the Scarecrow, the Tin Man and the Cowardly Lion that what they lack is not brains or a heart or courage, but faith in themselves. But he still agrees to meet each of them, giving them a placebo which brings out the qualities they had all along.

In order to help Dorothy and Toto get home, Oz realises that he'll have to take them home with him in the same hot air balloon in which he arrived. Just as they're rising into the air, however, Toto leaps from the basket to chase a cat and Dorothy goes after him, leaving the Wizard to rise and float away.

The citizens of the Emerald City suggest that Glinda, the Good Witch of the South, may be able to send Dorothy and Toto home. At Glinda's palace, the travellers are greeted warmly, and Glinda reveals that Dorothy had the power to go home all along. The special shoes she wears can take her anywhere she wishes to go. Dorothy tearfully embraces her friends — all of whom will be returned to their homes too. And Dorothy and Toto return to Kansas and a joyful family reunion, because there's no place like home!

The Eternity moment occurs when Dorothy realises what home means to her. Home existed in Dorothy's heart all along, but she needed to leave it to finally find it. Home is where the heart is, but sometimes we get lost along the way. Life is a journey and some have a longer journey than others.

Home

'Home! And this is my room — and you are all here!
And I'm not going to leave here ever again, because I love you all!
And ... Oh, Auntie Em ...
There's no place like home!'

— DOROTHY —
THE WIZARD OF OZ

THERE IS NO PLACE LIKE HOME.

During my Uncle's last week on earth he repeatedly asked to go home. Home is the only place he wanted to be. He was sick of doctors, sick of hospitals, sick of being sick. He yearned for home. Whenever we are vulnerable, afraid or insecure, that is the time when, more than ever, home is where we long for because home is our haven. Even those whose homes are full of turmoil and strife still yearn for home; to find a place where they feel that they have *come home*. It's difficult to articulate why home is so important to so many. Nevertheless, it is.

Home is where the heart is, both here and in Eternity. Home is an open door behind a fence of security. Within its walls are peace and love, people and mess. Home is the embodiment of all our dreams and the realities of life. A home is a place of companionship with people in it who love each other, who are harmonious and closer with one another inside it than they are with the outside world. A home is a place that is so magnetic it is difficult to leave. Home is where love, kindness, sharing and appreciation are found, and the inhabitants help one another. It is a place of selflessness and togetherness, where everybody has time for everybody else. In a home, guests are treated like royalty as they share in the qualities that lie within. Home is a place where you're at home and you know you're home.

Home is more than a physical or geographical place. It is a place that can be found emotionally and spiritually. Home is both our place of origin and our ultimate destination. The meaning of home to us is both what we remember and what we become. Home is not only the place we grew up in, but is also a reflection of the person we eventually become. Regardless of what home means to us, we are on a lifelong search to make home a place of wholeness, comfort and serenity for ourselves and those we love. Each one of us carries deep within our hearts and minds an image of the ideal place, the one true home where we belong.

I realise that my description of home is not everyone's reality. Home for some is anything but peace and tranquillity, family and fun. Home for some is pain, anxiety, fear and dread. But home can be something that we find amidst our circumstances. Just as we don't need a roof to build a home, we also don't need a perfect family to build a home. Home can be a state of our heart that lets us know that we belong.

Even those living without a physical place of shelter can find home in their hearts and in family or friends — togetherness. Families are designed to transcend building structures and to embody *home*. Such a family is at home wherever they are. A roof is not needed to make a family or a home. Some 'homes' become like a hotel lobby or a transit lounge. Dad works. Mum works. Mum, Dad and the children pass each other like ships in the night. The truly homeless are those who have lost the essence of home and the quality of family life.

Every individual has a deep inner longing for home. Consider the homing pigeon and how it knows how to find home. It has an inherent drive that brings it from wherever it has been taken to, back home again. The secret of homing pigeons is that they use their own navigational system (an inbuilt homing device) when making long-distance trips or when a bird embarks on a journey for the first time. Their uncanny ability to find their way home is also part of the pigeon's habit. When they have flown a journey more than once, homing pigeons establish a habitual route. They know how to get home. Home is the goal. Home is the prize.

Anyone who has done any kind of travel will be able to relate to the heart of the homing pigeon. I have done my fair share of globetrotting, and am always glad that the final destination on my ticket is *home*. Home is definitely where my heart is.

❖ Home is a place of refuge.

❖ Home is a place to laugh.

❖ Home is a place to express.

❖ Home is a place to sleep.

❖ Home is a place to reside.

❖ Home is a place to embrace.

❖ Home is a place to relax.

❖ Home is a place that is mine.

❖ Home is a place that is ours.

Home contains cherished childhood memories and dreams for the future. Home contains disappointments and pain wrapped up in bandages. Home has my favourite food in the fridge and my favourite seat in front of the TV. Home is loving and forgiving. It is shelter from the elements — wind, rain, criticism and strife. Home is where we belong.

Family structures may vary around the world, and yet the value of home endures. Healthy individuals within healthy family homes are at the core of a healthy society. It's in everyone's best interests, then, to help create a positive environment for all families. This can be a labour of love for all in the 'building' process. Home is our most intimate social environment. It is the place where we begin the vital processes of socialising our children, teaching them how to relate, survive and prosper in the world outside its doors.

Home here prepares us for home in Eternity. Families who understand the value, power and significance of home are families that, when faced with loss and tragedy, seem to pull through with a strength and resilience that they would otherwise not have had. This comes not only out of their faith but also out of the strength of *home* and what it has brought to their lives and relationships. In a similar manner, for those who are leaving loved ones behind, the value they placed on home and what they put into building their home will be something that they will experience around them when they go into Eternity.

I used to wonder why my mother never wanted to move out of the house she grew up in, that we grew up in. The older I get, the more I understand the dynamics of home and the security it brings. One could think that she and my Dad deserve an 'upgrade' in life. But home is where their heart is and their home is a place full of amazing memories.

Growing up in such a close family caused me to value home above just about any other aspect of life. We were living with my grandparents while my parents saved to buy a house, when my Grandfather — Poppy — passed away. Because we were so close, we didn't want to leave Nanny on her own so we decided to stay. There were three generations under the same roof. That was interesting a lot of the time, but home was always full of love.

Mum and Dad never set out to stay at home once they were married, but it is something that has become a very important part of who they are as people and how we all relate to each other now. Even though I don't physically live under that same roof any more, it still remains home to me. Even though my postcode is in another suburb, the place of my childhood memories will always be home as well to me. Home, you see, is not limited to geography.

Some of my friends at school lived in beautiful mansions, but they did not constitute a home. Many of these mansions were full of distance, not closeness. An upgraded house is not necessarily an upgraded home. You can buy a huge modern home with all the amenities that come with making lots of money, but there is always a greater cost involved. Some sacrifice home for house, when the ultimate prize is found in sacrificing house for home.

The trend started to shift a number of years ago with the idea of 'downsizing'. People who had traded the concept of home in on a bigger house were determined to get back what they had lost — home, spouse and family. Many people are now returning to the importance of home instead of chasing the illusory dream of a bigger and better roof overhead. Home holds something different for everyone. When interviewing a number of different people about their idea of home, I got many consistent responses: warmth, fireplace, family, movies, hot chocolate, holidays, cuddles, security, peace, unity, consistency, protection. Love, safety, peace and rest, sanctuary, being carefree and truly happy. Sleep. Comfort, relaxing. Shelter. A place of my own.

I love my home. I shed more tears over this chapter than any other chapter in this book because home means so much to me personally. One of the most difficult things we face is coming back to a home that we once shared with a loved one who won't be coming home again. My husband Jonathan's Mum passed away a number of years ago quite suddenly. He was living in Australia and she was living in England. When he first found out that she had a life-threatening illness, he was going to fly over to see her straight away. However, the doctors and family told him he didn't have to fly over immediately. Suddenly her condition changed and she went very quickly. Jonathan had planned to be there but now had to leave knowing his Mum had gone out into Eternity. That was an incredibly painful flight home for him. The first time he walked through the doorway into his Mum's home after she passed away he broke down and wept. The last time he had seen her, she had been standing in that very same doorway saying goodbye, and now she wasn't there and everything about the house reminded him of her and home.

Walking back into our home, into familiar surrounds when part of our home is now missing, is an incredibly painful event. It's now up to us to embark on the difficult and painful journey of transition to a life at home without the one or ones who made it what it was. It's up to us to continue building our home. Home is a very personal world, filled with family and friends so important to the one that has left, and it is so important to them that we continue to go on building our homes. Home is a place that should reflect the good times that have been as well as being a place to dream positively about our future. Let's take a walk through home.

❖ The front door

When you enter your home, you are entering into the atmosphere created by those who live and lived there. Every time a person comes home they also bring an atmosphere with them as they walk through the front door. Perhaps there were special routines relating to the way in which your loved one arrived home from work or from school, and that front door that once brought you so much joy now brings you great sorrow. Consider your front door in a new light. Consider that you have been left on earth to walk through it and into your future.

I bought a beautiful handmade card on a trip to New Zealand once. It featured a magnificent old door, slightly ajar, on the front, with the words 'Sorry you're leaving!' written underneath. The good news is we can have hope that through that door is the light of Eternity, which will bring our loved one complete joy, peace and no more sorrow.

❖ The living room

The living room has pictures on the wall, on the sideboard, on the table. The living room has magazines and a collection of memorabilia that is altogether you and yours. Comfy old sofas that have seen better days, gaudily coloured rugs and mismatched cushions; popcorn under lounges and tea-dribbles on the carpet. Living rooms usually reflect a whole lot of living.

I don't know about yours, but our living room is always a place of noise and interaction, of people coming and going, phones ringing, TV roaring then softening, of movie nights, laughter and tears, and cuddles on the couch. The living room is the place where we get to chill out and be completely relaxed and where we get to enjoy the benefits of home. It's where there's usually a special chair that we love to sit in and a place where we know we might get a foot rub or a shoulder massage. Perhaps there is a place that is now empty because it's where your loved one always chose to sit. Be assured that although that chair may now be empty, it is still filled with special, precious and important memories and it can become a great source of comfort when the next generation in your world sit back and relax in it.

❖ The kitchen

Our kitchen is the centre of the universe in our home. With a growing family, the fridge opens and closes several times a day and there is a well-worn path to the pantry. Our kitchen is the place where we prepare food, not just to satisfy hunger but to express love to our family. Our kitchen is a place that unites us all. It is difficult to come to terms with the fact that certain foods may no longer be bought because your loved one was the only one who liked them. Or perhaps kitchen time was special talk time between the two of you.

The kitchen is a very special place because in it we can touch not just our family's stomachs, but our family's souls. If you are now living on your own, try to sit around the kitchen table with family and friends. Jonathan talked about how healing it was when he got home to England after his Mum passed away, and all his family sat around the kitchen table, talking about his Mum. One minute they were all crying, the next they were laughing, and these times enabled them to process their emotions and walk through the reality of losing someone they all loved so much.

❖ The dining room

Dining-room time is very high on our priority list when it comes to hanging out together as a family. We saved up and bought a magnificent fourteen-seater Henry VIII-style dining table with bench seating to ensure that as our family and friendships grow, we can always enjoy mealtimes together. I understand that the more wonderful memories we create, the more we'll have for Eternity.

For some, mealtimes are now the hardest time of all — especially if they have always been a special focus of your home. I want to encourage you to keep celebrating the family you have. Keep cooking up a storm and remember that there are always plenty of mouths to feed and plenty who need a home.

One thing is for sure, there will be no 'dining for one' in Heaven ...

'We are our dinner tables.
Each family reveals itself by how it gathers around the table,
Where everyone sits, what is said, who serves,
who speaks, how people listen,
Whether they linger, and how they feel when it is over.'

— LETTY COTTIN POGREBIN ✧

✧ Your bedroom

Your bedroom is your private living space. It is a place that
signifies intimacy and vulnerability. If you have lost your
partner, then your bedroom — the place you shared together
so intimately — will never be the same again. But it is also a
place that you will need to keep living in, so it's up to you now
to make it a place of sweet dreams, tranquillity and wonderful
memories. Introduce music, candles and beautiful photographs.
Our bedrooms are an extension of who we are so it will take
some time for you to get used to occupying that space alone.
It's up to you now to fill the room with hope for the future.

✧ Their bedroom

Facing the bedroom of your loved one is incredibly difficult
and painful. Whether your loved one was ill and spent much
time in that room or whether they left for work one day and
never came home, their bedroom is a place like no other that
will cause you to miss them incredibly. I found it helpful to
go into my loved one's bedroom soon after they passed away.
I could see them in there, and their scent still remained. This
space causes us to feel the greatest amount of loss as it has
been an extension of who they are. All their personal
belongings matter, and sorting through everything will take
time and much emotional energy.

Try not to throw everything away and try also not to feel like you need to create a 'shrine' room — not moving anything. If your loved one were able to let you know what to do, they would probably suggest you make the most of the opportunity to have a big spring clean. Hang on to what's dearest, give away the rest. Paint the walls, buy a new bed cover and consider letting that room — be a blessing to others in your world.

❖ **The office or study**

One thing is for sure, bills don't stop rolling in just because you lost a loved one. In fact, they seem to come in thicker and faster than ever. Administration is something that you will eventually have to get on top of, but you will need to allow yourself time to breathe. There will be letters to write, cards to send and all sorts of businesses and governmental departments that will need to be notified, but once this is done, try to work on a system that you can maintain for the future. In our family my Dad is the admin person, so I can't imagine what Mum would do with all the paperwork. Becoming familiar with the necessary admin processes will help you cope with everyday life.

My Aunty Norma spent several weeks writing letters and cards to thank people for their kind thoughts when my Uncle Bruce passed away. She also had a large amount of other official correspondence to take care of, which was an enormous task for her. The good side of it was that it was a way to fill in the days, but the downside of any 'official' paperwork is that it can be impersonal. This I know was painful, as she had to correspond 'factually' about her loss, even though it was very personal to her.

❖ The laundry

There are seasons in life for everything. When we first start
out in life, our laundry is done for us; some don't even
venture into the laundry until they leave home and then
they have to work out how to wash clothes without ruining
them! Then there's the season where you could have up to
six loads a day (which is where I'm at, with a young family),
and that's when we can start resenting each and every dirty
sock, and the fact that each family member seems to use
three towels per day. Then the season comes when laundry is
down to just two of you. That's when you miss it most. Half
a load once a week makes you realise that you wish you
were doing six loads a day again. I try to encourage other
women in the season I'm in to be grateful for the workload
that our precious family brings because it merely reflects an
aspect of home that requires extra super-duper love!

❖ The garage or shed

Our garages and sheds are filled with many things, and
sometimes a car or two. When I think about our garage, I
think about my Dad's tools and his amazing collection of
antiques that he acquired over the years because people
couldn't see the value in old stuff. I think about him working
until late into the night and I remember the time he cut the
top off his finger and had to rush to hospital. He had a
miracle that night as that finger started to mend and heal
back together without needing surgery. I can also remember
when my Dad was trying to give up smoking when I was a
teenager and he used to hide in the garage to sneak a few
puffs. He had a miracle there too, and has been a non-
smoker now for over twenty-five years. Our garage is Dad's
special domain and it is a place with cherished memories

that will live on in my heart long after he's enjoying his new tool shed in Heaven (with no spanners missing!).

❖ The back yard

Perhaps your loved one really enjoyed gardening and being outdoors. Perhaps they were the king or queen of the barbecue or pool party. They would want you to continue doing their favourite things, so it's important for you to feel that you can enjoy your back yard like you used to. The back yard is our little patch of recreation where we teach our kids to walk and ride their bikes, and where we sit and enjoy the sunshine. It's also where our pets enjoy running around. Perhaps you have a patio of reflection. Our back yard is a place where lots of fun memories can still be made.

❖ The veranda

Our veranda was where my Nanny used to sit and read the paper. She would have her cup of tea without milk and with one sugar. That's where she ate her honey wholemeal toast and where she relaxed in the sunshine. That's where my Nanny put on my wedding shoes to stretch them out a little on the morning I got married. Verandas are places of contemplation and reflection. Even if you don't have a veranda, try to find a place where you can sit and dream about better days to come. A place that's quiet for you to read and meditate; a place where you can get a vision for your future life.

> 'In my Father's house are many mansions;
> if it were not so, I would have told you.
> I go to prepare a place for you.'

⌐ JOHN 14:2 ⌐

THE BIBLE

Home, precious home. We all long for a place where we are welcome, accepted, loved. Warm, relaxing, open — that's home. But not all homecomings evoke such memories. And while coming home often brings high expectations, it sometimes doesn't live up to them.

When this happens, we grow restless. That's because deep within each of us is the longing for home the way it should be, and some of us will experience that kind of home only in Eternity. For others of us who are blessed enough to be experiencing the goodness of a happy family home I exhort you not to take it for granted.

Sometimes we may feel lonely, but we are not alone. Many people today feel far from home. Perhaps they are divorced or widowed. Maybe they live a long way away from relatives. Even people who live close to their family often end up not seeing much of them because of work commitments. We have to slow down and make time to *build* our home. The reality is that this side of Eternity, nobody, not even the Brady Bunch, has a perfect home where people always listen and understand each other, take care of each other, or even like each other. Yet most of us keep looking for just that — a place where we are appreciated, where we can be comfortable, where we can be truly ourselves. Understanding this human dilemma, St Augustine once said to God:

'You have made us for Yourself, and our hearts are restless until they find their rest in You.'

As wonderful as our home here on earth might be, even the best of homes cannot bring abiding peace to our restless hearts. But we can set up home in the heart of God, where there is plenty of room, plenty of love, plenty of conversation, plenty of peace, and all our family and friends right by our side.

My Heavenly Father's home has many rooms — plenty for everyone. My Heavenly Father's home is safe and built to last for all Eternity. It is a home of lasting value and precious dreams. My Heavenly Father's house is filled with family — my family. All you need to do to live in this special home in Eternity is to accept the place that your Heavenly Father has prepared especially for you. Home is what we make it here and what we get to enjoy in Eternity.

'A man travels the world over in search of what he needs and returns home to find it.'

—◦ GEORGE MOORE ◦—
IRISH WRITER (1852–1933)

Jessika's Story

Mum was an amazing woman and I know I could never really put into words how amazing she was — and still is.

The Disney character Tinkerbell was always so full of life, adventurous, and so bright, leading so many people with her light, and not to mention so tiny! I can recall numerous times when my Mum, a 150-centimetre-tall lady, would say to me, with her New York accent, 'I love Tinkerbell — we are a lot alike — she is so small on the outside, but so mighty on the inside — that's me, tiny but mighty.' Here is the legacy and life of my amazing mother ... my best friend ... my Tinkerbell.

I lived in New York for the first three years of my life. In 1987 we moved from busy New York City to sunny Southern California. My sister and I have always grown up with the privilege of having a stay-at-home Mum. She used to say, 'Staying home and taking care of my family was the best thing that God could ever grant me.' I thank God for allowing her to be at home every day when I got back from school. Each day I would come home and she would be waiting at the door for me, with open arms and a big kiss. Everything I needed I had, and everything I wanted, my parents made a way.

Throughout my high-school years, I got very involved in all the activities in school. My family was at every event. My Dad and Mum joined the hospitality team and made sure every person at every event got fed. My school recorded all performances and guess who would be at the front of the line to purchase a tape? My Mum! Sometimes I would come home and find her curled up on the couch — thinking she was watching a movie, but there I was on the screen, singing my heart out — 'Somewhere Over the Rainbow' from *The Wizard of Oz*. I would say, 'Mum, what are you doing?' She would say, 'I'm just watching your tape ... again!!' My sister and I would crack up laughing. She was our biggest cheerleader.

In December 2001 my Mum encouraged me to apply for Bible college in Sydney. She believed in me and she knew that she and my father had raised a mature, strong woman. She also made a deal with God, saying to him, 'All right, God, I will let you have Jessie in Australia for two years. After that she has to come home ... please don't let her stay and get married there. I want my grandchildren here in California, I want my baby home.' She was too funny. I can imagine her, a little Italian Mamma, on her knees having a conversation with God. She was one hilarious, faithful, strong woman, who prayed all the time for everyone in the world, especially her family. I ended up staying in Australia for two years, coming home to visit every so often.

I went home for my sister's wedding. I was there for two weeks. It was the first time in a long time that everyone from my Mum's side of the family and my Dad's side of the family got together; there were over 200 of us, it was amazing! I flew back to Australia and I started a third year at college. Almost every day I talked to my Mum; I felt such an urgency to call her and tell her I loved her. One time in the phone conversation, I started to cry and I kept repeating over and over again, 'Mummy, I love you, I love you, I truly love you more than a daughter can love a mother, more than a friend could love a friend ... I love you always and forever!' She started to cry and she said in a gentle, loving voice, 'I know you love me, Jessie, and I will always love you too, no matter what.' I never knew why we had that conversation until three weeks later, when my life took a turn that I never, ever thought it would take.

Never once did my family talk about what would happen if one of us passed away. I guess you could say it wasn't a relevant thing to speak about. We always hoped and prayed that we would go to Heaven together, as a family. Everyone knows one day you'll pass away, but when it actually happens to someone you are very close to, reality hits you like a train.

I remember clearly the night I got the phone call. I was getting back from a fun trip in the city with my girlfriends. It was about twelve o'clock at night and the phone rang; it was my Aunt from Tennessee. I was pretty confused about why she would be calling this late. When my room-mate handed me the phone, my Aunt immediately asked me how I was doing, and then reminded me that my Dad had had eye surgery a few weeks earlier. She said, 'He needs to go back because they think there could be an infection.' She told me she wanted me to come home right away and that I would need to pack my bags for a good three weeks. She said it would be best to come home and help around the house.

I left Sydney and arrived in California. I was so excited when I got off the plane, I couldn't wait to see my family again. But this time my Mum and Dad didn't know I was coming home. My Aunt said not to call the house; it was going to be a surprise. I didn't realise until later the real reason why I couldn't call. When I walked off the plane I saw my brother and my cousin. They were so excited to see me, they acted normal and everything was fine. We got into the car and for the whole hour's drive home we chatted. I remember asking them at one point if we were going to stop by Mum's work and surprise her and tell her that I was here for three whole weeks. I could picture exactly what she would be wearing, her face when she saw me and what she would say. They didn't really respond to my question, but at the time I didn't even realise they didn't respond, I was just so in awe that I was back at home for a couple of weeks.

My brother and my cousin later told me it was the hardest thing they ever had to do, to watch and know that what was going to come around that corner in my life was going to have a major impact on me forever. As we got closer to home my brother rang the house and told them we were almost there. I didn't think anything of it; to me everything seemed normal. We pulled up to our driveway and I was so excited to surprise my family, I jumped out of the car. Just before I ran into my house, my brother gave me a big hug and then my cousin. They both told me how they missed me so much. I was sort of confused because I had seen them only six weeks ago at my sister's wedding. I left them and ran to the door. When I opened the door I saw my Dad standing in the doorway. I smiled really widely. I was shocked to see him out of bed and at home; I thought he would be at the hospital.

I soon heard the words that I never imagined I would hear ... 'She's gone, she's gone.' All I could do was stand in confusion. Who's she? Who's gone ... the cat? What is going on? Then I saw my sister come out from behind my Dad and her face was full of tears and black mascara running down her cheeks. I looked to the right of my Dad in our lounge room and standing there were some of my Aunts and Uncles, who lived on the other side of America.

I then realised, wow, could it be ... Oh God. I turned
around and ran outside into the middle of the street; I fell
to my knees and raised my eyes to the sky. My entire
family ran after me and embraced me. But for that
moment, everything around was mute. I didn't feel anything
or hear anything. When I looked into the sky the only
thing I remembered was some words I had spoken on the
plane. Over and over again I repeated those words in my
heart; they were so loud and clear: 'You'll never leave me
nor forsake me, no matter what!' Since then I have never
stopped holding on to that truth.

Everyone knew that my Mum had passed away, all my
family and friends in Australia and in America, except me.
My family didn't want me to know when I was in Australia
because I would have had to fly fourteen hours in agony,
by myself. Dad wanted to fly out and tell me, but my
family knew I would have wanted to know in my old
home, where I felt safe. Being the baby in the family and
being so far away and so very close to my Mum, everyone
knew that it would be the hardest thing for me to find out
and for them to witness my reaction. My family wanted to
do everything to try and protect me from the pain. But as I
learned at age nineteen, there are some things in life you
just can't control, and death is one of them. I learned that
life is a choice; the one thing I do have control of is my
decisions in life.

For weeks I felt numb; all I wanted was to feel
something. Empty and hollow on the inside, shocked and
lost on the outside. Every time someone would walk into
the house I would think it was her. While everyone was
asleep at night I would lie awake thinking about the last
conversation we had. I would close my eyes and imagine

her right next to me, holding me and praying over me. The love that my mother gave me was a love that was unconditional. It was a love like no other. She gave me enough love to give to the world and still I would have enough left over for myself. I was so blessed to have a woman like that in my life. Everyone that knew her loved her. With Mum, once she met you, you weren't just a friend, you were family. Her heart grew each day she was alive. The more and more people she encountered, the more she loved. She passed away from an enlarged heart. no-one knew she had it. One night she just went to sleep and took her last breath here on earth and the next breath was taken in Eternity.

At her funeral, no-one was allowed to wear black, for we were going to celebrate her life. My family and I knew she was dancing and singing in Heaven, rejoicing with the angels in the choir. At her funeral there were over 400 people, some of whom I had never met. Each person came with so much love and tears of compassion and hope for me and my family. It was such a beautiful day, there was so much food ... what can I say, we're Italian! But I didn't eat any food that day, nor did I have an appetite for another two weeks. I remember clearly that after the men in our family carried out the casket my brother and I went outside and we both took a deep breath; in silence we stood there gazing out into the sky. Two little butterflies fluttered by and my brother said, 'Look, Jessie, it's Mummy and Jesus.' That put a smile on my face and made me giggle. It was a funny thought, but since then every time I see a butterfly I think of Mummy and how she is flying free.

As the grieving process went on, the emotions came like waves: some would hit harder and stronger than the others.

Every time I would grieve I would get frustrated. I knew that after I was done crying my eyes out, Mum would still be in Heaven and I would still be here on earth without her; nothing could bring her back. But I soon realised that as I continued to grieve and allow what I felt to be expressed, whether it was anger, sadness, or shock, slowly but surely more healing was taking place.

Many memories passed through my hands for the first year or so. I found many cards and letters that Mum had sent me here in Australia. I found birthday cards, and letters that had a countdown of how many more days till I got home to visit. She was cute like that, always making everyone feel special and important. She had such a way about her which drew out the best in each individual she encountered. As holidays, anniversaries and birthdays pass, the pain of missing her doesn't go away — I tend to miss her more — but the sense of wonder and questioning has died down. I have come to realise each day that I have this moment, this day to make a difference; yesterday is history, tomorrow's a mystery, but today is the day that I am alive and I have now!

I know she is in Heaven preparing a home for me and my family. She is probably on the hospitality team, making sure the food is prepared and Heaven is sparkling clean! Here on earth, I don't think she slept much. She was a woman on a mission, always giving of her time and her life, always looking for a way to bring Heaven to earth. She knew her value and walked in confidence.

Each minute that passes is one minute closer to the ones we love, who have made it home before us.

Eunice's Story

My story began on 28 November 1997. Our son Andrew was married to Dominique on this day. Little did we know what lay ahead for us. I call this moment in time 'the four o'clock knock'.

Just three weeks after their wedding, on 21 December, we were woken up just before 4 a.m. and found the police at our front door. This is probably every parent's worst nightmare. We looked through the window and saw a police vehicle with its blue light. We knew immediately that this was bad news of some sort. Not for one moment did we think of Andrew and Dominique.

Then we heard the words 'Your son and his wife have been killed.' I felt certain that someone had made a mistake, and that the police would find it was a case of mistaken identity.

Our beloved son Andrew, twenty-six, and his wife, Dominique, twenty-seven, were young doctors. They had joined Westmead Hospital as interns the year before. They were still on honeymoon leave and had been driving home from Carols by Candlelight in the Domain when their blue Daihatsu sedan collided with another car being driven on the wrong side of the M4 freeway.

The other car's forty-year-old male driver and an eighteen-year-old female passenger were trapped in the wreckage for two hours before being freed. The woman was in a critical condition and the man, awaiting an interview by police, had severe bruising and cuts. His own brother died in the accident as he sped the wrong way along the M4. He was unlicensed and drunk, with a blood alcohol reading of 0.207, but he had no prior record. A father of ten, he was in Australia on a three-month study visa but had overstayed to remain here with his dying mother. She had died ten days before the accident.

The driver and his passenger were admitted to Westmead Hospital, where Andrew and Dominique worked. The hospital staff were incredibly distressed. Westmead is a large hospital, but the staff still share a sense of family. They had just lost two young doctors in a tragic accident who had only just started their married lives together, and it was Christmas. It was front-page news. The Christmas road safety blitz had just begun and it was off to a tragic start.

The judge who ruled in the case said that in their short lives both doctors demonstrated they were on their way to distinguished careers in medicine. He also said that their deaths were a dreadful loss to the community.

The man who was responsible for the accident was ordered to stay behind bars for at least four years. The judge said that although the man expressed considerable remorse, he must suffer the penalty of his folly.

When asked at the time about the sentence, my husband responded. 'It can't bring our children back.' How true. It was so hard coming to terms with the fact that we were never going to see our son and daughter-in-law again on this earth. In fact, the word 'forever' suddenly took on a whole new meaning. We were never going to see the children they may have had, never going to see them fulfil their purpose on this earth.

No parent is ever prepared for the loss of a child, irrespective of age. I remember a few years ago, while visiting a nursing home, I met a ninety-year-old lady whose seventy-year-old daughter had just died, and for her, as she expressed it, 'She was my baby, my only child.' As I hugged this lady, I knew that her grief was the same as mine.

During the very early stages following our tragedy, I knew that God was going to use our experience to touch others who were also going through grief following the death of someone very close to them. We are so grateful to God that both Andrew and Dominique are now in Heaven with the Lord.

Some time later my husband Keith and I were invited by a pastor to facilitate a grief support group at our church, which we have done for over four years now. It is a blessing to be able to help other people receive hope in the midst of their bereavement. We are thankful that God is using our sorrow to help and bless others.

Home, Sweet Home

- **Take the opportunity to make beautiful the place you love most.**
  After any life-changing experience, returning home can be traumatic or it can be something to look forward to. Over time, allow yourself to dream about how you want things to be. Remember, you won't take any of the 'stuff' with you when you go, so make it beautiful but don't attach any eternal value to it. Remember, it's those who live in the home that make it what it is, not the décor.
- **Become an observer.**
  Make note of what catches your attention. Look through magazines, watch decorating shows on television and give your tired furniture a lift. Use a combination of the colours you love with the colours that have always made your house a home. If you want a second opinion, ask an expert.
- **Take an honest inventory.**
  Decide which room or rooms you would like to improve and those that you want left alone. Don't allow family or friends to force you into changing things that you like, even if they think it would make you feel better. Rushing into it will only cause you to regret it.
- **Work towards a goal.**
  Determine how long it will take for your project — six weeks, six months or a year. Enlist the help of family, friends and tradespeople if necessary and make sure that whoever

starts to help you actually stays around long enough to help you finish the job!

⬧ **Balance practicality with flair.**

This may be your opportunity to try some different decorating ideas that allow for your personal touch in turning ordinary things into things uniquely your own. You could use a beautiful blend of old with new to give you the best of both worlds.

⬧ **Give change a chance.**

Redecorating can be as simple as just removing a piece of furniture, although the most dramatic change usually comes from introducing a strong new colour or a different pattern. Just remember that all change, even for the better, requires a period of adjustment. However, most people who have decorated their home or any portion of it will tell you that they should have done it sooner.

⬧ **Find joy in doing.**

Home improvements are a great way to take your mind off your problems. For some, home improvements give them a whole lot of new problems to worry about. Laugh — these problems aren't eternal, they're just about stuff and sometimes stuff is good for us, as long as we look at it with an Eternity perspective.

Wrinkles

Well, old Bob hasn't got much, but he values his boots
He values the time he spends growin' flowers
He still loves his babies that grew to be men
He recalls all the days 'n' nights and the hours
When he and his woman worked on the land
In the heat and the dry, in the cold and the wet
He still picks her a rose and his old heart still races
She's still the most beautiful girl that he's met
And you ask is he happy . . . and you ask is he happy . . . ?
He's got wrinkles from smiling, he feels lucky and free
And he knows what it means to live here in the sunshine
He's got wrinkles . . . from smiling . . .
He walks with Amelia down to the store
With a little cane basket for the bread and the daily Sun
Still hand in hand like babies in the meadows, and young faces turn
Love is so beautiful, it can be so deep
And a man is a king when he has his own princess
Bob wears no crown, no long flowing robe
But there in his mind he still rides on his black stallion
Then a cold winter came, and Bob was alone
His beautiful princess had flown with the angels
He faded so quickly, the man became old
And the wandering dew soon covered the roses
First just a cane, then a strong stick for walking
Then just a chair with a grey old man dying
All that he lived for was always beside him

So Bob left in peace, to join his lady
And you ask is he happy . . . and you ask is he happy . . . ?
He had wrinkles from smiling
He felt lucky and free
And he knew what it meant to live here in the sunshine
He had wrinkles . . .

∽ JOHN WILLIAMSON ∽

CHAPTER EIGHT

Memories

that never fade

'What we have once enjoyed we can never lose.
A sunset, a mountain bathed in moonlight,
the ocean in calm and in storm —
we see these, love their beauty, hold the vision to our hearts.
All that we love deeply becomes a part of us.'

⚬ HELEN KELLER ⚬
WE BEREAVED

The Notebook

The Notebook is a movie about a summer romance between two young lovers, Allie (Rachel McAdams) and Noah (Ryan Gosling). Noah grew up not having much, but enjoying the simple things of life. Allie, on the other hand, came from an upper-class background, never truly knowing what it was to work for something she really desired, but always wanting to experience freedom. As love blossomed challenges came along, but no matter the distance between them, their love was stamped on each other's hearts forever. Allie soon faces a decision that will alter which path her life is to follow: a choice between her soulmate and her class. An older gentleman (James Garner) faithfully tells this tale to his companion (Gena Rowlands). Together they unfold this beautiful love story, and healing and hope begin to take its place in these two hearts.

In this movie, you begin to fall in love with Allie and Noah right from the start. Their love is full of life and spontaneous events. You actually begin to experience the joy of these two lovers. This movie triggers something inside the hearts of all who watch it. You begin to relate it to a situation you have been in or you try to picture yourself as one of these characters.

Towards the middle of the movie and definitely at the end, you start to feel the aching in the characters' hearts. Their love for each other is so full and strong that it will last through anything. Towards the end of the movie it is revealed that the older gentleman and his companion are in fact Noah and Allie. Allie has Alzheimer's and Noah reads to her each day and night from her notebook, which she has kept since the two of them met so many years before. This helps her remember their love. Every once in a while she remembers Noah and their life together, but only for a short time. Soon she falls back into forgetting. One night he goes into her room to visit and she remembers his familiar face. As they look at each other you begin to feel the pain and the longing that they have to be together.

The Eternity moment that surpasses them all is when Allie and Noah lie down together and go out into Eternity, in the same beautiful breath.

At the end of the movie you come to realise what's really important in your life: family. And we are reminded once again how powerful love can truly be. Their love made miracles, it brought joy and it never ended. The power of the human memory is astounding. Even through a debilitating illness such as Alzheimer's, glimmers of hope shine through.

We must strive to have great memories to look back on, treasure and leave behind.

Memories

Memories are life's living library.

WHEREVER A BEAUTIFUL SOUL HAS BEEN, there is a trail of beautiful memories.

My Aunty Eileen was a very special woman. She was diagnosed with Alzheimer's disease not long before she passed away. A widow of just a few years, Aunty Eileen never had children because she was unable to. An only child herself, she had found herself alone in her old age, though not because she didn't want a family. I loved my Aunty Eileen. She was completely eccentric and very sociable. She dressed up to go to the theatre but she also dressed up to go grocery shopping — never without a full face of make-up and a fur wrap. Hers was a timeless glamour! It was sad for us as a family when Aunty Eileen seemed to be losing her memory. She had coped so well on her own at home, even though we knew she missed Uncle Horry more than we could ever imagine.

Aunty Eileen was ninety-three years old when she was finally moved into a nursing home. She forgot so many things, not least of which was to eat. It was necessary for her to be cared for properly, but she was so unhappy with the move. I remember the day that she moved into the same nursing home as my Nanny. Mum thought it would be a good idea to have the two in the same place so that she could ensure that Aunty Eileen received regular visits from our family.

It wasn't long, however, before Aunty Eileen went missing. She had walked two kilometres in her dressing gown and was found back at her home, the place she longed for — the only place that she felt she belonged. This was really interesting for us, as we had been told that she had lost her memory and that she wouldn't know us or much about anything from the past. She knew my Mum, she knew my Dad, she recognised my niece Sarah and she walked all the way home in her dressing gown and slippers at ninety-three years of age. The memory is a powerful force, even in one diagnosed with Alzheimer's.

The night that my Nanny was rushed to hospital was the same night that Aunty Eileen was admitted to the same emergency ward. It was a harrowing night to say the least. Aunty Eileen was very sick with pneumonia but was still able to communicate. My Mum and sister Kathy sat by Aunty Eileen's bedside and talked to her and consoled her. Mum was told by the doctors that Aunty Eileen probably wouldn't make it, so in the time that she had by her bedside, Mum asked Aunty Eileen if she had made her peace with God. Aunty Eileen replied in a surprisingly lucid manner, telling my Mum that she had once been a churchgoer and that she had once been a Christian and that her Mum was a Christian and always prayed for her.

Mum asked Aunty Eileen if she could pray with her and if she wanted to make her peace with God right then and there. Aunty Eileen told Mum that yes, she wanted to make her peace with God, so Mum prayed with her and at the end they both said, 'Amen!' (so be it). Mum recalls those precious moments as being extraordinary because of how completely 'with it' Aunty Eileen was. She spoke so fondly of her own mother and of her desire to connect back with her Heavenly Father. These were not the words of someone who was out of their mind. She knew what she was saying and she spoke from her heart.

These precious words that Aunty Eileen spoke were the last words she ever said. That evening she slipped into a coma as fever came over her body. Aunty Eileen lasted a few days but never communicated verbally again. When I saw her after she had lost her ability to speak, she communicated with me through her eyes and her touch. I could see the peace of God was very present in her life even though it was evident that her time here on earth was coming to an end.

It was a cold winter's night and I had been running up and down between the third and sixth floors of Concord Hospital in Sydney, as the doctors and nursing staff called us to let us know one was slipping away, then the other. It was a surreal experience. This one time, however, we knew this was it for Aunty Eileen. We hurried up to her room and stood by her frail body. She was breathing so softly that we thought she must have already gone. Her passing was to be any moment. 'God is faithful, Aunty Eileen. We love you. I love you. Goodbye, precious lady.' She was gone. I couldn't believe that she was gone. The incredible relief of knowing she had peacefully gone to Heaven was the only thing that got me through that night.

After we had said our final goodbyes, we walked down the corridor, entered the lift and headed back to Nanny. I still to this day cannot believe that both these precious women (married to two brothers) were to depart from here to Eternity within a few hours of each other.

As we stood numb with pain, one of the nurses kindly handed me a bag of Aunty Eileen's belongings. I took hold of the bag and began to sob as I thought about its contents: her toothbrush, hairbrush, dressing gown and slippers. That was all that was left. That plastic bag could have been filled with diamonds and it would have made no difference to me, because she was gone and anything left just didn't matter. Tears are streaming down my face as I remember that night as though it were yesterday. I can still remember that moment when Aunty Eileen breathed her last on earth before her spirit soared into Eternity; that miraculous moment so special it's impossible to articulate in words.

'All my possessions for a moment of time.'

—∽ LAST WORDS OF QUEEN ELIZABETH I OF ENGLAND ∾—

Soon after Aunty Eileen passed away, Mum offered to help clean up the home that had been built for her and Uncle Horry. A number of relatives, nephews and nieces were on the scene to help with the cleanup. Aunty Eileen's home was filled with memorabilia from trips she'd had overseas. There were some lovely antique pieces and other beautiful belongings, but there was also a whole lot of stuff that just got taken to the tip.

The following weekend I arrived at Aunty Eileen's to see Mum and to help with anything I could. I asked Mum who was going to take the beautifully framed portrait photographs of Aunty Eileen and her parents and was shattered when Mum told me that no-one wanted them so they were left to go to the tip. I was so upset, I collected some and took them home. To me these memories were so precious because they were all that was left of her. I wanted to keep them to remember her by.

Mum recalls a time when Aunty Eileen was desperate to be remembered, saying, 'Lynore, will you remember me? Please remember me. Tell me that you will remember me.' Because she didn't have any children of her own, she was concerned that no-one would remember her. Mum promised to always remember her. I promise to remember her. Aunty Eileen mattered and the memory of her matters. Those words, 'remember me', are words that I will never forget.

Everybody needs memories and wants to be remembered. Memories are like precious pictures in your mind that never fade. Not only are we able to receive comfort through our five senses, we also collect memories through them. We remember how people look, how their skin felt, their scent, how it tasted when we kissed them, what their voice meant to us.

Good memories are powerful and healing reminders of people, places, events and experiences. The key to our ongoing healing is to hold on to our favourite things and to let go of memories that cause recurring pain. I call it 'living like we've never been hurt'. If we can go on living like we've never been hurt, we will be able to make the most of our favourite memories, as the pain of what we've been through slowly but surely fades away. Living like we've never been hurt is not denying that we have been hurt, it's just a choice to live in a different frame of mind. We get to choose good memories or bad memories.

Fortunately, when it comes to the passing of those we love, remembering the good times is often easier than when they were with us. For most, positive feelings stick around longer than negative ones. 'People have an inherent bias to view their experiences in a positive light,' says psychologist Richard Walker. The reason for this is that most of us go through more positive experiences in life than negative ones. The good news is that happier emotions have a longer shelf life in our memories and negative emotions tend to fade out over time. This fading effect, however, works differently for those suffering from depression, who tend to have both positive and negative emotions fading at the same rate, and are pulled more towards negative memories.

Memories of youth and young adulthood are likely to be amongst our clearest and fondest recollections; memories of our first car, our first home, our first job, our first love. 'Memories tend to cluster in the years between ages ten and thirty,' says Professor David Rubin of Duke University. People tend to recall things that happened during that time because many of these experiences were firsts and the novelty of them made them highly memorable.

What makes these experiences memorable are the feelings attached to them. Memories are stored and beliefs are formed as a result, especially during our young adult years. We're at our sharpest mentally when we're young, so we have more mental resources to store information efficiently. That, in turn, makes memories easier to retrieve and enjoy reminiscing over later. And that's why our parents and grandparents have a tendency to speak about the good old days with such fondness.

'Autobiographical memories'[7] that tell the story of our lives are always undergoing revision, because our sense of self is too. We are continually extracting new information from old experiences and filling in gaps in ways that serve some current demand. 'Autobiographical memories' may be accurate without being literal. They may also represent the personal meaning of an event at the expense of accuracy. Times and locations are usually inferred rather than pinpointed with accuracy. Things that happened are often open to interpretation rather than absolute fact. Imagination is used and the experience of remembering is always present, with the memory lasting for many, many years.

That is why some people seem to have selective memory. It's not even that they are lying or making up stories, it's just that we all tend to record and recall life's experiences very subjectively. If your loved one perhaps didn't treat you very well, and their life here on earth was fraught with dysfunction and pain, you will probably be recalling some of that past pain in a different way now that they are not here any more to cause it. And that's why it's easier to let go of hurt and to hold on to the good memories that you'll never allow to fade.

What's also true is that we tend to remember recent experiences more accurately, and tend to become increasingly vague the further back in years we reach. We use our imagination to tweak our memories for a number of reasons. We rely on memories of the past to help us imagine and make sense of the present. We then tend to develop and rehearse scripts of certain kinds of common experiences so we'll know how to act in future situations. That is so we can minimise pain.

Sometimes people use their imagination to make sense of (and sometimes make excuses for) someone else's past. There are times when imagination gives memories a positive spin. As we age, we tend to cast earlier hardships as experiences that made us stronger. But imagining a better past isn't always helpful, especially if it makes us deny that we've been hurt or that we've hurt others. Of course it is possible to forget traumatic events. However, ask most people who have survived the horrors of war, tragic accidents, sexual abuse or any other kind of abuse, and they will tell you that the pain of the trauma has faded but the memory of the event remains. That's where our relationship with God is so important. He is the healer that brings restoration to our soul and healing to our memories.

Some people may be predisposed to imagination-based false memories, and this can be dangerous — especially if 'truth' is manufactured to annihilate someone. But some consequences of memories that have been influenced by imagination are not as serious as others. So at your next Christmas dinner when your relatives start with their version of a family story, you can laugh along with everyone else, even if it's not all true, and especially if it makes for a funny story. What is important is the fact that you're all together, laughing and enjoying each other's company. Too many relationships have been spoiled and too many people have been hurt because some party-pooper in the group refuses to allow a little imagination latitude or a 'different perspective' that would hurt absolutely no-one.

Perhaps you haven't been left with beautiful words or wonderful memories and now you need to work on sifting through all that's in your mind in order to bring to the forefront those memories that will bring you most comfort at your greatest time of need. The human mind is a remarkable part of our anatomy that bring us blessing and healing once we understand how it works. We can set it on the right course for our future.

Loss is a time for grief but also can be a time of relational tension. Once we understand more about memories, I believe it helps us understand people and relationships a whole lot better. According to Daniel Schacter, author of *The Seven Sins of Memory: How the Mind Forgets and Remembers,* the 'sins of memory' can be divided into the following areas.

'Transience
Transience is a basic feature of memory and the cause of many problems. It is the failure to bring to mind a desired fact, event or idea because of a weakening or loss of memory over time.

Absentmindedness
Absentmindedness involves a breakdown between our attention and memory. For example, we lose our keys or glasses or forget that we have an appointment, usually because we are distracted or preoccupied with something else.

Blocking
Blocking involves a foiled attempt to find information that we may be trying hard to recall. An example is trying to put a name to a face. We know that we know but we can't recall because our memory is blocked.

Misattribution
This involves assigning a memory to the wrong source, or incorrect filing of information. It mistakes fantasy for reality and is a far

more common problem than people realise. In legal terms, misattribution can cause an innocent person to lose their life. In social terms, misattribution can destroy relationships.

Suggestibility
Suggestibility occurs when memories are recorded as a result of leading questions, comments or suggestions when a person is trying to call up a past experience. The ramifications are similar to those of misattribution when it comes to legal and social issues.

Bias
Bias is the powerful influence of our current knowledge and belief system or perspective that filters how we remember our past. Bias allows for editing or completely rewriting our previous experiences, unknowingly and unconsciously, in light of what we now know or believe.

Persistence
Persistence is something that we would banish from our minds forever, if we could. It entails disturbing information or events being played out over and over again; remembering everything we wish we could forget. Everyone is familiar with this problem, and it usually hits us in the middle of the night. In some extreme cases, persistence can be debilitating and even life-threatening, especially for those who suffer from depression.'

I hope this information will shed much-needed light at this time, to help you with people in your world and also to help you recognise what you may be going through. Our minds are incredibly powerful, and with God on our side, regardless of all the thoughts that are currently in our minds, we can be assured of a renewed mind and a positive collection of memories.

Even though the seven areas of memory may seem like our enemies, they are actually a vital part of our mind's function because they help our memory work well. These aspects illuminate how memory draws on the past to inform the present, preserves elements of present experience for future reference, and allows us to revisit the past whenever we like. Memory's weaknesses are also its strengths, elements of a bridge across time that allows us to link the mind with the world.

Women are far more inclined to be ruminators than men: stressing about problems, disappointments and encounters and getting stuck there. Women tend to dwell on the symptoms, causes and consequences of their loss, whereas men tend to ignore them. Women tend to go over and over their negative thoughts and feelings, examining them, questioning them, kneading them like dough. And like dough, their problems swell in size.

When something happens that causes a halt in our normal daily activities, many of us become flooded with anxiety and emotions, causing us to feel out of control. We are basically experiencing an 'epidemic of morbid meditation', says Dr Susan Nolen-Hoeksema, author of *Women Who Think Too Much*.[8]

As you ruminate, you run faster and faster around the treadmill of your brain, deepening the grooves and intensifying levels of anxiety and despair. This kind of thinking needs identifying and it needs to be dealt with, otherwise it will get even harder to cope with your grief. Overthinking is something that we might have a natural tendency towards — using our memory to rehash and punish us and everyone around us in order to try to somehow deal with thoughts that simply won't go away. There is a better way. Overthinkers are not standard worriers. Regular worriers worry about what may happen to them in the future; overthinkers go over and over what happened in the past.

I for one am prone to overthinking. The way that I have to combat this natural tendency is to fill my mind with healthy, positive words that have the power to renew my mind and change not only my thoughts but also my thinking habits. The way I do this is by reading my Bible, as it contains words that promise life and a renewed mind. Reading my Bible has literally changed the way I think, the way I record and the way I recall memories.

The reason women tend to be overthinkers is that they pour a lot of time as well as mental and emotional energy into processing the myriad details surrounding all the people in our world. Sometimes they think and think and think until they simply cannot act, because they become frozen in their thoughts. Men tend to take the opposite tack, at times seeming to launch into action without very much thought at all! That's why men use outlets that aren't related to their problem to solve their problem, such as sport, entertainment or window-shopping for expensive cars and big boys' toys!

We can learn from each other when it comes to thinking styles. The following thinking strategies can help you improve the way you handle your thoughts when facing difficult situations.

❖ **Identify**

Identify whether you are an overthinker — rarely, sometimes or always.

❖ **Assess**

Time yourself the next time you face a difficult thought. If you don't have a way forward by the end of five minutes, you are probably overthinking about it rather than assessing the thought for positive action.

❖ **Focus**

You will know whether you are trying to squash your thoughts out by how much time you spend purposefully trying to avoid facing them. Overthinking is not healthy, but neither is repressing thoughts that need to be worked through.

❖ **Action**

It's important to develop some healthy strategies of distraction when you know you are going down the overthinking road. Exercise is great, so too is cooking (as long as you are not eating too many comfort foods — which is a whole other problem you don't want on board!). Another action I have found really helpful is keeping a journal. For many of the brave people who have shared their personal stories throughout this book, keeping a journal has been a key to their healing.

'The thoughts and memories stored in our brains don't sit there in isolation; they are woven together in intricate networks of associations,' Dr Nolen-Hoeksema says. 'When you are in a bad mood of some type — depressed, anxious, just altogether upset — your bad mood tends to trigger a cascade of thoughts associated with your mood. These thoughts may have nothing to do with the incident that put you into a bad mood in the first place, as when a poor job performance causes you to think about your aunt who died last year.'

In a season of mourning your loved one, you may find that you are constantly thinking about what has happened, perhaps reliving memories in your head or even talking to your loved one as if he or she were in the room with you. The full realisation of your loss may make you feel hopeless, depressed or as though life is not worth living. This is often the most difficult stage of grieving, but it is part of the healing process and will not last forever. Given time, you will be able to think more clearly and you will begin to feel better again. It takes time and you need to take as much time as you need. Pressure to feel better doesn't help the healing process. Relaxing your mind will help give you the space you need to move on.

To help us free up our minds so that we can enjoy the memories that will bring us much joy for many years to come, it's important to work through the clutter in our minds. You may need help with that process, so if you find you are caught on a thinking treadmill and you simply do not know how to jump off, talk to a qualified professional and get some help. Remember, when you are moving forward, you will always be going in the right direction.

Understanding the triggers that make our minds and memories work will help us free up positive space and arrest the negatives that come our way.

❖ **Environment**

When we are helping family or friends come to terms with their loss, it's important to understand the things that may be influencing their memories. To begin with, the environment or circumstances surrounding the passing of a loved one will be influencing their thinking. If it was a slow, painful passing that meant months, weeks, days and hours sitting in a hospital room, memories of this will take time to fade. Or if it was a tragic sudden loss, the mind can create scenario after scenario to try to come to terms with what it must have been like for the loved one who lost their life.

If the person grieving was particularly close to their loved one, it will simply take longer for their mind to settle at a place where they can get on with normal thinking again.

❖ Spouse

The loss of a husband or wife is particularly hard. The surviving partner has to deal with decisions and arrangements, finances and paperwork that can be all-consuming. They may also need to tell children and other family members what's happened, and the recalling of detail can cause them to feel they are in mental meltdown. Memories that they wish they could forget must be recalled in order to relay information.

❖ Child

A child's death is a devastating event that overwhelms a parent, regardless of the cause of death, or the age of the child. In losing a child, parents may feel that they have lost a vital part of themselves. Feelings of desolation may be combined with the sense of injustice for a lost future, particularly in the case of a young child. Sometimes parents find it difficult to console each other when a child has died, as women and men express themselves differently. Marriages are vulnerable when parents go through this trauma, so abundant and ongoing support will be needed.

❖ Parent

Although it is natural for parents to die before their children, it is still an extremely painful loss. Anyone who has lost a parent may feel as though they have lost part of their past or part of themselves. They may also feel frightened about the future, especially if they are still young and dependent when their parent passes away.

If the parent has been living with you, it can be very difficult to adjust to their absence. In addition to dealing with your own grief, you may now have to support or care for a surviving parent.

❖ Suicide

For every one person who commits suicide, there are many others around them who suffer intense grief: parents, partners, children, siblings, relatives, friends and colleagues. The people left to pick up the pieces can suffer not only from loss but also from guilt and shame. We need to support those going through this kind of loss and allow people time to work through their pain.

❖ Family pet

The death of a pet will often mean the loss of a cherished family member and can bring great heartache. Some people find it difficult to understand such a reaction to what they may see as the loss of 'just an animal', and they may therefore be less understanding. However, losing a pet that you and your family have loved will be very difficult and you need to allow yourselves permission to mourn, especially where children are involved. Not long before we lost our beautiful Nanny, our cat Princess was hit by a car. It was our children's first loss and the pain of telling them was just awful. They sobbed their little hearts out. We had a burial service for Princess and talked about Eternity. This experience helped a little to prepare the way for what was ahead when they lost their beautiful Nanny only four weeks later.

❖ Anticipated loss

When we know that we are about to lose a family member or friend, we will begin the grieving process even before the person we love has passed away. Our hearts and minds become flooded with thoughts and emotions as we come to terms with the impending loss. The most important thing to remember at this time is to spend as much time as you can with your loved one; say all the things in your heart about your love for them. Ensure that you are not left with empty regrets, but that you have made the most of every moment you have. Say 'I love you.' Say 'I forgive you.' We only have one life, so make every moment and memory you have count.

Not everyone is able to be with their loved one when they pass on. Jonathan wasn't able to be there when his mother died. He wished so much that he could have been there, but he was able to call and speak to her just hours before she passed away.

The most important thing to remember if this has happened to you is to keep an Eternity perspective. If you could have been there, you would have been there, but most times we won't know when that important moment will be. Remember the fond conversations and remember past happy farewells you were able to share.

I can't encourage you enough to talk to your family while they are still around to share their memories. Everyone deserves to have their memory live on. Everyone who ever lived had hopes and aspirations, and had an impact on other people's lives. It's up to us to ensure their memory lives on.

Something beautiful to do to keep the memory of your loved one alive is to tell stories and pass on history to your children and grandchildren, so that they can get to know them too. Create a family tree and take time to explain to the next generation who each person was and what they were like. I sat with my Nanny a number of times and asked her to tell me about who everyone was. And my kids sit with my Dad and ask him to tell the same old stories of when he was a fireman, over and over again. There's something precious about the retelling of memories.

Memories are one of the best legacies our loved ones leave when they enter into Eternity. Treasure the memories that comfort you, and take time to work through those that concern you. Even some difficult memories can help us to heal when we face them. Share memories with those who listen well and support you. Your memories may make you laugh or cry, or sometimes both. Whatever the case, memories are a lasting part of the relationship we had with our loved one. You may also gain comfort from finding a way to honour your loved one's life.

It's important to remember that healing doesn't mean forgetting. We must remember the one we love and lost. The jokes they retold, the meals they enjoyed, the way their arms felt around you, or their scent as they held you close. Give yourself permission to remember and hold your memories deep in your heart.

> *'When your days on earth are over*
> *and life's weary pathway trod,*
> *May your name in gold be written*
> *in the autograph book of God.'*

> ~ AUNTY EILEEN'S MOTHER ~
> 26 APRIL 1925

Alex's Story

'Two big bangers, please.' I sank further into the passenger seat of our 1976 white Kingswood while my father yelled our order into the speaker at the local McDonald's drive-through. It's true that he had a thick Slovenian accent and that he hadn't quite mastered the Australian vernacular; however, I was convinced that he was calling burgers 'bangers' in an attempt to embarrass me — and it was working. Being a fourteen-year-old private school girl transported around the finer parts of town in an ugly, cheap car was damaging enough to my precious ego — having to endure my father's bad English at McDonald's was too much for this teenager!

It wasn't until many years later that I understood my father cared more about my education than he did about what kind of car he drove or how silly he appeared in public. I cringe now when I think about how ungrateful I was and how painful it was for me to climb out of that car in front of the other schoolgirls.

In addition to the sacrificial and extravagant education policy that my father implemented in my life, he also believed in raising his daughter with the strictest of rules. Discipline was his favourite word. This meant that I was not permitted to have a social life. When I was eighteen, I won the Miss Slovenia Australia crown and everyone went out to a disco afterwards to celebrate. When I completed my final lap around the hall, my father took me firmly by the hand, led me to the dreaded Kingswood and took me home. I was in bed before midnight and awoke the next day unable to see out of my puffy eyes: I sobbed the entire night. I felt like a princess locked in a prison. It was excruciating.

A few months before my twenty-first birthday my relationship with my father grew tenser. I wanted my independence. I wanted my freedom. I wanted to be recognised as a woman. Everything in me wanted to rebel. I was very angry with my Dad all the time. I think that he was so worried about what the big bad world would do to his daughter, and out of that fear he forced me to live a sheltered life. I remember very few pleasant words passing between us at this time.

One Sunday afternoon, Mum and I returned home and as we walked into the hallway we found Dad collapsed on the floor. We called for an ambulance and within minutes Dad was on his way to hospital. It all happened very quickly and I don't think Mum and I had time to think about what was going on.

Mum and I visited Dad later that afternoon and the doctors told us that he was just dehydrated and had a bad bout of the flu. He would be home in a couple of days. Mum had been planning a social event at our home for quite some time that was scheduled for the next afternoon. Dad absolutely insisted that she go ahead with the luncheon. So, the next day, Mum and I entertained forty ladies from church. Towards the end of the meal, I excused myself and Mum explained to the guests that I wanted to hang out with my friends. I said goodbye and drove myself (in the Kingswood) to the hospital.

I wasn't prepared for what I was about to experience. Dad looked very bad. He was struggling to breathe through the oxygen tube and I'll never forget his desperate, sad eyes. My father had always been strong, strict and in control; now he looked helpless and lost. It broke my heart to see him like that, but due to the pride that was in me and in him, I acted like everything was just fine. Pride is an awful thing; it robs us of sincerity and truth. After about half an hour, I couldn't handle being there any more and I made up a ridiculous excuse to escape. Dad asked me to fill out his dinner menu before I left. He wanted soup and orange juice. I ticked the boxes on the form quickly and turned to go, tears streaming down my face. He grabbed my arm and whispered, 'Anita, Daddy's gonna be all right, don't worry.' I couldn't look at him. I nodded and blurted out an annoyed 'I know!' and left the room.

That was the last time I saw him alive. Two hours later, I returned to his hospital bed — he was lying still, no longer struggling to breathe with the oxygen mask. There was no life in him. He didn't look at me. On the table by his side was his dinner: soup and orange juice. He would not eat that meal.

I bent over and kissed his cheek. I couldn't remember the last time I had kissed my Dad. He didn't move. He was dead. I no longer had a Dad. I never told him that I loved him, I never said goodbye, and I never told him 'thank you'. My world was instantly and forever changed.

For the next decade, I ran around the globe trying to escape the pain of the loss of him. I longed for love and acceptance and went looking for it in all the wrong places. I ran away from my family, my friends, from Australia and from myself. The pain followed me everywhere I went. The numbness that the drugs and alcohol provided only lasted until the sun came up the next morning. Over and over again I had to face the hurt and brokenness inside me. But I didn't know how to face it, so I kept running.

A peculiar thing happens when you lose someone you love — you think you keep seeing them. I remember being in Paris and I could have sworn that my Dad was crossing the street and coming towards me. I stopped in the middle of the road ready to greet him. He walked right by me and of course it wasn't him. This occurred several times, and to this day, on the odd occasion I think I see my father here in Sydney.

In time, I found myself living in London and then in New York. I had an amazing career and my social life rivalled those one reads about in the magazines (actually, sometimes I was in the magazines!). During my time in New York, my workout schedule was full and in the middle of an intense workout session I snapped my right achilles tendon. I spent days in hospital and had surgery, and for the first time in my life was forced to spend months in bed recovering. I thought I was going to kill myself from sheer boredom. I remember screaming into my pillow one night, 'God! I give up! I'm done ... I can't do this any more. If you exist, help me!' It was a heartfelt plea and I cried myself to sleep wondering if my life was ever going to feel like it had any purpose at all.

A few months later, I accepted a job transfer to Houston, Texas. I was still in rehabilitation and I started meeting with a specialist trainer at a downtown gym. During our second training session, I noticed that he wore a small gold cross around his neck and I asked him why he did that. He told me that he loved God and wore the necklace as a small statement of his faith. Having been raised in a Catholic home, I was sure that I knew all about his faith. However, over the course of the next few months I learned that his faith was not based on rules, expectations and guilt like my childhood faith, but rather on a concept called grace.

Sean had a peace about him that I couldn't figure out. I made it my personal mission to find out how Sean could have this kind of constant peace and contentment. Sean started teaching me about having a relationship with God. He took me to meet some of his friends and I connected with a wonderful group of women who all shared this same peace and joy. The way these people lived fascinated me, and for the next three months as my leg healed I found that something inside me seemed to be healing also. For the first time in my life, the empty space inside me was being filled. God was revealing His true nature to me through these people. After several months I was no longer satisfied with using their faith as a way to have peace. I wanted my own! So I said a very simple and somewhat unsophisticated prayer asking Jesus to come and live inside me.

My life started to change and I started to change. I gradually stopped seeking self-gratifying ways of making myself feel better. The more I released myself to the service of others, the more I experienced the love and acceptance I had been yearning for. When I stopped focusing on me and started to figure out how I could help others, a peace and contentment entered my life. It was a miracle!

I still miss my Dad, but I remember him fondly. I don't have that awful pain or bitterness in my heart. Now I wear my heart on my sleeve and am always telling my family and friends that I love them and treasure them. My life is full of adventure and love. I know I will see my Dad again one day and we'll laugh and hug each other and there will be no pride separating us. And I will probably kiss his cheeks for hours! These days, whenever I go to the McDonald's drive-through (which is not very often!) I think about my funny Dad, in our funny car ordering big bangers and I am thankful for the memories.

Making Memories

The loss of a loved one can make us remember just how much they mean to us. One great way of keeping their memory alive is to create a memory book.

- Begin by collecting your materials — photos, theatre and airline tickets, newspaper headlines, the receipt from your first mortgage payment, a menu from your favourite restaurant.
- Look for some different items such as pieces of material, or favourite perfume or cologne sprayed onto paper.
- Choose the size of the folder or book depending on what you've collected. Check the number and size of the pages you need.
- Arrange your items, thinking about how they will go together and how many will fit on a page.
- Attach the items to the pages of your book using glue, staples and tape.
- Add words to your book in silver, gold or your loved one's favourite colours.
- You could also send some blank sheets to friends and family members for them to contribute their words, thoughts and pictures, so that you can include them in the memory book.
- Choose a favourite photograph that reflects a happy memory and have it enlarged on a colour copier to use on the cover.
- You may want to have this book electronically scanned, so that you can send it to family and friends.

CHAPTER NINE

Time

changes everything

'Though nothing can bring back the hour
Of splendour in the grass, or glory in the flower;
We will grieve not, rather find
Strength in what remains behind ...'

— WILLIAM WORDSWORTH —
'INTIMATIONS OF IMMORTALITY', 10

Cocoon

A group of senior citizens find their lives turned upside down after they are offered the gift of eternal youth by benevolent aliens in Ron Howard's wonderful movie tribute to the human spirit, *Cocoon*. Brian Dennehy is Walter, an alien who returns to earth to rescue twenty of his friends now hibernating in cocoons off the coast of Florida.

With the help of a charter-boat captain, played by Steve Guttenberg, Walter stores the cocoons in a deserted swimming pool. When three men from a nearby retirement village sneak into the pool for a swim, they discover what seem to be oversized oyster shells in the water. Suddenly they feel physically and spiritually rejuvenated, and believe they've found the elusive Fountain of Youth.

The men's frisky behaviour causes something of a controversy in the retirement village as residents are given the choice of a second youth or accepting the natural ageing process.

Cocoon ponders the price of immortality and the power of everlasting love. The movie's Eternity moment occurs when the newly rejuvenated retirees are forced to choose between living out their lives on earth with their families, or leaving with the aliens and attaining immortality. More character-driven than dependent on the incredible plot, the film's charm comes from the wonderful cast, including Don Ameche.

What sets this movie apart from other science fiction movies is the portrayal of events affecting people in the latter part of their lives. *Cocoon* is a social comedy that appeals to virtually all age groups on different levels. It appeals to the elderly with its semi-serious look at ageing and the pros and cons of reversing the process. It tackles the subject of ageing, asking the question: is growing old a bad thing and to be avoided, or is it an honour to be entered into gracefully?

Time waits for no man, so the choice to flow with it is ours.

Time

'Time heals what reason cannot.'

⁓ SENECA ⁓
ROMAN PHILOSOPHER (1ST CENTURY A.D.)

TIME CHANGES EVERYTHING. THE BEGINNING of life sees our hourglass full on top and the end sees the last grain of sand drop to the bottom. The falling sands of time have given poets a favourite metaphor for the passing hours. In England, hourglasses were frequently placed in coffins as a symbol that life's time had run out. 'The sands of time are sinking,' went the hymn, 'the dawn of Heaven breaks.' The wonder of time and Eternity is that when our time here on earth is up, the sand in our hourglass rises, this time never to fall again.

Time is brought into sharp relief when someone comes to the end of their life. How little time is left, how fast time has gone, how relative time is, how time has been spent, and what really matters in the time that we have. All of these things become very real issues to the individual and their family and friends, as time runs out.

Time belongs to both God and us. Time reveals truth, and time softens many things. It is one of life's great teachers, preachers, counsellors — and friends. Time, if we value it, will make a way for us to understand fully the hope we have. How we measure time is sometimes as subjective as trying to measure a piece of string. *Forever* means 'always, eternal, everlasting, continual, perpetual, ever and ever, for ever more'. Forever, however, does not necessarily mean endless. When it comes to the subject of time, it's good for us to know the differences that forever can bring.

To me, the word forever brings with it thoughts of Heaven, of dwelling in the presence of God, of a place where there are no more tears, no more pain of any kind. Many of us long for that kind of forever, especially those of us with family and friends who we know await our arrival.

However, forever does not always stir up positive and blissful emotions in everyone. For many, forever is a term that brings along with it dread, pain and even despair. For those who don't fully understand Eternity, who don't believe in Eternity or believe any of the many other opposing beliefs, 'forever' has been a source of much dread and worry. The idea of spending an unending period of time *anywhere* seems ridiculous and a state of utter boredom is sometimes all that they can think of.

Sometimes three days or a single moment can feel like forever, especially when we are in the middle of a crisis or significant tragedy. Forever can also mean a time that exists until another time takes over. When we say 'I do' on our wedding day, we are saying this forever. But forever is only as long as 'we both shall live'. Whether we choose to remarry again one day or not, the promise of forever is until one passes from here to Eternity.

The average time that we have on planet earth these days is longer than it was a hundred years ago. The only person to live beyond 120 years was a Frenchwoman named Jeanne-Louise Calment, who was born in 1875 and died in 1997 at 122 years of age. She rode a bicycle to the age of 100 and once met Vincent Van Gogh in her father's painting shop. Her longevity was most likely linked to her genes as well as her lifestyle and the advance of medical technology during her lifetime. Her father lived to the age of ninety-four and her mother to the age of eighty-six.

Not all of us will live to enjoy 122 years of life here on earth. Regardless of the number of years we have, time is something that we need to hold dear and make the most of while it is on our side. The subject of time should not be one that is pondered in the dying moments of an individual's life; it should be a subject that motivates us at any time or season to maximise our lives.

With time comes seasons and with seasons come opportunities for us to grow and learn. Without winter, we wouldn't enjoy the blossom of spring or the warmth of summer. Without summer we wouldn't appreciate the cooling of an autumn breeze. We need to read the times and the seasons of life in order to make the most of them. Life is short, so understanding the seasons of our years helps us to know what to expect and should inspire us to maximise each season we're in.

❖ **Infancy and early childhood (ages 1–6)**
Children acquire their unique view of the world in the first six years of their life and it is during this time and this season that they gain the confidence and curiosity to venture beyond the family. This is a time of wonderful growth.

❖ **Childhood and adolescence (ages 6–20)**
After learning cultural skills, traditions and information in early childhood, a dramatic move of the biological clock brings on puberty. These formative years bring the stress of moulding an identity while the biological and social clocks are out of rhythm. This is a time when much room and space are needed.

❖ **Early adulthood (ages 20–40)**
It's in this season that young adults hear the first of many urgent messages from the social clock: to separate from family, get a job, find a mate, set goals, and face the realities of life. This is a developmental period of intense social growth. This is the time when we set our course.

❖ **Middle adulthood (ages 40–60)**
While some people in middle adulthood have attained their goals and achieved personal success, others have experienced

losses that prompt changes in direction. In this developmental season biological and social clocks fade in importance, and the psychological clock has greater influence. This is the time for increased thinking.

❖ **Late adulthood (ages 60+)**
In late adulthood, the psychological clock becomes even more dominant as the biological clock begins to wind down. This last season of human development is a period when people evaluate the stories of their lives and wonder what they might do to change or add to them.

Each season has a special beauty and usefulness of its own. Life is the same. Each era of life has its own contributions and compensations. Problems arise when we fixate on only one value or purpose in life so that we don't enjoy the characteristics of all seasons.

❖ familiar seasons
❖ festive seasons
❖ family seasons
❖ fun seasons
❖ forever seasons
❖ fearful seasons
❖ fighting seasons.

If we believe that a certain period of life is the only good time, we will forever be discontent when we are not experiencing those years. There will be times of shading and sheltering other people as well as experiences of barrenness and rest, getting ready for another cycle of life and growth. As we understand each season, we will better understand ourselves and the people around us.

During our early twenties, our whole life is ahead. This is the time and season for forming dreams and setting direction. It's the time for deciding on values relating to career, relationships and what's important to you. Our twenties is a time marked with many changes because of establishing the *dream*. This is when many people start their careers, find a partner for life and start a family.

By thirty-something, that dream is under evaluation. This is when time seems to become pressing. We realise we want a home and we want to make sure the career we've chosen is actually what we're meant to be doing with our lives. This is also the time when our circle of friendships changes as friends marry and children start school.

When we're younger, we tend to have higher expectations of what the future will bring — after all, we have all our life ahead. Life can sometimes feel tough when we're young and trying to get ahead, but really, looking back at that period in my life now, it was easy street, with less responsibility, more flexibility, more energy and more time.

Our early adult years are marked by hope, a future-driven outlook, a dream, and a good amount of physical and emotional energy. At that time in our lives, the limitations come in the form of lack of life experience countered with the tendency to feel as though we know it all.

As life and time progress, we experience a higher level of productivity that usually comes with a higher level of responsibility and, sometimes, much anxiety. As we enter this time in our life, the takeoff and landing in our thirties and fifties is when we feel the biggest stretch. We somehow get to enjoy life more during our forties, as we steadily cruise along at a higher altitude.

In our busiest times of life we are most productive, but we also tend to focus on the immediacy of what's going on, rather than looking long-term at what really matters. Many men can seem to focus on career almost to the point of ignoring family time. Women may have to focus on a wider range of areas, as their role often involves multi-tasking career, family and home. This is the season where time flies by: we can't believe another birthday has arrived and that our kids have outgrown the clothes we just bought them.

Once we've passed through our midlife season of re-evaluating what's important, we have more experience and hopefully more wisdom to ensure that our life from now on makes a significant impact. Priorities are settled and those things that are unnecessary obligations have been cut off. This is the time to focus on achieving the dream that was set perhaps twenty or thirty years earlier.

There are times in our life where we can do everything at once, with an abundance of energy and opportunities. Then comes the time in our life when wisdom overtakes energy, and we become even more accomplished. The more time you have lived, the less you will feel the need to compete and the more you will be able to reflect and relax. You will also carry with you a wealth of understanding and wisdom that you simply cannot buy, as time is the only provider of such wealth.

Women and men see times and seasons of life quite differently and tend to peak in these periods at different intervals. Regardless of when that peak hits us, we will all ask the questions, Who am I? Why was I born? What am I meant to be doing with my life? We will assess the direction of our lives several times over our existence here on earth. These assessments come when we marry, have children, look at our career, become empty-nesters, in-laws and grandparents, and then when we face the loss of our spouses. When we're young, we look towards the future. During midlife we tend to concentrate on the present, and the reflective years at the end of our life are made up of the full spectrum of past, present and future focus towards our Eternity.

My great desire is to help you understand the time you have so that you can make the most of your life here on earth. For this to happen we also need to understand the process of sowing and reaping, as these are principles of time that have the potential to change our lives. You may have heard of the saying, 'What goes around comes around.' This is merely a modern expression of the ancient wisdom that says, 'Whatever you sow, that you will also reap.'

When it comes to the passing of your loved one, you can either sow this loss into helping others, or keep it to yourself. Every day you can sow good seeds in all areas of your life. Think of all you do as seeds sown into not just your future, but the future of others.

Dear friends of ours lost their son through cancer; their Eternity story is at the end of this chapter. Marion writes courageously:

> 'People say, "How did you cope?" I would say my faith in God was the biggest thing that kept me sane. I had faith in the fact that God is in control — even if I didn't like what was happening. I believe we don't know everything and God does! Simple — but I can't explain it any other way. Do I still trust God? Yes. We miss Andrew terribly, terribly, terribly, but we know he is in Heaven and one day we will see him again, and my mother and my father and my friends' children (several of them) who have also gone there before us.'

With that perspective in mind, Marion's husband Steve has set out to ensure that the seed of his precious son's life is sown into the future generations. Steve is on a mission now to invest into one thousand young men, to empower them to live lives that make a difference on the earth. He may have lost his son, and Andrew can never be replaced, but Steve is going to make sure that Andrew's death is turned around to help others.

Sowing and reaping are unchangeable principles that help us value each period and season in life. As you face need, sow seeds and look to God as your source in this cycle of life. The following words reflect the process of time.

> *'Sow a thought, and you reap an act.*
> *Sow an act and you reap a habit.*
> *Sow a habit, and you reap a character.*
> *Sow a character and you reap a destiny.'*

—✧ CHARLES READE ✧—
ENGLISH WRITER (1814–1884)

You may be currently sowing in tears, but be assured that through faith you will one day again reap in joy. Sow today but remember it takes time for you to reap. If you sow hundreds of seeds today, you will harvest thousands in the future. The principle of sowing and reaping is not just limited to production of fruit, it is also the key to multiplication of fruit.

If you sow kindness, in time you will reap kindness. If you sow bitterness, in time you will reap bitterness. Similarly, sowing hatred will reap hatred, not compassion, and real love is the only thing you can sow to produce real love in return. By understanding and applying the principles of sowing and reaping we can make a difference to our lives and future. The biggest test we will face is the season of *time in between*, however long that may be.

Because of the gap in time, we sometimes fail to see how our actions and their results are connected. When you make a conscious choice to plant a flower in your garden, the connection between the care you give to the flower and the results you receive is obvious. However, we make countless unconscious decisions every day. Sadly, we often don't value the time and season at hand. When we understand and value the process of time involved in sowing and reaping, we will also understand the value of small things having great impact.

The world in which we live reflects what we sow. If family members or friends are making life difficult for you at this time and you are feeling bombarded with negativity, the most powerful way through your situation is to sow positive actions. Make time to change the way you respond and watch how you enjoy the difference.

Time may cause our body to age and our eyes to grow dim, but it works wonders on our soul. We must take one day at a time. Don't look back and long for a past that has gone and try not to be troubled about the future which has not yet arrived. Live today with the time and opportunity in your hand, ensuring that you sow into a life that will be beautiful and very worth remembering.

Time is a valuable commodity and we need to manage and maximise it as best we can during our lifetime. We need to see our container of life filled with things that matter. Picture a container and put in it as many big stones as will fit. These large rocks are like the areas of your life: spouse, children, career, finances, house, church life, social life, family, friends. I'm sure your container is looking pretty full right now but in fact there is more capacity in that container than you probably realise. Next thing to do is throw in some small stones until you can't fit one more in. Just when you thought that container was as full as it could get, go ahead and add sand right up to the top. All that's left is to try to pour in water and just see what a mess it will become!

❖ **Big stones**

The *large stones* in our life represent our most important priorities. These things are simply not negotiable.

❖ **Small stones**

The *small stones* in our life represent things we may enjoy doing, like some recreational activities. These things are important to us but not necessarily at the top of the list.

❖ **Sand**

The *sand* in our life represents things we have to do, like paying bills and other mundane duties that come our way.

❖ **Water**

The *water* in our life represents those things we don't like doing and really don't need to do. These things usually clutter up our lives.

It's wonderful to have our priorities in place. Sadly, however, this sometimes doesn't happen until it's too late. We may know that it's important to spend time with our family, but we may simply do nothing about changing our priorities. That's why when we face the loss of a loved one, all that really matters is brought into sharp focus. Perhaps now is the time for you to look at the big stones, smaller stones, sand and water and make some decisions and choices about the way you spend your time.

Now may be the first time in a long time that you have considered your own life in the light of Eternity and how you can ensure that every moment counts. When we decide to prioritise our time, we in turn increase our effectiveness and therefore reap the rewards in our relationships, our career and our finances. The reality is, we can't actually manage time as time passes beyond our control. What we can do, however, is manage ourselves and make the most of our lives. Here are some practical ways you can manage yourself in the time you have.

- Create a to-do list.
- Set goals.
- Be proactive.
- Look for opportunities that will bless others as well as yourself.
- Work harder at understanding others.
- Improve yourself, perhaps by returning to study or by getting in shape.

Focusing your mind on maximising your time will help you make the most of your future. Aim high and try to visualise your goals, then focus on just one area at a time. If you want to lose weight, change jobs, move house and get married, then take on one thing at a time. This will help you reach your goals. It may help for you to share your new goals and commitments with someone you trust. Stay positive and keep active. Be happy about your successes, but just as importantly, learn from your mistakes.

Although time passes at the same pace for everyone, we can feel that it slows down and speeds up at different points. For instance, when you are doing something for the first time it can seem longer than the second or subsequent times because of the amount of focus your mind gives the task. It may take exactly the same amount of time each and every time, but it just feels different. When your mind is focused on something other than the passage of time itself, you can think that time has flown. That's why it's important to try to get your mind off the stopwatch of your heartache and onto your future, your family and your friends as soon as you can.

Time certainly seems to go faster as we get older, so we need to ensure that we are making the most of every moment that life grants us here on earth. Someone once said that growing older is like accelerating past a picket fence: each year flashes by faster and faster.

There are cultures on the earth that don't use words for *minute* or *hour*. In these cultures a moment can last an entire day. But we in the time-impoverished Western world live in a culture of juggling balls and spinning plates, hoping that we won't break anything or anyone in the process. There must be a balance between super-activity and stillness and it's up to us to find the middle ground.

Sometimes those things that are supposed to aid us in productivity simply produce more activity for us, causing the speed and anxiety of our lives to increase. We learn to go faster to try and get more done so we can take on more responsibility and get ahead further. We try to jam more big stones into the jar.

Something very interesting happens as the pace of our lives grows faster and faster — our definition of a moment becomes a smaller piece of time and life. By living the way many of us do, we only allow for the 'moments' to appear in short bursts, rather than creating a culture of living meaningfully in the moment called life. This incredible pace at which we live causes aspects of our future to arrive quicker than we expect or want them to. As well as not savouring the moment called life, many of us spend our time being present in body but absent in heart and mind.

Each of us lives in a particular time tank; a culture with its own beat. It's important to ensure that whatever pace you're living at, you measure your time with the inclusion of Eternity. Having an eternal perspective allows us to measure and allocate our time very differently than if we just finish the race of life at, say, eighty years of age. What we spend time on now we will get to enjoy in Eternity.

People do tend to focus on the past as they grow older. They enjoy reruns on television, old music, looking through old photographs — and they also seem to value relationships more with each passing year. Problems only come if we look back at our past and it is empty of what matters and filled only with career accolades and a garage full of material possessions. The past, after all, is a reflection of how well we have lived in the moment called life and how much of life's emotions and experiences we've incorporated into who we are today; how much good we have sown. We spend our lives waiting for the important events to take place, rushing through the moments. Yet the reality is that these moments actually give meaning to our existence. Allowing ourselves to experience the moment called life is what makes us alive and keeps us young.

The urgency of time is released in Eternity. No-one knows the time or the hour of our eternal moment, so we need to make the most of each moment that presents itself to us.

Steve's and Marion's Story

'When the way ahead looks dark and foreboding
And every step seems covered by shadows
When the light you once knew seems so far removed
And your testimony's shaken and your faith's being proved
Its time to dig a well
When your days become repetitive and dreary
And your mind is filled with questions
How long will this valley continue to go on?
Until the well gets deeper and the sweeter your song
Keep on digging your well
As my well gets deeper and my faith gets stronger
I see the wisdom of God in all that I do
And I pray for those who will follow behind me
May they drink from this well and find strength to go on
I've finally dug my well.'

—◦ STEVE PENNY ◦—
JULY 2003

What do you do when unforeseen circumstances invade your world and turn it upside down? In 2003 our family went through the worst eight months we could ever have imagined. In just eight short months our eldest son Andrew went from being a healthy, strong young man to a wasted human shell ravaged by the dreaded disease called cancer. Then, on 4 September of that year, we watched as our son died before our eyes.

Despite all our best efforts at trusting God, we watched as the cancer in Andrew's body came back after each round of chemo, to challenge our faith again. We never once gave up hoping for a miracle, but at the end of it all our son died and we were left heartbroken. We wondered how God could allow such a thing. We felt as though we had given faith in God our best shot and it hadn't worked.

Since then we have tried to keep our faith strong, and to go on trusting God even though it seemed everything we believed in had been taken from us. We decided in the early stages of our trial that whatever the outcome, it would not change who we were.

Since Andrew's death, we have also decided that we will not allow ourselves to become people who retreat from life because of the apparent 'failure' of our faith in God. Our faith in God did not work the way we wanted it to, and because of this our commitment to live a life of absolute faith was challenged for a period of time.

However, we went searching for some answers and God is always there for those who seek Him. The answers we have found have been a remarkable help to us as we have endeavoured to go forward in life and live with fresh hope for the future.

We learnt so much during the time of Andrew's sickness and in the months following his death, and we're still learning, as we try to focus on our future. My Eternity story is not just about our son Andrew, or the difficult season our family has endured. It is about believing when there is nothing else left to do but believe. About hoping when all hope is gone, and trusting God when all seems lost.

There was a defining moment in this journey when the doctor told us that the chemo was not working. Andrew broke down and cried, saying, 'Where is the miracle? Aren't we hoping for a miracle?' These words were to become the challenge that would haunt me after he died. Where was the miracle? There had to be a miracle or my faith was not worth having. Ours is the story of how we found our miracle and came to understand more fully God's incredible love for us all.

My wife Marion was born to help others, and when Andrew became sick she just rose up and became an absolute angel of mercy and care. Not once during the whole time did she ever want time out and she resolutely continued to tend to Andrew's needs whenever she could.

Our loss is immense. There is still not a day that goes by without moments when I think Andrew should be included in my activities, and fresh tears overflow like a river, reminding me again of our earthly loss. I find it so hard to play golf now, as Andrew was my golfing partner. I still start crying for no reason whenever I play and I look up expecting to see Andrew enjoying the game with me. He and I loved to watch sport together on TV and now there is an empty chair in the room. The loss of a dear companion and friend is like a dull ache embedded in the soul.

However God was gracious to me in a most unusual way in giving me a glimpse of Eternity to assure me of our son's blessed state. I was in the city of Bergen in Norway in February 2004, just five months after Andrew died, to speak at a church conference. During a worship session, I had a vision that was totally unexpected and quite amazing. I saw my son Andrew riding on the backs of two angels. He was straddling the two angels and holding on to their wings as he left the earth's atmosphere and flew into the clouds above. It was remarkable, because he looked so frail and sickly as he started his ascent, and then he became progressively stronger and more majestic as he rode on the angels' wings up into the Heavens. As he disappeared from view he looked just so glorious. By the time he had reached the clouds he looked like an ancient gladiator in a chariot.

I just burst into tears and then felt embarrassed as I looked around and found myself back in the worship service, realising my emotion didn't fit the order of the service. I had not been thinking about Andrew, so the vision had come as a complete shock to me.

No sooner had I stopped crying than God opened my eyes again and I saw another vision. This was a scene of people sitting around the throne of Christ in Heaven. I didn't actually see the Lord on His throne, but just knew it was Him. Seated around Him were many people singing with all their might. But my attention was drawn to a person in the front row. It did not look like Andrew as I had known him, yet I just knew it was him, and wonder of wonders, he was singing his lungs out in worship to the Lord.

Just as I began to comprehend the scene, Andrew turned around. He saw me and gave me the biggest grin. It was the smile of a child who has been given their greatest desire. Then he turned back towards the throne of Christ and continued singing with enthusiasm and joy. Finally the scene vanished and I was again back in the worship service in Bergen.

For some reason God had allowed me to see my son enjoying Heaven and it has had a remarkable impact on my life. I can never be the same. Every prayer we have prayed for him, and every moment spent with him sharing about the Lord, has been more than worth it. No one can boast of tomorrow, and Eternity becomes so much more real when someone you love has crossed over. The most wonderful thing about the Christian faith is the fact that death no longer has any finality about it. Death is simply a transition to a new dimension to spend the rest of Eternity in the presence of God and His angels. We knew that Andrew was ready to meet his Saviour, and the truth is, our sorrow was more about us and our loss, rather than for Andrew who we knew had received great gain.

To have seen just a glimpse of Heaven has more than satisfied my soul that it will be worth it all when we finally get there and meet our Saviour face to face. I can rest confident that the first member of our immediate family is already in Heaven catching up with his grandparents and other loved ones.

Whatever experiences we may have here on earth, I can assure you that there is nothing to compare with the amazing sense of completeness and fulfilment you feel in the presence of Christ. If I could put into words the highest sense of accomplishment I have ever felt on earth, it would pale into insignificance compared with the brief moment I experienced in my vision of Heaven.

Being touched by death in such an untimely way has changed how I look at life. Even though I became a Christian as a young boy to escape hell and its eternal torment, I live today as a Christian because I want to spend Eternity with Jesus Christ. My understanding of the Christian life is so different since I have witnessed a little bit of Heaven. Nothing can ever satisfy you on the inside like a moment in the presence of Christ.

I have at times wanted to go to Heaven since I saw those visions, but I know that my work on Earth is not yet finished and that we have two other wonderful children whom the Lord has given us to care for. We want to help them fulfil their godly destiny and make a difference on this side of Eternity. It is too late once you cross over.

There are no dress rehearsals in life. I have realised that it is actually about preparing for Eternity and so I am even more committed to serving God here on earth before I go to Heaven. My passion now is to help as many people as possible live life on earth with the blessed assurance that Heaven is their destination. I want to leave the fingerprint of God on as many lives as possible before I go and enjoy extreme bliss and fulfilment forever and ever.

Where's the Miracle?

'When the trials of life surround you
and your eyes no longer see
And the hope you once held strongly
seems a distant memory
Its time to lift up your head and shout out His name
I'm not just a number and life's not just a game
All my days have been counted by my Father above
So I'll focus again on faith, hope and love.

When the pain you feel increases
and there's no relief in sight
When your path seems filled with sadness
and your days like darkest night
It's time to lift up your head and shout out His name
I'm not just a number and life's not just a game
All my days have been counted by my Father above
So I'll focus again on faith, hope and love.

When your dreams no longer stir you
and no hope they ever bring
When your soul no longer lifts itself
to fly on eagle's wings
It's time to lift up your head and shout out His name
I'm not just a number and life's not just a game
All my days have been counted by my Father above
So I'll focus again on faith, hope and love.'

--- STEVE PENNY ---

Take Time

Since all of us feel pressure, we forget that the way we allocate our time can be changed and shifted. Learning how to 'shift time' can bring both health and longevity.

- ❖ **Engage the moment.**
  This entails finding a balance between super-activity and non-activity without feeling lazy or inefficient as we take a moment to engage.
- ❖ **Make a date.**
  Set aside some time and make a date with yourself. Try to make it a part of the day that you know is least likely to be interrupted. Don't answer the phone or look at your emails. Go for a walk and think about good things.
- ❖ **Be spontaneous.**
  Make no plans for an entire day. Just go off and have an adventure. No time limits, no maps — just enjoy some new territory.
- ❖ **Retreat.**
  Find a special place where you can have regular holidays. Have at least one holiday per year that involves you doing nothing!
- ❖ **Spoil yourself.**
  Do something you love and don't feel guilty about it. A moment can last a whole morning when you're doing something you love. Slowing down is a good way to appreciate the present moment.

❖ **Drive slower.**
For many of us, this will simply mean sticking to the speed limit. And take a moment to enjoy the scenery on your way to work.

❖ **Enjoy a moment's entrée.**
Take a moment before eating. Saying grace or just sitting quietly gives us an opportunity to appreciate and enjoy our meal.

❖ **Speak to your neighbours.**
Spend a moment doing more than waving at your neighbours as you leave or arrive home. Take some time to have a brief chat.

❖ **Do something well.**
Honour the process of doing something well that you normally rush to get finished.

❖ **Have an Eternity perspective.**
Time on earth seems to move slower than we'd like at some periods and faster at others. There is, however, a divine pace that we need to step into.

CHAPTER TEN

Angels

in our midst

'Love your neighbour as yourself.'

~ JESUS ~
MATTHEW 22:39, THE BIBLE

Pay It Forward

In this drama, a young boy stumbles upon a simple way to change the world. Trevor is a bright eleven-year-old boy who comes from a troubled home; his mother Arlene is an alcoholic trying to hold down two jobs to support her son, while Trevor's father left his family behind some time ago.

At school, Trevor's class is introduced to their new social studies teacher, Mr Simonet, a guarded man with severe facial scars. Simonet gives his class an unusual assignment: to think up a practical way to make the world a better place, and put it into action. Trevor comes up with the notion of 'pay it forward': do a needed favour for three different people without being asked, and then ask them to do the same for three others.

Trevor starts by letting Jerry, a junkie living on the streets, stay in his home. Next, he tries to fix Arlene up with Mr Simonet, since both seem to be lonely and the clean and sober teacher might help Arlene stay away from alcohol. Finally, he tries to rescue one of his schoolmates, who is constantly tormented by bullies. Later, journalist Chris Chandler finds himself stuck on the road without a car late one night when a man stops and gives him the keys to a new car, asking him only to pay the favour forward to someone else. Astonished, Chris wants to find out where this philosophy came from.

There are many Eternity moments throughout this film. Trevor knew what it was to live a challenged life, and he decided to put that experience to good use. He did three important favours for people who needed them.

Then, instead of allowing them to pay it back, he asked each of them to 'pay it forward': to do three favours for other people, and then ask them to do the same.

The theme of generosity between strangers, or *human angels*, is powerful. Helping people for no reason brings with it many rewards both here and in Eternity. We know that as we receive hope and comfort from family, friends or complete strangers, we too can offer that same comfort to family and friends, or, just like the movie, we can 'pay it forward' to people we don't even know.

Angels

'And surely I am with you always,
to the very end of the age.'

—◦ JESUS ◦—
MATTHEW 28:20, THE BIBLE

I ONCE BOARDED A FLIGHT on my way home from Coffs Harbour on the New South Wales north coast after speaking at some regional women's events, and I was looking forward to getting back to Sydney. I wasn't very enthusiastic about the flight home in the little plane, so I hoped that someone interesting would sit next to me so we could talk away the hour. I was just settling into my seat when someone walked on board that seemed more than vaguely familiar to me. I thought to myself, 'I know this guy.' Know him! I had got to know him over many evenings at home, as he delivered television commentary on my husband's favourite sport, soccer. I thought to myself that it was very cool that I was on board the same plane as someone my husband really admired. However, I hadn't anticipated what happened next.

'Hello, love. I think I'm sitting here with you,' said the charming man. I turned and said, 'Hello.' I then thought to myself, 'Jonathan will be very impressed!' Not only was this man, whose name I couldn't remember, flying back to Sydney in the same plane, but now he had sat himself down right next to me. He was the company I had hoped for.

On my lap was a beautiful set of pale pink angel's wings that belong to my daughter Bella. I had taken them to my speaking engagements to use as an illustration of how people perceive us when we are kind. When we do something so lovely that causes people to look beyond our humanity, they think we are angels. The angel's wings left a visual memory with people, to remind them to be kind and to love their neighbours.

The wings caught this man's attention. 'I hope we're not going to need those, love,' he said with a grin. I just laughed in reply. After takeoff, the man asked me what the wings were for, so I began to explain that I had been speaking to some groups of women and encouraging them to get outside their own lives and to be actively kind to their neighbours.

The man seemed interested and intrigued by what I was saying. I then asked him what he had been doing in Coffs Harbour and he told me that he was there to promote his new book, *Wogs, Sheilas and Poofters,* about the history of Australian soccer. The man then began to explain humbly who he was and what he did until I jumped in and told him that I knew who he was and what he did, and then, thank goodness, his name came to mind. This man was Johnny Warren, sports commentator and former Socceroo captain.

He seemed surprised and a little impressed that I knew who he was. We then spoke for what seemed like ages about soccer. I told him that he appeared often in our room in the early hours of the morning, at which he laughed. Because of all the time spent by my husband's side while he watched anything to do with his favourite game, I had learned a thing or two. I think Johnny was again surprised and a little impressed that I knew as much as I did about soccer. I became oblivious to the bumps of turbulence we were flying through. I was really enjoying the conversation and was suitably distracted.

He then got onto the subject of his book and he mentioned that it was going well but he wished it was going better. Once we started down the book trail, we discovered that he and I were not only published by the same publishing house, but that our actual publisher was the same person! That's what you call a small world in a small plane. We became friends that evening.

We got onto the subject of Eternity and he began to ask me

lots of questions. I answered him as best I could, trying to speak from my heart more than my head. I knew he was looking for answers that would connect him to Eternity. I even told him something funny that I had heard Jonathan telling people before, about how when God created the earth, he created it round, not oval, and that's why soccer is God's favourite sport. Johnny liked that and said he was going to use it.

I asked Johnny if it would be okay if I kept him in my prayers and he said, 'Would you do that for me?' I sure did. The plane started its descent as we exchanged contact details, and Johnny signed a copy of his book to Jonathan and our boys before the plane landed.

We disembarked the aircraft and walked into the airport terminal. Jonathan and the kids were there to meet me and I couldn't wait to introduce him and the kids to Johnny. Jonathan was blown away! We saw each other again briefly at the baggage carousel before bidding our final adieu.

It was World Cup season just a few weeks after our flight when I received a call from Johnny. We had talked about catching up and he asked if Jonathan and I would like to have breakfast with him while he was in Sydney doing the commentary for the soccer World Cup. It was the morning after the final of the World Cup and Brazil had won, so Johnny was in heaven. He loved Brazil and anything South American; it was in his blood. We had a great breakfast together and Jonathan was really enjoying himself, talking to Australia's best about his favourite sport. Johnny was a man with a mission, passionate about seeing Australia embrace soccer.

After several coffees we eventually said our goodbyes. Jonathan and I spoke with Johnny a couple of times after that. We had also been praying for him, knowing that he wasn't well. Johnny remained in our hearts as someone who knew what passion was all about; he had a passion that consumed him. He said to me that we were similar creatures because we were both on a mission. My mission, he said, was to tell people the good news about life and Eternity, and his mission was to tell people the good news about soccer — the game he called 'the world game'.

We knew that Johnny had become sicker and we had heard that it looked like he wasn't going to have long to live. We kept praying for a miracle and also praying that he would find that peace I knew he was searching for. I'm sure he did. I will never forget being overwhelmed with sadness on the evening of my birthday in 2004 when Johnny Warren passed from here to Eternity.

Family and friends were devastated by his passing. Although he had been sick for a couple of years and his impending departure was not a surprise, it doesn't make it any easier when such a great person dies. In the brief period of time that I got to know Johnny Warren I can say that he was a kind-hearted and sincere gentleman.

Of course I wished I had seen him more and talked with him more, and life is always full of regrets when we don't get to say goodbye, but I know that the brief time we had was significant. Sometimes we can devalue the *moments* in life that come our way as seemingly meaningless. What I really appreciated about Johnny was his transparency when it came to his life and those things that he struggled with. He was not just willing to talk but he was also willing to allow me to pray for him.

We have angels in our midst but sometimes we don't recognise them. They don't have wings or halos and aren't dressed in white. They don't sing and play harps. They are merely people who choose to live a life beyond themselves, showing love and kindness to others. There is one person in particular in my life who has taught me about the power of kindness and what an angel really is. That person is my elderly next-door neighbour Arthur, and I hope that this story encourages your heart as much as it has encouraged the hearts of the countless other people who have heard it.

It was a sunny Monday afternoon towards the end of winter. I stood in my kitchen staring out the window as I peeled vegetables for a roast dinner. Monday night in the Wilson household is family night. I came back to earth for a moment and noticed two things: one was that I had peeled too many potatoes and the other was that my neighbour Arthur had just returned home from work.

I left the vegetables and walked out the front door to greet Arthur. He hopped out of his car in the driveway and came across to see me. We chatted for a moment and then I asked him, 'Are you busy tonight?' to which he replied inquisitively, 'No.' I then said, 'Would you like to come for a roast dinner?' Instantly he responded, 'That would be nice, what time?' I told him to come any time from around 5.30 p.m. onwards. It was a done deal and now all I had to do was tell my husband that I had just invited someone around for dinner on his only night off in weeks!

Jonathan was not altogether happy with me and it had nothing to do with our lovely neighbour. He changed his mind after the kids all got really excited and started exclaiming, 'Arthur's coming for dinner! Arthur's coming for dinner!' It didn't take long before Jonathan decided to get into it too. At 5.30 p.m. on the dot, Arthur knocked at the front door. Jonathan let him in and I greeted him with a little kiss on the cheek.

We didn't really know each other except for many waves and the odd 'Hi — how are you?' In fact, the only other time I had hugged Arthur was when we returned from overseas to find that Arthur's beloved wife of fifty-nine and a half years, Violet, had passed away. Mum had told me what had happened but I hadn't

seen Arthur at home yet. I saw him at the supermarket and knew
he hadn't yet seen me. Everything inside me wanted to let him be
and not say anything because I didn't want to upset him, but
something came over me which caused me to be brave enough
to invade his space.

'Hello Arthur,' I said as I looked into his big eyes. I gave him
a hug and told him how very sorry I was to have heard about his
darling passing away. He held on to me tightly and said, 'Thank
you. Where were you?' Right then I realised that we were on the
map of his life. Up until that time, I didn't realise that we mattered
to him, but now I knew that we had become a ray of hope to his
life and that it was important for us to remain connected.

Arthur walked slowly across the lounge room into the dining
room and sat down. We offered him a drink and he sat chatting
with Jonathan while I finished preparing dinner. Jonathan was
interested in Arthur's knowledge of the area in which we now
live. He discovered that Arthur had been living next door since
the beginning of World War II. They chatted and chatted until
Jonathan asked Arthur something that no woman would dare! He
said, 'Gee, Arthur, you've been around a long time. So how old are
you?'

Arthur's reply is something that has become immortalised in
our hearts forever. He said, 'Well, actually, it's my eighty-eighth
birthday today.' No way! You could have knocked us all over with
a feather, and the *moment* didn't end there. The very next thing,
'Happy Birthday' began to sound out from the kids' organ that
had been set on 'autopilot'. Our home had been burgled earlier
that year and we still hadn't replaced our stereo, so the organ
provided musical entertainment for the evening. I managed to
find something that resembled a birthday cake and we sang to our
new-found friend. This was all too much. Wow, who would have
thought that a simple dinner could turn into a birthday

celebration that would end up forming a friendship that would be for Eternity.

We enjoyed getting to know each other more over the next few months, and then on Christmas Eve that same year I invited Arthur to come to a service with us at church. He accepted the invitation and seemed to really enjoy the night. I then asked Arthur if he wanted to come again another time, to which he enthusiastically affirmed that he would, and from that weekend until now, apart from the odd holiday, we have taken Arthur with us every Saturday night. The picture of him sitting outside the front of his house waiting for us each week is something that will remain in my heart forever. He once told us that he liked to look over at our place to see what he called our 'friendly light'. This was a little light we left on every night for the kids and we hadn't even realised that it lit up Arthur's world too.

One afternoon soon after Arthur's special birthday dinner at our place, he arrived on our doorstep with a beautiful bunch of flowers. They took my breath away. The flowers were gorgeous but the gesture was magnificent. He said, 'Thank you for being my angel.'

Arthur became part of our greater family and was soon 'adopted' as everyone's special neighbour. Young and old each Saturday night would come and greet Arthur and chat with him. Arthur has always said that he feels very special in that environment. Arthur may have called me his angel, but he has become one to me. This beautiful man's life has had an enormous impact on all who have heard his Eternity story.

A human angel is a messenger of love, created to bring good news from God to man and also to bring good news from man to man. These angels are not only our family and friends who reach out to us in our greatest time of need, they can also be complete strangers. Think of the times in your life when you have been touched by an angel of timely kindness. You may be easily able to identify these kind angels in your life, but even if you can't right now because of the fog in your life, know that they are around you just waiting to help make life better.

In the TV series *Touched by an Angel*, Tess, an angel played by Della Reese, makes her mark by bringing truth and hope to people's circumstances. Her role in the show is to be a messenger of God, bringing warning in times of danger and comfort in times of anguish. Her role is to take care of what the human eye can't see.

The angel (caring, benevolent soul) in you has much to do, especially when it comes to helping others at their greatest time of need. Most of the time, just being there and expressing words of comfort and support, such as a simple 'I am so sorry to hear about your loss', is what will help. Offering support to people who have lost a loved one requires us to try to understand where they are at and also requires us to give them not just support but sometimes space. Here are some ways in which we can be human angels in times of need.

❖ Allow the person to talk about and express their loss and heartache. Listen without interrupting them or offering advice.

❖ Patience will be necessary as you ride the wave of changing emotions. It is completely normal for someone suffering loss to move between anger and sorrow, numbness and acceptance; they may even have some memory loss.

❖ We also need to encourage the letting go of regrets and anything that cannot be changed and replace those feelings with forgiveness and peace.

❖ Please don't impose time limits on how long you think someone should be allowed to grieve. Telling someone to get over it will only cause them to be stuck in it longer as they try to deal with pain upon pain.

❖ Don't be afraid to ask what you can do to help them practically. Again, be patient as they try and work out if they need anything at all. You may know that they do, but they may not be able to register anything right now.

❖ Offer to do things that you know are immediate, like making sure there's milk in the fridge and bread in the breadbin. Also try to find out if your presence is helping or hurting. Sometimes people don't want people around and it's important for the one trying to help not to take anything personally at this time.

❖ Reaching out and touching, showing affection, hugging and holding a hand is always good medicine for a hurting heart. If the grieving person seems irritated by your touch, just minimise it but don't decide you will never try to hug them again. Remember their response right now is anything but usual, although it is completely normal in loss.

❖ In time, encourage your friend or family member to think about doing a course to help them through their grief, or encourage them to join a support group.

Remember, angels understand that there is no correct amount of time to mourn a loss. The grieving period varies with the individual. Be sensitive to significant dates such as birthdays, holidays and the anniversary of the death or loss, as the person left here will find these especially difficult times.

Reassure the person or people that you want to help that what they are feeling is normal, regardless of how normal you think it is. Also encourage them to keep busy, to get on with as much as they can to help soothe the pain of nothingness that will be very present at this time. Busyness will not fill the empty void — only

God can do that — but it will help to occupy a mind that could well do with some healthy distraction.

Try not to say things like 'I know how you feel', because even if you have lost in a similar way, everyone feels differently. Instead, ask them how they are feeling and give them time and space to express.

Some people won't express their feelings until long after they have experienced the loss of a loved one. Where possible, help steer the person you are trying to help away from alcohol or taking medication that hasn't been recently prescribed from their doctor. They should also be encouraged to wait a while before making any big decisions. Just be a guiding voice to help them through this tough time.

What made my personal journey of loss something I'll remember and treasure forever were the precious angels who knew what mattered, who knew what to do and how to love. On page *v* of this book, I pay special tribute to those in my world who have been angels without even realising it.

Angels appear but they are not what you think. I pray that you are able to find the angels so you too can become the angel to bring hope to someone else's life and walk them over Eternity's rainbow.

The Invitation

'It doesn't interest me what you do for a living. I want to know what
you ache for and if you dare to dream of meeting your heart's longing.

It doesn't interest me how old you are. I want to know if you will
risk looking like a fool for love, for your dream, for the adventure
of being alive.

It doesn't interest me what planets are squaring your moon . . .
I want to know if you have touched the centre of your own sorrow,
if you have been opened by life's betrayals or have become shrivelled
and closed from fear of further pain.

I want to know if you can sit with pain, mine or your own, without
moving to hide it or fade it or fix it.

I want to know if you can be with joy, mine or your own, if you can
dance with wildness and let the ecstasy fill you to the tips of your
fingers and toes without cautioning us to be careful, be realistic,
remember the limitations of being human.

It doesn't interest me if the story you are telling me is true.
I want to know if you can disappoint another to be true to yourself.
If you can bear the accusation of betrayal and not betray your own soul.
If you can be faithless and therefore trustworthy.

I want to know if you can see Beauty even when it is not pretty every
day. And if you can source your own life from its presence.

I want to know if you can live with failure, yours and mine, and still stand at the edge of the lake and shout to the silver of the full moon, "Yes."

It doesn't interest me to know where you live or how much money you have. I want to know if you can get up after the night of grief and despair weary and bruised to the bone and do what needs to be done to feed the children.

It doesn't interest me who you know or how you came to be here. I want to know if you will stand in the centre of the fire with me and not shrink back.

It doesn't interest me where or what or with whom you have studied. I want to know what sustains you from the inside when all else falls away.

I want to know if you can be alone, with yourself, and if you truly like the company you keep in the empty moments.'[9]

— ORIAH MOUNTAIN DREAMER ~

Wilma's Story

'If your heart is broken, you'll find God right there;
If you're kicked in the gut, he'll help you catch your breath.'

–◦ PSALM 34:18 ◦–
THE BIBLE

I can't remember the exact time when my son Adrian
phoned; it must've been around 11 a.m. It was Saturday,
30 December 2000, and a glorious summer's day under our
African sky. Life was good until I heard my son's voice say,
'Mum! Shannon's drowned! Where's Dad? Please, Mum, ask
Dad to go to the hospital and pray for him. Let me know
what happens.'

Adrian was in another city hours away from our
home and he was referring to his little boy. I immediately
called Andre, my husband, to tell him that 'Grandpa's boy' had
drowned in a friend's pool. We were both numbed by the
news. Andre drove to the hospital and prayed for Shannon in
the hope that he would be restored to us. It was too late.

I stood by our little Christmas tree and looked at
Shannon's birthday and Christmas gifts, still underneath.
Shannon's Mum was on holiday with him, so we had not had
the chance to give them to him. Oh, my heart was breaking.

Shannon was a healthy, outgoing three-year-old. He
brought a lot of joy into our lives. His parents never
married and he lived with his Mum. We often had him stay
over for the weekend so that he could be part of our lives.

We took him to church on Sundays and he really enjoyed himself. As the pastors of the church, it was a joy to us every week to watch our precious little grandson take hold of Jesus at such an early age.

His favourite treat on Saturday mornings was when Grandpa made him heaps of crumpets with honey. He could speak from an early age and no word was too difficult for him to pronounce. I can still hear his little voice as he came walking on his toes calling me 'Granny'. We taught him about Eternity and he sometimes asked questions that surprised us. Several weeks before he passed away, he found a dead bird in our garden (our cats often hunted for birds). Shannon asked, 'What happened to the birdie? Where did it go, Grandpa?' Andre explained to Shannon about Heaven and his face lit up as he listened.

Shannon's father, Ady, was very successful in the music scene in South Africa, heading up the opening band for acts such as Westlife and Savage Garden. When he told us that he and his girlfriend were expecting a baby, we embraced them, even though we were, in our hearts, disappointed that our son hadn't embraced some of our values about marriage and family. As pastors, this was going to be a difficult time for us because we knew that some people would judge our family. We knew, however, that this little boy was meant to be.

We found ourselves to be young grandparents at the ages of forty-three and forty-four. Our hearts were open. After Shannon's birth, we watched our son grow incredibly, and we saw that those values we had held so dear became important to him also. He was growing into a fine Dad. As far as we were concerned, Shannon was not a 'mistake'. This precious little boy had a purpose and a destiny.

Deep mourning, pain and a lot of tears followed in the days after Shannon's death. Not only were we surrounded and strengthened by our family and friends, but we found enormous strength that can only come from our Heavenly Father. Yes, we had questions. We even blamed ourselves for not doing more. 'If only I had phoned to have Shannon for that weekend! Why did I not phone more?' I realised that all these questions were a normal part of the grieving process. I had some of his clothes, a blanket and toys in our guest bedroom and found myself holding them and smelling him every now and then. I found every new day was easier to cope with than the day before. Acceptance of what had happened sunk in, except for a few lapses of emotions, especially when I came across a photograph of Shannon or when I read about the tragedy in our local newspapers or magazines.

Our eldest son Donovan and his beautiful wife brought Kane, our only other grandchild, to us every day for two weeks so that we could hold him and love him. Family is very important at all times, but more so when you face a tragedy like this. You have a renewed appreciation for each other. We had meals together, played peaceful instrumental music and reflected as flowers, plants, cards, food, friends and condolences poured in. Kane was only two months old at the time of the accident. Shannon could never be replaced, but it was a comfort to hold another child in my arms. Kane now has a little sister, Ashley, and I love my grandchildren dearly.

I am incredibly grateful for Eternity, knowing that one day I will see our precious angel Shannon again. There is no doubt in my mind where Shannon is. He's in Heaven. I feel sad now and again knowing that I won't see him grow up and develop into an awesome man, but then again I know he is awesome right now in Eternity.

My husband Andre conducted Shannon's funeral, which was the hardest thing he has ever had to do. He did it with supernatural ability and grace. It was sad, but beautiful. Shannon loved sunflowers, so there were sunflowers. We had the very last photograph taken of him with 'Father Christmas' on the big screen. One of the songs we sang was 'Jesus Loves Me', chosen by his Mum.

Andre said, 'The soul of a baby is pure and untouched, bringing lasting love into your lives even after he is gone. Because of his soul, Shannon will always be. Although there is much sadness amongst us, there are no tears in Heaven.'

Shannon's Dad, Ady, wrote and recorded a song for Shannon for the funeral called 'My Angel', which was re-recorded soon after and went to number two on the Top 40 chart in our nation. Most people thought it was a romantic love song. It is a love song, but for Shannon. A bright, light song because that's what Shannon was like. Ady worked with Variety Club, the world's largest children's charity, on a campaign called The Adrian Shannon Drowning Awareness Campaign in association with Swimming South Africa's Learn to Swim program, helping parents and children's caretakers understand the danger of water, and not just swimming pools. He donated all the royalties from the single to the fund. It was money and hours well invested and it was good to see him pour energy aroused by his grief into something worthwhile.

The life and death of little Shannon has had an impact on our lives. We have found different ways of expressing our love for him and remembering him.

My husband wrote a book dedicated to the memory of Shannon, entitled *Finding a Way to Win*. In a section called 'Expect the Best from God', Andre tells his version of the tragedy and how he bounced back. God has been very real to us during our months of sadness, and truly, He is who He says He is: 'The God of all comfort.'

In 2001 I launched a women's conference and I had the privilege of dedicating the first conference to the memory of Shannon. I also wrote a song dedicated to Shannon which we sang and recorded at our church.

Shannon's Dad Ady got married in May 2002 to Claire, a lovely young woman, and now they have a precious son, Aidon Shannon, born in November 2004.

A funeral company approached Ady's recording label, Sony BMG Africa, to use 'My Angel' for an advertisement on television. They had no idea that the song was written and sung for a funeral, let alone the songwriter's own son's funeral. He agreed, and was paid a substantial amount for the use of the song. This became a wonderful example of the principle of sowing and reaping. Ady sang the song for Shannon to say goodbye, and now, with part of the finances, he could give his new son a beautiful nursery to say hello.

We have experienced much healing and know the power of Eternity working within. Shannon will always be in our hearts. I have learned that life is rather short and that we should welcome each new day as a gift. Someone once said, 'that is why today is called the present'. We understand sadness better, but we also understand wholeness better, and we know that Eternity has made life better.

My Angel

'Can't escape
The way that I'm feeling
Tomorrow will never be the same
How I wish that I could wake up from this dream
I want to start all over again
And I fall asleep
And I dream you're here
Forever
I'll love you
You'll always be my angel
And all my dreams of you and me
I'll hold till we're together
Nothing will
Ever take your place
And the things we had in your time
All your smiles would melt my heart
Like when you put your hand in mine
Someday I'll be coming home to you
Like we were never apart
And every time I lose my way and wish for you
I'll find you in my heart.'

⭑ ADRIAN SHANNON ⭑
2001

Julie's Story

When my husband said to me, 'You need to ask that girl over for dinner', I looked across the church car park to see who he was talking about. I saw an attractive Titian-haired young woman called Jenny. Though I had never actually spoken to her before, I knew a few things about her. Fact one: she was a great musician. Fact two: she was a school teacher. Fact three: she had an entirely professional air about her. So it was with some trepidation that I walked up and asked her over for dinner, never expecting her to say yes. She happily accepted the invitation and when she did, Jenny simultaneously accepted a friendship that would span four years.

I look back and see Alex's suggestion as a God-ordained idea that resulted in a very dear and close friendship. It was a friendship for all of us, Alex and our young children included. Jenny would go on to become one of the family. Her visits became more frequent and her company was always welcome. She and I both played the piano and had music in common, but apart from that we were like chalk and cheese. Where I was intuitive, she was intense. Jenny was a deep thinker and would transform a light-hearted conversation into something challenging; I would return it to something light. If her thoughts became too heavy I would happily bring Alex into the conversation and leave them at it! Jenny and I were good for each other and benefited from seeing things through one another's eyes.

One afternoon I received a phone call from her physician, Dr Lee, asking me to go to his home, where Jenny was. He had some test results following a recent checkup. Over the phone, he informed me that he had some very grave news concerning her. As I drove there, I considered what the problem could be. I was aware that she was never quite well. It seemed that she had one complaint after another. Till now she had never been able to find out exactly what was wrong.

I sat across from Dr Lee with Jenny beside me. He explained the test results: a melanoma had surfaced years ago on Jenny's arm during a trip to Italy. It had never been properly treated and now it meant Jenny had cancer. As the words came out of his mouth, it all sounded surreal. At thirty-four, Jenny had cancer. It had begun to affect other parts of her body. There would be treatment to follow but nothing was promised. We sat in stunned silence for a while, then Dr Lee and his wife, who were also friends, began to pray. In their lounge room was a beautiful grand piano. As their prayers for Jenny intensified I sat down before the keys and began to play a tune. I didn't know what to say so this seemed the natural thing to do. The prayers and the music became a cry from our hearts for Jenny's wellbeing. All the time Jenny somehow remained calm and said that she deeply felt God's peace.

The next few months were filled with intensive treatment. They were also a time of frustration as news of improvement following chemotherapy would be replaced by news of unfortunate relapses. Jenny was in and out of hospital and this took a toll on her body. At the same time family and friends rallied around her, offering her strength and faith. One of her college friends, Todd, visited her in hospital dressed like Elvis. Armed with a tape player, he would dance, sing, and generally make a clown of himself — so much so that it would reduce Jenny to roaring laughter.

Around this time, I had my third child. It became difficult to visit Jenny as regularly as I had. Once a week seemed like a long time between visits. However, it was heartening to see many church and college friends encouraging her along the way and she definitely drew strength from that. Times such as these showed me the value of being part of a church family.

Throughout this crisis, Jenny's faith had been tested and to this point remained strong. However, she soon received news from doctors that rocked her. A tumour was developing in her brain and she needed immediate surgery. The operation left her energies depleted and rest was called for. The Sacred Heart Hospice in Sydney was the very place.

We would go to the hospice and the children would lie on Jenny's bed while she read stories to them. It was much easier to encourage her when the children were at my side. They had a vibrancy about them that would draw the best from Jenny. She was always interested in what they had to say and share. I found her very brave and cheerful in spite of her pain. She had the most musical laugh and eyes that fairly sparkled. I would come away feeling happy that I had seen her but despondent with her condition. It was hard to believe that so quickly I was losing my friend.

Jenny remained steadfast, believing that the day of healing would come for her. And ultimately it did. One spring morning, a mutual friend of Jenny's met me and took me by the hand. She said, 'Jenny's gone. She went this morning.' I had known the day was coming. Jenny shed her sick body and stepped into glory.

I met a lot of Jenny's friends through this time and they became my friends. We would talk and fondly laugh as we reminisced about her strong character. One would say, 'Jenny will be singing in the choir right about now.' Another would reply, 'No, Jenny would be directing the choir!' And knowing her, that's about right!

I found the passing of Jenny a difficult time to come to terms with. There were lots of questions with 'why' in them. Didn't we have enough faith? Should we have done more for her? I was upset with God.

'If the earthly tent we live in is destroyed, we have a building from God, an eternal house not built by human hands.'

—∽ 2 CORINTHIANS 5:1 ∼—
THE BIBLE

I was blessed knowing Jenny in my life. My family was blessed to have known her. We have friendships that still continue to this day as a result of this chapter in life. In my heart, I know that God has the final word and knows things we don't. He sees the big picture; I only have a glimpse of it.

My five-year-old son put it in perspective for me. 'Mummy,' he said. 'Jenny is now an angel wearing a beautiful crown.' I smile when I think about that. Jenny was such a girl, I know she would love that!

Human Angels

Our role on earth as human angels is to communicate good news to people through deliberate acts of kindness. Here are some ideas.

- ❖ **No reason**

    Write a 'no reason' card to as many people as you can think of that you know who would be blown away that you have thought of them.

- ❖ **Time**

    Take time to spend time with someone you know will value it most.

- ❖ **Gifts**

    A gift opens the heart of a person if the giver's motivation is to be a blessing.

- ❖ **Home improvement**

    Offer to make someone's home brighter by bringing in new cushions, or offering to help rearrange some furniture to bring a new outlook.

- ❖ **Spring clean**

    Roll your sleeves up and initiate a big cleanup. This is a task that can either seem overwhelming to someone who is grieving, or can be something positive for them to put their energy into.

- ❖ **Gardening**

    While mowing the lawn, why not mow the nature strip on both sides of the fence as well? This is a great act of kindness without being too intrusive. One day you may even be able

to mow your neighbours' lawns and surprise them
completely!

❖ **Flowers**

If you can't afford to send bunches of flowers to as many
people as you'd like, why not buy a bunch, tie a ribbon
around the stem of each flower and take the time to hand-
deliver them with a card.

❖ **Food**

Food always works! Bake something or cook something to
communicate your love and care for someone.

❖ **Listen**

Shut down your computer, make a cup of tea and pick up
the phone. Be prepared to listen to your family or friend
who may just need to talk.

❖ **Give**

Perhaps you are able to contribute financially to an
individual or an organisation. The most powerful way of
doing this is anonymously. If you do make yourself known,
allow the benefactor space to come to terms with your
generosity.

❖ **Babysit**

I have always found that those most willing to help look
after my children are those who have children of their own.
Offering to babysit is a wonderful thing to do, especially if it
is done so the parent or parents can have a nice night out
and not just when they need help because they need to
work.

❖ **Pray**

One of the greatest things we can do for another human
soul is to pray for them.

CHAPTER ELEVEN

Farewell

until we meet again

'See you soon.'

— NANNY —

Beaches

CC Bloom (Bette Midler), an aggressive and outrageous Jewish girl from the Bronx, meets Hillary Whitney (Barbara Hershey), a shy and proper WASP from San Francisco, on the beach in Atlantic City when they are both eleven years old. Although they come from very different worlds and have nothing in common, they share a deep yearning for a close friend. The two begin a correspondence that continues over the years.

One day Hillary, now a lawyer, shows up in New York City and meets CC at a nightclub where she is singing. The two friends experience the ups and downs of living together until CC gets a big break in her career, and Hillary returns to California to take care of her dying father. Hillary is later diagnosed with cancer. As Hillary is slowly and tragically dying, CC comes out to care for her and look after Hillary's daughter Victoria, as well as spend the last days of Hillary's life with her. It is during this time that we see the greatest and final test of their friendship.

Mary Agnes Donoghue's screenplay for *Beaches*, based on a novel by Iris Rainer Dart, charts the emotional high points and the painful low points in this friendship as it shifts gear through marriages, divorces, career changes and pregnancy. Director Garry Marshall accentuates the special problems and challenges in maintaining a lasting friendship.

Beaches portrays the desire that each human being has for a lifelong, strong friendship that nothing, even death, can end. The sadness of CC and Victoria after Hillary's death is undeniable. But notice that neither of their lives stop when hers does. CC actually chooses to draw strength from the tragic loss of her dearest friend. She continues life stronger than ever and chooses to live on the 'high road'.

I believe the Eternity moment in the movie is when CC has to deal with the fact that Hillary is dying. We watch as her heart breaks for her friend. One of the main 'common grounds' we all find during this movie is in the complete helplessness of CC to stop what is happening to Hillary. Sitting by and helplessly watching someone suffer on the way to death might actually be the worst part of death. If you could pay for a cure, you would; if you could magically make their pain go away, you would; if you could give your life to save theirs, you would. But most times there's absolutely nothing you can do to help them other than to pray (which is actually doing a great deal for them and not to be underestimated!) and hold their hand.

In *Beaches* we see true friendship and true love survive the most difficult circumstances one could face. It is happy, funny, sad, challenging and inspiring all at the same time! It is a movie that every person can relate to in one form or another.

Farewell

'Only in the agony of parting do we look into the depths of love.'

⤙ GEORGE ELIOT ⤚
ENGLISH NOVELIST (1819–1880)

IT WAS TIME TO SAY GOODBYE. I held Mum's hand and said, 'It's time.' We gathered around Nanny's sleepy body and told her how much we loved her. With my cheek on her cheek and my hand on her heart, my tears drenching her white pillow, I said over and over, 'He is faithful, Nanny. He is faithful, Nanny.' I knew that she was sure her loving Heavenly Father was faithful to take her by the hand and lead her blissfully into Eternity with him — the place that she had longed for; the place where she would be reunited with her beloved husband and her precious Mum and Dad and brothers. Oh, what a party would be held to usher in this beloved princess.

The final hour before my precious Nanny slipped from here to Eternity, I had no more words to say, but so much more to express. I went downstairs to the hospital newsagency and bought a notebook and pen. The words in the paragraph above were just some of the sixteen pages I wrote, until I knew it was time — her time.

Saying goodbye is never easy. I prefer to say 'See you soon', just like my Nanny always used to say. With an eternal perspective, 'see you soon' makes sense. Goodbye is so final and there's not much 'good' about it, especially if you are having to say it to someone you love. Bye bye, *au revoir, auf Wiedersehen, aloha, ciao, sayonara, ma as-salaamah, joi gin, arohanui, até a vista, adieu, fir milaan ge, poka, adiós, do pobachennya,* see you soon. Whatever the language, goodbye carries with it a vast array of feelings for us all.

When Nanny said goodbye to her own mother, she found words of comfort and kept them with a photograph by her bedside. This photograph and these words now bring comfort to my Mum.

'They say that you are gone, and nevermore your voice will sound
within these walls, your step approach the door.
And yet I know you still abide, and when the shadows fall, and all the
world is hushed to rest — I hear your spirit call.
I see you in the empty chair and watch your loving smile — and so I
know that you are there, just with me for a while.
And so it is, through happy tears, born of life's joy and pain,
My spirit leaps the vacant years, and we are one again.'

—◦ AUTHOR UNKNOWN ◦—

There is a deeper meaning to 'goodbye' than just a simple 'see ya later'. 'Goodbye' is actually a contraction of the phrase 'God be with you'. It is a blessing we pass on to someone as we part ways with them, trusting them to God's constant, eternal presence.

Goodbye is a process that we can live through in turmoil or release, and it's basically up to us to choose the way we farewell. The picture of a child on their first day of school gripping tightly to Mum's legs, not wanting to hear those words, is one visual reminder of a painful goodbye. Another is when we see someone walking out the door, never to return, because they want to live a separate life. We can chase them, begging and pleading for their return, but if their heart is not willing, there is not much we can do other than release them. When the time comes for us to farewell those we love from here to Eternity, we need to do it well for their sake, our sake and our family and friends' sakes.

Airports are places we are easily reminded about painful goodbyes, as family and people in love part, perhaps not knowing when next they will meet. Although airport farewells can be quite dramatic, especially where large families are concerned, there is something truly lovely about people caring so much for each other that they simply don't know how to let go. We should live like this. Not with wailing and physical gripping, but in our hearts. When we leave for work in the morning, say goodbye and part in a way that will leave you and those you say goodbye to at peace until you meet again. For some, that will be the last time those words are said.

Goodbye is in our reach, regardless of whether we have notice or not. If you have suffered the unthinkable in losing a loved one without the opportunity of saying goodbye, or perhaps your goodbye wasn't on such a great note, then take the opportunity of saying goodbye now. It's never too late.

When a father walks his little girl down the aisle on the day of her wedding, there is a goodbye involved that only fathers and little girls can truly fathom. Although they are together in the same family still, the process of farewell is a necessary part of the next generation getting married and starting a family of their own. It is a positive, natural part of the cycle of life, but it is not easy. Even those who end up getting fantastic sons- and daughters-in-law still grieve at least a little deep down, in the final farewell at the altar.

Farewell is graduation time. Graduation from nappies, graduation from school, graduation from college or university, graduation from one home to another, graduation from one job to another, graduation from work, and, eventually, graduation from here to Eternity.

When my little girl Bella was born I can remember feeding her in hospital and holding her little hand in my hand. I stroked her tiny ring finger as a tear rolled down my cheek at the very thought of the day she would get married and leave home. For that moment in time I grieved her pending departure, even though she was just a couple of days old.

My eldest son Ben has wanted to be a pilot since he could talk, which he has done a lot of since he worked out how! The day will come when my beautiful son will need to leave home and spread his wings, personally and professionally. For Benny's sake, I promise not to be a pathetic clingy mother who makes her son feel guilty for having a life. At the same time, I will ensure that he knows how much we'll miss him when he's gone and I will also make sure that when we part, we do so in peace and much love.

Then there's his twin brother Beau, the artistic sports hero. Goodness knows what he'll become, but I'm positive that the world will be his for the taking and it will only be a matter of time before he too will need to spread his wings and embark on his own life adventure. I love my children so much my heart aches, but I love them enough to release them to live and to be free to be all that they were created to be.

Bella has the softest heart and we just know that she will devote her life to making other people's lives better. She could be a doctor, but may find her life more effective being a nurse. She may become a teacher. Who knows? What I do know is that Bella knows the power of goodbye and simply insists on the ritual of hugs, kisses and 'I love yous' before she goes anywhere.

Then there's Rachel, our eldest daughter. Social justice is in her heart and I'm sure it's only a matter of time before she'll be making a difference to women's lives in some Middle Eastern country. Rachel is an adult now and we don't get to see much of her these days. Nevertheless, goodbye is still important and her daddy insists on a kiss and a hug and an 'I love you' before she leaves or goes to sleep. While you have the opportunity to farewell your loved ones properly, don't miss a single moment.

Every single night bedtime is a very special time in our home when we kiss and hug and say, 'see you in the morning', before saying faith-filled prayers and going off to sleep. Because of how we farewell each day, I am praying that the learned art of goodbye will remain a tradition for our children's children and their children. The words 'I love you' are the most universally important words to say when parting, either in person or by phone, email or snail mail.

Saying goodbye when it's the last thing we want to do leaves a gaping hole in our hearts and lives. Time is a great healer, however, and after a while that void will begin to lessen and sorrow will eventually dissipate. This process is not quick, but it is inevitable. Eventually things will change. What was once a bleak absence can soon become a warm presence. Those who have departed can return to your heart in a nurturing way that transcends humanity.

When your loved ones were still alive, you may have deeply loved each other, but, as with all families, that love came with some form of tension and imperfection. Relationships, even those steeped in love and concern, always carry an element of hurt, shadows, some resistance and irritations. That's family and that's normal. In this present life, there's no such thing as intimacy without some pain. No matter how much we love someone, we will always experience some feelings of resistance, disappointment and misunderstanding, of not being properly valued, of needing space at times. We are all human and our love, as deep as it is, is flawed.

Eternal love, however, is very different, and when a beloved one departs this world and enters the next, their love returns to us devoid of their humanity and abounding in all things wonderful. Their love for us and their presence is able to flow into our lives in a way beyond humanity's tensions. Their love can be felt without shadows and hurt.

We know that absence makes the heart grow fonder, and although everything inside us wants that absence to turn into physical presence, we can find incredible comfort in the knowledge that absence can indeed make love more present, in the light of Eternity. Sometimes when we are physically present we cannot give each other what we need to and we must go away, at least for a time, in order for that to happen. Sometimes only our absence can deepen our presence.

As a parent, we experience this when our children grow up and move away. First there is the pain of letting them go, but eventually there is the joy of having those same children come back in a new way, as adults who can be with you in a way that they couldn't as children. But this can't happen unless our children first go away. Good parents know that by hanging on too tightly, by not giving our children the space within which to be absent, we not only stunt their growth, but we can deprive ourselves of eventually having a wonderful adult comeback with something deeper to give than the dependent love of a child. That is true in every relationship.

When it was Jesus' turn to depart this world, he spent many moments preparing his followers for his absence. He encouraged them repeatedly that although they would feel the pain initially, they would also benefit from His spirit returning to be with them after his death. When children leave home for the first time to begin lives on their own, they are saying to their parents what Jesus said to his disciples before leaving earth and entering Heaven: 'It is better for you that I go away. If I do not go away I cannot come back to you in a deeper way!'

Every family has a tradition of saying goodbye, though sadly for some that tradition is pain filled, as strangers under the one roof go through the motions of entering and departing home without so much as a word said. If this has been your experience, then I want to encourage you to create a new tradition of farewell, something that will build your family and relationships and that will give you cause to live without regrets.

'Don't let the sun go down while you are still angry.'

⁃⌒ EPHESIANS 4:26 ⌒⁃

THE BIBLE

It is not good to go to sleep on our anger. You and I both know how completely damaging it is to you and whomever it is you are angry with when you take all that baggage with you to bed and to sleep. When we sleep on our anger, we are giving it our place of peace, where it simply does not belong. Sleep is a time for us to close one day before opening another and the moments in between aren't meant to become a stewing pot of undealt-with emotions.

Whatever it takes, deal with your anger before you go to sleep. The simple words 'I'm sorry' don't take much effort if you understand the power and release they bring with them. Or what about 'I forgive you'? Asking for forgiveness and offering it are two very effective ways of ensuring a peaceful night's sleep and being able to awake to a brand-new day devoid of clouds in your heart.

When you live your life as a peacemaker, not just a peacekeeper, you are actively ushering in eternal love that will always transcend your own and others' humanity. It is up to us to make peace every time we depart. When we say goodbye understanding the origin of the word, I believe it helps us have an eternal perspective on this parting phrase.

When it comes to helping others say goodbye, we need to allow people to come to terms with their loss in their own way and in their own time. Not only will this help them accept what has happened, but it will also help them accept moving towards the future. The time of freedom from intense pain will come, but the memory of those loved and now gone will remain forever. We also need to be aware that saying goodbye is often hampered by a feeling of disloyalty. But we need to help people understand that when they say goodbye they are only letting go of the pain, not the beautiful memories that will be cherished forever.

One thing I took great comfort in when my Nanny passed from here to Eternity was to ensure that she had a magnificent farewell — to thank her for a life well lived and also to honour her family left here to go on without her. The handmade orders of service each included an actual photograph, so that family and friends could keep it afterwards. Because my Nanny was now in Eternity with my Grandfather, the photo I included was a beautiful portrait of them together in the prime of their life — because that's what I believe they will be in throughout Eternity.

The service itself was truly a beautiful moment in time. I remember family arriving at the chapel looking very sorrowful — some fearful too. Funerals are not events that people look forward to attending, as they simply cause us all to consider our own mortality. However, my husband Jonathan ministered love and hope at Nanny's service, and several people came up to me afterwards thanking us for making something so awful filled with such hope. One of my Uncles even asked if he could book Jonathan to take his funeral when he dies!

After a million tears and finally laying our precious Nanny to rest, we sang our last hymn, 'When I Survey the Wondrous Cross', before heading home, where a triumphant send-off would begin. My Nanny loved many things, including champagne and strawberries, curried egg sandwiches, and scones with jam and fresh cream. Thanks to the work of many kind hands, we had a first-class send-off for a first-class lady.

Nanny often said, 'Life is mainly froth and bubble, two things stand like stone, kindness in another's trouble and courage in your own.' I count it a privilege to have been able to pay tribute to such a brave and courageous woman who left an eternal mark of love and hope on us all.

At the end of the day, what mattered most to our loved one will become what matters most to us when it comes to saying goodbye. What mattered most to them at the end of their life is that they were loved by you and that you knew you were loved by them. The service, the flowers, the people and the party are all great ways of saying goodbye, but how goodbye fits in your heart is what really matters. That perfect peace that only comes from our Heavenly Father can fill your heart with an Eternity of love without the pain of goodbyes.

When speaking to an assembly of young women at the school I used to attend, about the importance of valuing their identity, I recalled my first day at school. It was a scary experience because I didn't know anyone and got completely lost. Then I recalled my last day of school: our entire year was a complete mess at the very thought of having to say goodbye. School wasn't perfect, but even so, saying goodbye was quite traumatic. Saying goodbye causes us to miss that which we didn't even really appreciate at the time.

The fact that we cannot see our loved ones or speak with them after they have breathed their last here on earth is no proof that they cease to exist. When we understand the magnificence of an Eternity in Heaven it will help us release our loved ones to enjoy the life through faith and hope that God has prepared for them. Ours is not to reason why or to call them home, but to release them to walk that great path of honour as they enter glorious foreverland to be reunited with family and friends who await their triumphant arrival.

Farewell beloved ones. We salute you. Heaven salutes you. Cheers for a life well lived.

Sue's Story

I wiped the tears from Joe's eyes and then, as my head rested on his bare chest, I heard him gasp his last breath. I kissed his bare skin, not willing to believe this was it. I held my breath listening for his heartbeat, but it did not come. I rubbed my face into his skin, breathing him in, tears dropping onto his smooth warm skin. I felt him slip away, gone from my loving grasp forever. I felt a sharp pain from my stomach, making me sit upright. I caressed my stomach, distressed, knowing that our baby would never meet its wonderful father.

Joe and I were high-school sweethearts. It was love at first sight. He made such an impression on me. In English, I would feel somebody kick me in the bottom. I would turn around totally annoyed to find Joe smiling innocently at me. I just loved his cheekiness; no-one could make me laugh like Joe. There was something very wonderful about Joe, something that reached out and drew me to him and I knew we would be together forever.

We started dating when I was just seventeen. In 1990 we moved to Sydney from Wagga Wagga. He had landed a great apprenticeship at Qantas. We loved our time together, and worked hard when we were apart. Once a year we would take about a month off and travel together. We travelled to Egypt, Africa, the United Kingdom, Europe and Hawaii.

Joe and I would soon be up for long-service leave in our jobs and I planned our last big trip prior to having kids.

I wanted to go trekking in the Andes but soon discovered I was pregnant. Shocked but delighted, I changed our trip, as trekking six months pregnant combined with altitude sickness didn't sound so great. So we changed our plans and went to Europe instead.

We spent four weeks in Europe before returning home. I felt so loved and lucky in love. The next week I went back to work; Joe had planned a trip away with some guys from work. At the last minute he changed his mind and decided not to go. I talked him into going as I thought he needed some time away with the boys and I knew that with the baby due soon, next year we might not be able to afford for him to go. Joe ended up going, but later I would feel a lot of guilt about convincing him to go. If I had encouraged him to stay home things would be different now.

On the morning he left I was very tired. I was finding it increasing difficult to sleep as I was really starting to get big, so Joe kissed me, said he loved me and to stay in bed. Over the next couple of days he rang me at least twice a day to say he loved me and to say what a great time he was having, but he couldn't wait to get home and feel the baby kicking.

The day before he was due home, I was sitting at my desk at work and the phone rang. I answered the phone and listened to Luke, a friend, tell me the things that you never want to hear. Joe had been in a road accident; he was unconscious and had been airlifted to the Alfred Hospital in Melbourne. This is the closest I have ever been to hyperventilating. I rushed into the toilets and splashed water onto my face. I tried to gather my thoughts and a plan of action. People don't get airlifted for a broken leg,

I thought. I heard a voice in my head, and it said to me, 'Prepare yourself; he is not coming home with you.' I instantly knew this would be true.

I raced home, grabbed a few clothes then raced to the airport and got on the first flight to Melbourne. I was a mess. Even though I was not a Christian I kept praying, 'Please don't let him die. Even if he is paralysed we will work it out.' As dread set in, I was praying, 'Please don't let him die until I am with him.' I arrived at the hospital at around 8 p.m., where other family members were already waiting to see him. After what seemed like an eternity, we were let in at about midnight. I was very tired and my back and body ached. Hospital chairs are not good for pregnant women's backs. They led me through a dim-lit room with lots of alarms and lights flashing. I could feel myself shaking uncontrollably.

They led me to someone lying in a bed. My eyes filled with tears and I stared, unable to see Joe. I looked at the man I had known for twelve years and I couldn't tell it was him. After a few minutes the nurse asked if I could tell if it was my husband. Finally I recognised his nose and I knew it was him. The reality then hit home; this wasn't a mistake, and it was actually him. I was in a state of shock. I just sat there staring at him, crying. Every half an hour they would check Joe's response mechanism. Every time there was no response it broke my heart a little more. I made several phone calls to family.

I tried to eat, but felt sick. The thought of food made me want to throw up. I think the family knew he wasn't coming home. The surgeon arrived soon after and wanted to have a meeting with us, to discuss Joe's injuries. He advised that Joe would not survive. We then had the option of turning the machines off, to be with him when he died. After much discussion and grief, we all agreed.

After watching all the medical dramas on TV, I believed that the respirator would be removed and the machines turned off and in a few minutes he would silently pass away. How wrong was I? It was the most traumatic experience of my life. I held my breath, listening for his heartbeat. I felt him slip away.

After sobbing uncontrollably for quite a while, I had this irresistible urge to get out of there. Cars still rushed past on the busy street. An ambulance rushed by, sirens blaring, and I imagined another life on the edge. It became very apparent to me that everyone outside was oblivious to my pain and what I was going through. Life rushed on around me. I was upset, angry and overcome with anxiety. What on earth was I to do now? The most important person in my life, the person you turn to when you want to share something special, the father of my child was gone. I wished my life away. Let me die young, so I can be with Joe again. Why was Joe punished? No, why was I being punished? Why was my unborn child being punished? Instantly I knew the road would be very difficult, but I knew God had left me with a gift, a very special gift. Our baby.

I went back to Joe's side and dedicated my love to him, kissed and caressed him for the last time. I called to him to give me the strength for the final goodbye so that I might have the courage to leave him. I stood tall in his love and walked out of that room, not turning back. I left Joe's family in their anguish to say their goodbyes and waited outside for them. I rang Mum and Dad and told them the terrible news.

Next morning I tried to eat something, for the baby's sake. Once back in Wagga, Joe's family came around to pay their respects. I remember walking in and seeing photos of Joe on the fridge. I was to start seeing photos in a totally different light. They have become such a precious commodity to me. I adore photos; they are everlasting memories set in time.

For quite a few months after Joe's funeral I had vivid nightmares. There are so many things you can't predict that will bring back all the heartache. I remember going shopping at Kmart. Out of the corner of my eye I saw a flash of blue Qantas overalls. I was so upset, I went home. They were so Joe.

On 23 July 1999, after a long labour, I gave birth to a beautiful baby girl. I was so thrilled it was a girl. I wanted my child to have its own identity, and I was anxious that if it was a boy it would always be referred to as 'Little Joe'. So a little girl was a true blessing. This was quite a stressful time for me. Going into labour in the middle of the night by myself, and through the labour process thinking that Joe should be by my side. Thankfully, my mother and my friend Alexis gave me strength and encouragement through this time.

Kirralee ended up being a very stressed-out baby. Not surprising really, considering all that I had been through. The first twelve months were very challenging for us. I found it very difficult that I didn't have that someone special to share those moments with, the staying up all night and all the milestones.

Joe touches my life every day. The special days like birthdays, anniversaries, Mother's and Father's days and of course Christmas are very challenging. They have become days of grief which squeeze my heart. As the years and anniversaries pass, Kirralee and I try and celebrate Joe's life and our life together with his loving influence on these days. This year on the sixth anniversary of Joe's death, we visited our old home in Revesby and released six balloons. Kirralee said a prayer and wished the balloons all the way to Heaven and into her daddy's heart so that he knows that he is loved.

About three years ago I decided that it was time to go to the site of Joe's accident. This insignificant piece of ground had become a source of heartache to me. It was a difficult trip, but one that was very necessary. I certainly felt close to Joe there. My brother had made a beautiful metal cross, so I erected a memorial for Joe at the site of his accident. The memorial is about nine kilometres outside a beautiful little town in Victoria called Buchan. The countryside is just beautiful, with its green rolling hills. Kirralee and I planted a tree next to the cross and we visit once a year as close to the anniversary as possible. Even though it is a sad reason to be visiting Buchan, each year it becomes easier. Kirralee and I have had some wonderful times there. We visit the caves and we just love the National Park with all its wildlife and walks. We have shared a lot of love and laughter on our trips there and Kirralee and I spend lots of time talking about her father.

Prior to Joe's death I felt very secure and happy about where life was taking me. I was married to a wonderful man, whose cheekiness made me laugh every day; we had a home together and were starting our family. After Joe's death I felt all alone in a dark hole, trying to see some light. I felt robbed of my happiness. I felt robbed that now I was wholly responsible for our child. Mother, father and provider.

Suddenly my life was totally different. I had dedicated my whole life to one man, till death do us part, and now I had to find out exactly what it meant to be without Joe. Many of my friends reached out and tried to comfort me and many just helped out or let me know they were around, but there are three people that comforted me the most.

The first one was a friend, Maria. I met her on one of the worst days of my life, Joe's funeral. Her husband, Pete, worked with Joe. I met so many people that day, but Maria was a standout. She was a breath of fresh air. About a week later she popped over, bringing me some food with a lovely note. When I arrived home to find this act of generosity I was bowled over. I was very emotional and filled with admiration for Maria. We became very close friends and she is now an inspiration to me. I would often wonder what made her so different. I found myself longing to be like her. Then one day it dawned on me that it was because she has faith.

Maria came to visit me when I was in hospital. She prayed for me and it was the most wonderful experience. Her church sent me some food packages, with lovely messages of hope. I found this very encouraging, and it still fills my heart with love and warmth every time I think of it. Maria gave me a special gift, the gift of faith in Eternity and friendship. For a long time I struggled, as I didn't know what to believe. I didn't have any set beliefs about what happens when someone dies. For the first time since Joe died I feel really comfortable about where I fit into this world. I feel comfortable about being a single Mum and what type of person I am. In fact I am proud of what I have achieved. I know this is because I now have faith, hope and purpose.

The second person I drew strength from is of course Joe. The love you have for that special someone doesn't die when they die. Love endures all. He gave me such wonderful memories and a wonderful life. His energy still runs through me and I draw from it often. I often think, 'I would rather have three minutes of my wonderful Joe than a lifetime of nothing special.' Joe certainly gave me the three minutes of wonderful, and he also gave me a lifetime of love with Kirralee. There will never be a day when I won't wish the world for him. Thank you for being my best friend, a good man, a worthy person, and such a wonderful husband.

The third is Kirralee. God gave me this very special gift and I intend to enjoy her. She gives me purpose, understanding and strength. Kirralee placed laughter and love back into my life.

Fond Farewell

How you leave says a lot about you, whatever the circumstances. The process of farewell isn't about packing up and moving to a new place. It's about sealing relationships. To stay emotionally grounded while saying farewell and beginning your transition, apply the following steps:

- Express appreciation and stay connected in your heart.
- Take time to reminisce with family and friends about special times you shared and joint accomplishments.
- Letting go, embracing a new opportunity and exploring the unknown takes courage. Focus on what is instead of what was.
- Unclutter your mind.
- Say farewell without strings attached. Neatly file away things you know you cannot change and only take things that belong to you now into your future.
- Value treasures.
- Keep positive memories, thank you notes and other bits and pieces that will supply you with enthusiasm, courage and hope in the future. Realise the difference the life of your loved one has made and will continue to make in other people's lives in the future.
- Don't hold on to hurt.

❖ Don't be critical. Avoid criticising anything to do with the circumstances of your loss and avoid participating in negative conversations about these subjects. You may feel upset and wronged but going over and over the negative things you can't change won't help you say farewell properly.

❖ Prepare, reflect and move on.

❖ Recognise that every experience in life has value, and view your experience as a bridge to help others in the future. Allow yourself to be excited and dream about what might be.

❖ Take time to play.

❖ Make time for some time out before beginning the next phase of your life. Consider taking a holiday. Even long leisurely weekends can provide opportunities to laugh again, become energised and relax.

❖ Recognise the value of friends.

❖ Take time to get over what you've been through but try not to neglect friends. This change may make you want to retreat into a corner. But contact with and reassurance from others is what you need most. You may be surprised to discover that many others have been through similar experiences. Identify supportive people and maintain contact with them.

❖ Be open to new possibilities.

❖ Change always comes with an armload of gifts and it's up to us to find them. Don't be so reluctant to embrace change that you can't see new opportunities that come to light up your life.

❖ Successfully farewelling a season of life will give you a good start in the new one.

Purpose

*'Without wavering, let us hold tightly to the hope we say we have,
for God can be trusted to keep His promise.
Think of ways to encourage one another to outbursts
of love and good deeds.'*

⤙ HEBREWS 10:23–24 ⤚
THE BIBLE

CHAPTER TWELVE

Life

your purpose remains

'For I know the thoughts and plans that I have for you ...
to give you hope in your final outcome.'

— GOD —
JEREMIAH 29:11, THE BIBLE

Schindler's List

Based on a true story and adapted from Thomas Keneally's novel *Schindler's Ark*, Steven Spielberg's *Schindler's List* stars Liam Neeson as Oskar Schindler, a German businessman in Poland who sees an opportunity to make money from the Nazis' rise to power. He starts a company to make cookware and utensils, using flattery and bribes to win military contracts, and brings in accountant and financier Itzhak Stern (Ben Kingsley) to help run the factory.

By staffing his plant with Jews who've been herded into Krakow's ghetto by Nazi troops, Schindler has a dependable unpaid labour force. For Stern, a job in a war-related plant could mean survival for himself and the other Jews working for Schindler.

However, in 1942, all of Krakow's Jews are assigned to the Plaszow Forced Labour Camp, overseen by Commandant Amon Goeth (Ralph Fiennes), an embittered alcoholic who occasionally shoots prisoners from his balcony. Schindler arranges to continue using Polish Jews in his plant, but as he sees what is happening to his employees, he begins to develop a conscience. He realises that his factory (now refitted to manufacture ammunition) is the only thing preventing his staff from being shipped to the death camps.

Soon Schindler demands more workers and starts bribing Nazi leaders to keep Jews on his employee lists and out of the camps. By the time Germany falls to the allies, Schindler has lost his entire fortune and saved 1100 people from likely death.

In one of the most dramatic scenes, an incredible Eternity moment, Stein hands Schindler a gold ring with an inscription of a Talmudic adage which says, 'Whoever saves one life, saves the world entire.'

Schindler drops the ring, then slips it on his finger, thanks Stern and shakes hands with him as an equal for the first time in the film. Then in an emotional parting speech, Schindler berates himself for not having saved more lives as tears flow down his cheeks. He looks at the eyes of the workers, seeking their apology for not doing more, saying, 'I could've got more ... I could've got more, if I'd just ... I could've got more ...'

Eleven hundred people were saved because of him, but he knew he could have done more. 'One more. One more person. A person ...'

Schindler's List was nominated for twelve Academy Awards and won seven, including Best Picture and a long-coveted Best Director award for Spielberg, and it has been praised as one of the finest American movies about the Holocaust.

Every life is precious (one more ...).

Life

'I saw the departed, both great and small, standing before the throne.
And the books were opened, including the Book of Life.
And the departed were judged according to the things
written in the books, according to what they had done,
according to their whole way of feeling and acting,
their aims and endeavours in life.'

REVELATION 20:12
THE BIBLE (PARAPHRASED)

'LIFE GOES ON' IS NOT what we want to hear after losing someone we love, but the last thing our loved ones who have departed this earth would want is for us to spend the remainder of our days here pining for them instead of maximising the gift of life that we still have to live. Our life needs to be committed to the generations after us.

An Eternity friend, Darlene, is a beautiful example of someone who chose life after they faced the loss of an unborn baby. Darlene tells the story.

'I was twelve weeks pregnant with a child we had planned for and waited on for a very long time. Three days before we were to leave on a trip to the United States, my husband and I went to the obstetrician and found out that the baby had just died in my womb.

I was shattered and broken-hearted; the agony of that moment was indescribable. It was an awful and terrible loss. We had taken separate cars to the doctor, so I had to drive back to the house by myself with my husband following me. I got in the car, and I just didn't know what to think or do. I felt the depth of my sadness would become too heavy to bear. Then I heard a word in my heart whisper, 'Sing'.

In that moment it was absolutely the last thing I wanted to do. Sing? I couldn't think of anything that I felt less like doing. But again I heard the word, 'Sing'. So after years of learning it is much better to obey that 'voice' quickly, I started to sing. My head didn't sing, and I do not even know if my heart sang, but my soul sang. It was almost involuntary. I sang two songs. The first song that I heard coming out of my mouth was the hymn 'How Great Thou Art', which really surprised me, as this was a song we sang at my father's funeral. The lyrics are about putting God above anything we could be humanly facing and being triumphant in Him.

By the time I got home something had definitely transpired in Eternity. I had spoken many times on the power of singing to God through a trial. I had done this myself in varying degrees, but never before had I experienced the power of God so sovereignly fulfilling His promise to heal me.

I still had to go through the physical ramifications of losing a child, the operation, telling our girls, telling our church family (and the rest of the world), who had been so excited for us, and hours and hours of tears. I found my healing in the arms of God, and even though grief still took its natural course, I found the truth in singing through my barrenness. I will always treasure and thank God for the child I carried only twelve weeks.

One day in Eternity I will be united with my baby. So many women have lost their babies before birth or at birth, but one day they will have them in their arms in Heaven.'[10]

Loss of life can cause us to ask some serious question about life itself. My Eternity friends have shared their loss, but they are not despairing or hopeless in that loss. They understand that Eternity holds so much more for them. Following are some stages we need to pass through in order to refocus our lives.

❖ **Shock and numbness**
Everything seems to lose its importance for a while.
❖ **Emotional turmoil**
This is when you'll need support and a listening ear.

❖ **Emptiness**
Loneliness follows loss, so keep people closer than ever.
❖ **Acceptance**
In time a renewed outlook on life will follow your loss.
❖ **Purpose**
Turn your pain into purpose to give another person hope to live again.

In this final chapter I want to present to you a life that awaits you in all its fullness. There is in fact life after death, not just for those now in Heaven, but also for those of us left here on earth.

There is a purpose for my life. There is a purpose for your life. I am a wife, mother, pastor, author and speaker. I am a woman, a daughter, a sister and a friend. For many years I spent my life helping people get in physical and emotional shape and as a result have gained entrance into people's lives to help them with their spiritual lives too. As we are body, soul and spirit beings, we need to look after the health and wellbeing of each aspect of who we are.

I was invited to take part in Channel Nine's *A Current Affair*. My role was as 'life coach', helping a woman to regain the figure she once had before the birth of her three children. The goal was for Elise to be in shape by her twenty-year school reunion; we had our work cut out for us, especially Elise. We had just eight weeks to make a significant physical transformation take place and due to Elise's diligence and my coaching from the sideline, she did it magnificently.

Over one and a half million people viewed that show the night it aired and I recall the emails that streamed through to my desk over just a few hours. One of the emails I received was from a woman called Anna.

Anna's email said: 'Hi, my name is Anna and I am thirty-three years of age. I have a four and a half year old boy and since his arrival I have been unable to lose weight. I have fallen pregnant four times since Jayden, but unfortunately have lost each baby, and sadly six weeks ago I lost my daughter at twenty-five weeks gestation. My body is like a yoyo, from pregnant to not, and this time around it's hard because I have no baby to show for my increase in weight ...' Anna went on to ask for advice on how to get back in shape before signing off her email with the following words: 'Could you please help me? Regards, Anna.'

An opportunity arose for me to be part of another television program called *Body+Soul* on Channel Nine. I was invited to join the *Body+Soul* team as series life coach; this time I wasn't limited to just helping people get in physical shape, but I was able to help them body and soul.

I had contacted Anna after her initial email to me, encouraging her in the situation she was in, and I gave her some practical advice on how she could get back in shape. When the producers of *Body+Soul* asked me if I knew of anyone who could really do with a body and soul makeover, Anna was one person who stood out.

I will never forget my first conversation with this remarkable woman. We began talking about what she wanted out of the program and it wasn't long before we progressed from body to soul and then to spirit. Anna began sharing about the loss of her precious baby just a few weeks earlier. She told me how the doctors had determined that something was wrong and that it was a rare genetic condition that neither she nor I had ever heard of. Anna began to cry on the telephone as she was sharing because she told me how she felt that she was left without a choice when it came to the eventual fate of her precious daughter.

It was great to get to know Anna and it was an honour to help her shed the three sizes that she hoped for. That was the easy part! My goal for Anna's soul was for her to be able to smile again. After a few weeks and good progress with the physical challenge presented to Anna, we began working on her soul. Anna took me to a very special place in her home where she said she often sat or walked around and listened to the song that was played at her daughter's funeral, over and over again.

Although I felt quite out of my depth with Anna's circumstances, I knew I needed to do something to help her. My 'prescription' for Anna's anguish was to bring in some laughter therapists to present an option for Anna to remember! The laughter therapy took place in the same location as Anna's near–ritualistic walks. The purpose in all this was never to try to minimise Anna's loss, but to give her options to fill her mind and to give her future memories of some good times.

The laughter therapists, Todd and Scott, were absolutely fantastic. They not only had Anna laughing until she was crying but they had all of us rolling around, including the camera crew. All of a sudden Anna's breakthrough gave us all permission to join with her in a glimpse of a happier future for her and her lovely family. It's no secret that laughter can help heal. Sometimes, when emotions are raw and despair is deep, a good laugh is good medicine. It helps to put things back into perspective. After the crying has stopped, acceptance and laughter can begin.

That wasn't the end of the story. Anna lost the weight; she looked and felt fantastic. She laughed again and began to smile more than frown from that day on. I knew there was more on offer, however, so in our last week I had a chat with Anna about Eternity. 'Do you sleep, Anna?' I asked quizzically. 'No!' she exclaimed. I figured that this woman that I had got to know over the past few weeks was still suffering from anxiety about what had happened and I figured she probably wasn't getting much sleep.

I asked Anna if she would like to know how to get more sleep to which she immediately responded, 'Yes.' We had a talk about peace. We then got on to the subject of Eternity and Anna was very responsive. The next week I spent some time with Anna and it was then she asked how she could have a personal relationship with God. We talked more about Eternity and she prayed a simple prayer one morning that changed her life and brought faith into her world like never before. At the end of this chapter, you can read Anna's amazing story of faith and hope.

Anna lives in my heart. I believe that through faith and hope we will have the privilege of communing with those in Heaven who have lived in our hearts here on earth. I believe it is important for the physician to care for people as well as to heal people and for the preacher to love people as well as to save people. The place that a person holds here in our hearts will remain throughout Eternity.

Growing up, I saw my parents lovingly care for all kinds of people, including an old man who lived next door to us. His name was Mr Gordon. The house next door was a large Victorian mansion with some fourteen bedrooms that had been converted into a boarding house. Mr Gordon occupied one of the rooms. Mum and Dad befriended him and soon Mum was cooking dinner for Mr Gordon every night and we all took it in turns to visit him, taking him some of Mum's best home cooking. It was something that I remember fondly. I can still smell the liniment oil that he used on his tired old body. He was a dear sweet man and we were so sad when he finally entered Eternity.

When my own children take meals, cakes or treats into our neighbour Arthur's place, it often reminds me of a similar period in time when Mr Gordon was the object of our family's affection. I pray that my babies catch the spirit of what life's truly about so that when they are grown up with children of their own, they will be looking to the needs of others — those right under their noses!

The week that I lost both my Nanny and my Aunty Eileen was the same week that our neighbour Arthur turned ninety. It was a big week for us and certainly we would have been excused for not having time or emotional energy to celebrate a ninetieth birthday in the middle of it all. Even though it was a very difficult week, I was very aware of Arthur as he was feeling vulnerable too. So we celebrated and it was really rewarding. I went out and bought a new cardigan for our dear friend and a little cake. The kids gathered around and we sang with great gusto! Who would have thought that moment would have meant so much to him.

It wasn't very long after, on our way to church one Saturday night, Arthur asked Jonathan if he could possibly say a prayer with him about Eternity. We had hoped for this moment for such a long time, but this was something that Arthur had to decide for himself. You see, we can have Eternity in our hearts, on our lives and in our hands, and we can offer it freely to everyone we come into contact with, but at the end of the day, only the willing choose to receive. I am so glad that Arthur was willing to receive the gift of Eternity, the wonderful gift of eternal life.

We were born with a purpose that is greater than ourselves. When we tap into the very reason we were born, we have the privilege of living a life of significance, regardless of what we go through along the way. Knowing your purpose for living and having a cause to focus on ensures that life's disappointments don't throw you off course. If you were to ask me what my cause is, I would simply say, 'To love God and to love people.' How I go about doing that in my everyday life is up to me, but one thing's for sure — the power of a cause is something we need to lay hold of if we want our lives to count.

In the very first chapter of his bestselling book *The Purpose Driven Life*[11], Rick Warren talks about how life is not about us. 'It's not about me!' This is a profound thought. If life is not about me, then who is it about? It's about others and our positive contribution to other people's lives. The most remarkable people we know are those who give to others when it is they who deserve to be on the receiving end because of the hardship they have to live with. Sometimes the most selfish amongst us are the ones who have the least amount to complain about. Be assured, there is always someone worse off than us.

I was speaking once to a mother who had lost not one but two daughters in the Bali bombings of October 2002. Others who had also lost children and other relatives in the same blast determined that their loss must somehow be less than this woman's loss because no-one could begin to imagine losing two children in the same tragedy. This amazing woman told me how she had consoled these people by saying that loss is loss regardless of how much you go through. She didn't know what it felt like to lose just one daughter, because she lost both, but she did say that she couldn't imagine being less grieved by the loss of even one of her children. Loss is loss and most painful to the individual suffering from it. Regardless of whether our loss has been great or small, while there is still breath in our lungs we need to make sure the remainder of our life here on earth counts for something. Many people turn their pain into purpose by starting causes and foundations to help others going through similar circumstances. This is a good way of making your life count. In the light of Eternity, just remember that whatever you do, make it count not just on earth but also in Heaven.

A legacy is an intentional gift that we spend our lives creating for others. It is not only politicians, athletes, movie stars and social activists who leave legacies. Everyone will leave something behind and it's up to us while we're still here to make it something magnificent. What will you leave behind for others? Are you leaving the legacy you really want to leave?

Throughout our lives we enjoy the benefits of those who came before us and sacrificed to make what we do more meaningful and significant. We have all been affected by the legacy of others, both positively and negatively. When we intend to leave behind something of eternal significance, we need to create a life plan to make it happen.

My Dad is a wonderful example of someone who has intentionally worked his entire life to provide a lasting and eternal legacy for his children. He and my Mum have spent their entire married life building a legacy of real estate here on earth, but have also spent their lives as our parents, building a legacy of a wonderful loving family with an incredible perspective that Eternity is our home.

I thank God for having a natural father who so beautifully reflects my Heavenly Father. I am sure that is why I have always found it completely natural to have faith in God, because of the wonderful example of my own father. Whether your natural earthly father was a good reflection of your kind Heavenly Father or not, be assured that in the light of Eternity, you can experience that love and legacy in your lifetime, and also learn to leave something that you never had, for others to benefit from.

It is true that we hope to be remembered with fondness when we pass from here to Eternity, but the real question remains: what are we doing about it now while we still can make a difference? If life hasn't been kind to you so far, consider what good things have come from your pain and what good things are yet to come from your pain. There is much gold hidden in the rubble of our lives. Decide what legacy you want to leave behind as a sign of hope to others.

Here are just five ways that you can begin to make your life count.

❖ Look around and get involved in your community. Are people hungry, homeless or ill? Are parks or schools dirty or neglected? No matter where you live, there's a need nearby. Do you have a lonely neighbour?

- Consider working with other organisations who are already involved in making a difference in the area you're interested in. Rather than reinventing the wheel, you may be able to jump on board and make a greater impact as part of an existing team.
- Roll up your sleeves and act alone or enlist your friends and family. Tell others what you're doing and ask for their help.
- Prepare a comprehensive 'to do list', gather 'tools' and ask for donations for your cause in helping others.
- Share your story with others to give them hope for their future — not so you get glory for what you've done, but so that others can be inspired that life can and should go on — for Eternity's sake.

If your identity has been wrapped up in someone who is no longer here to do life with, now is the time for you to find out who you really are and why you were born. This is your time to live, your time to make your mark.

Sometimes the silence of Heaven can be deafening if we sit around waiting for God to drop His will for our lives in our lap. His will for our lives is all around us. We have many opportunities to make our lives count for something greater than ourselves. We have the opportunity and ability to climb many mountains in our lifetime, even when making it over small bumps in the road is at times all we think we can do.

What about when you see a person lying in a doorway, and you know that they will be there all night. What do you do? Finding shelter for a person who has none is a basic duty of humanity. How wonderful the world would be if we had the same determination to clothe, feed and provide shelter for others as much as for ourselves. That is what is meant by loving our neighbours as ourselves.

Look for opportunities to serve others. Associate with all age groups. Younger people need to be able to talk to older people. New mothers need help. People need encouragement. Volunteer to help whenever help is needed. Don't just sit around waiting for someone to ask you to do something or to go somewhere. Be the most concerned, the best neighbour in your street.

People are looking for something deeper and more meaningful in their lives, but don't know where or even how to look for it. There are many communities of hope to which you can belong, including many great churches. I know first hand the incredible strength that my church family offers. We may be several thousand members strong, but there is a phenomenal sense of intimacy in relationships because of the love and care of the people who are the church. When a group of people with the same heart and spirit hold Eternity dear, it offers a richness and quality beyond itself that is able to impact the saddest of situations and ushers in hope.

Your future is grand. Walk tall into all that God has prepared for you.

> *'Never let the fear of striking out*
> *keep you from playing the game.'*
>
> — BELLA WILSON (AGED 7) —

Anna's Story

My beautiful son Jayden was born at forty-one weeks, weighing a healthy 2.63 grams. With tears, joy and anxiety I finally met the one who was kicking me all those months. What a day, what an experience, what a fantastic journey. Two years later Joe and I decided to try for another child. We wanted four children altogether. I fell pregnant and was thrilled. At eight weeks, I miscarried. Anger, disappointment and confusion were emotions I became familiar with. There was no reason for this to have happened. 'It was one of those things,' I heard the doctor say, and it wouldn't be the last time.

October that same year, I was expecting again. My first ultrasound at six weeks confirmed that I was having identical twins. I was the most thrilled, elated and surprised woman in the world. Joe and I were so happy and excited about this challenge coming our way. But the twelve-week ultrasound revealed that the babies had died in utero. My children had died. 'It was one of those things,' I heard the doctor say again. In six months, I had lost three babies. Unfortunately, if you miscarry less than three times, investigations aren't warranted. I had to lose more babies before I could find out the probable cause.

The following year I became pregnant once again. You can imagine the excitement, then the grief when at twelve weeks an ultrasound confirmed that this baby had also died in utero. By now, I was mortified and frustrated. I knew it was 'one of those things', but why, and why me? What was wrong? Why was I being punished? I repeated the questions in my mind over and over again.

Thorough investigations showed no abnormality. I was young and healthy, and — according to the doctors — there was no explanation as to why I was miscarrying. They told me that it is quite common to lose consecutive pregnancies, and to try again when I felt ready. In a very short period of time I had lost four babies, so Joe and I decided to wait a while, to deal with the losses and to get my body and mind into a healthier state.

The following year, I became pregnant once again. This time, I insisted the pregnancy be managed regularly. I had an ultrasound fortnightly I was excited, scared and anxious. I kept hoping that this baby would be 'the one'. I knew I had to reach twelve weeks to feel safe. It was a milestone that I reached without a hitch. I made it past the first trimester. I was thrilled and looking forward to the next six months of pregnancy. At nineteen weeks, I went to have an ultrasound. All was well. I was almost halfway to meeting this little being. This was the one. I knew it. I felt it.

The next evening after the ultrasound, my doctor contacted me at home to tell me there were problems found in the ultrasound scan. I froze. I was booked in for an emergency amniocentesis the next morning. Although the procedure went well, I was told that my baby was growth-restricted — although I was nineteen weeks pregnant, my baby's growth showed sixteen weeks. The results of the amniocentesis were clear, but they believed that the placenta was not functioning properly, hence my baby was growth-restricted. My baby was a little girl.

I decided to contact a specialist in placentas and I made an appointment to see her. After thorough investigations and extensive ultrasounds, the specialist was convinced that the placenta was working fine. In fact, if anything, according to her analysis of the results, it was my baby that had the problems. I was told that my child had a genetic disorder and wouldn't survive because of her size.

Each week that went by felt like a month. It was the most agonising and confusing experience of my life. The joy and happiness I felt each time she kicked me, then the torture of knowing that she was dying. The feeling is too hard to describe.

What added to the heartbreak of knowing that I would not be taking my baby home was the need to find the right words to explain it all to Jayden. He was so excited that he was going to be a brother and each night would kiss my stomach to say goodnight. When I told him what was happening and what was to happen, he didn't cry, which amazed me. Instead he was angry. He felt that he was being denied a brother or sister.

Weeks went by, and at twenty-five weeks my baby was growing at a slower rate. The ultrasound confirmed that she was stressed and the level of amniotic fluid was decreasing. My baby was dying. There was no hope.

I kept praying and begging for everything to be all right. I wanted a miracle. I wanted to go to my next ultrasound and hear that the baby had miraculously grown to a weight that was safe — but that was not to be. At twenty-six weeks, we made the agonising decision to terminate the pregnancy based on the baby's growth restrictions, her size and the high probability of genetic disorders. I was numb. I remember feeling an incomprehensible amount of deep sadness, yet I still didn't believe that this was happening.

One of the hardest things for me was when I would go

out to collect my son from pre-school and I would see a lot of pregnant women. They would look at me and we would exchange smiles, yet no-one had any idea I had a baby in utero that was dying. The pain was unbearable.

I was booked in to terminate the pregnancy. It was the most tormenting day of my life. When my husband and I arrived at the hospital, we walked past a man holding his newborn baby girl. I couldn't bear to look at him. For the first time, I felt sorry for myself. I was about to lose my little girl, and there this man was holding his. It just didn't seem fair.

I was told just before theatre that there would not be any medical intervention. To be honest with you, I didn't even think about this before. I assumed that she would either be born lifeless or die a few minutes later. I was so confused. I was going to give birth to this baby and basically wait for her to die. At twenty-six weeks gestation, my baby's size was that of an eighteen or nineteen week old. She was so tiny and doctors were convinced that even with medical intervention, she would not survive. It was time to go to the operating theatre.

I remember hearing my husband Joe beside me calling my name. I didn't want to wake up. When I did wake up, and opened my eyes, I saw Joe staring at me and I automatically bellowed a moan. I remembered what I had come into hospital for. Joe grabbed my hand and told me our daughter was beautiful. I cried and cried and was presented with this little bundle. Her name was Jacinta Mary-Anne, born at twenty-six weeks, weighing 310 grams. I held her, touched her mouth and cried. She looked perfect but small, and yes, she was beautiful. Jacinta was lifeless, my angel was gone.

I only held her for thirty minutes as she had to be rushed to Westmead Hospital for an autopsy. How do you say goodbye? How do you give your angel to a stranger to take away forever? I had no choice. This baby was not coming home with me. I was holding my baby, my beautiful baby. My baby, whose presence I had felt in my body for six months, was now lifeless in my arms. My body ached and craved for her and today my body still craves for her. The loss was unbearable. After the birth, I stayed in a room in the maternity ward, which was just total heartbreak. I didn't leave the room for three days, but I heard the wonderful sounds of crying babies. I was discharged from the hospital and had to explain to Jayden that Jacinta was in Heaven now. He cried and continued to kiss my tummy.

Funeral arrangements had to be made and I had to make the choice of which music we would like played at the service. It was heart-wrenching, but I managed to do it for Jacinta. My husband and I went to purchase her a beautiful wrap and teddy bear to place in the coffin. That was so hard to do.

Just before the service my husband arranged that we would see her for the last time, as I didn't have much time with her after the birth. I couldn't wait to see her again. I know it sounds strange but it was true. The mind can play all sorts of tricks. There were times before the service that I would tell Joe that we needed to go to the morgue to cover her up because she may be cold; once, I wanted to stay with her in case she was scared in a strange place. I had to quickly snap out of it or else I would completely lose it.

It was time for the service and our family members inside the chapel greeted us. The service went well until the music played and then it hit me that this was the real goodbye. The curtain closed slowly and I watched the coffin disappear. I cried and cried until I could cry no more. The pain that went through every part of my body was indescribable. In my mind I was yelling for it all to stop, but I knew it wasn't meant to be. I kept telling her that I loved her and would talk to her every day forever.

Life was different for me now. I had to be strong for my little boy Jayden. I somehow accepted Jacinta's death and knew in my heart that she was with me. I talked to her each day, and after crying I would feel a little bit better.

Six weeks later I saw Di Wilson on television helping a mother of three get back in shape, so I emailed her to ask if she could help me. I needed to get back in shape, yet had no little baby to show for it. Di really helped me, body and soul. I dropped three sizes and found myself able to smile and laugh again. She talked to me about Eternity, and helped me find peace and hope for the future.

Months later, we decided to go overseas for a holiday and when we came back I was pregnant. I was so excited. I was pregnant for the sixth time. Twelve weeks into the pregnancy, I lost the baby. It was a boy. My dreams of having another baby were diminishing. But I was determined. After meeting Di, I started to read books on healing and positive thinking. I began to change my way of thinking to a more positive outlook.

I knew that Jacinta's death wasn't punishment but a path that led me to turn to Jesus, God and all the angels and saints, and to regain my faith. I prayed constantly and read more literature, and day by day my faith increased. I was feeling good, positive and focused.

Joe and I decided to paint what would have been Jacinta's bedroom and convert it into a meditation room or

a 'chill-out' room. We purchased a large comfortable chair
and would sit in the room each night with lit candles
and fantasise about having a baby. I would visualise the
pregnancy, the birth and my life after the birth. It made me
feel relaxed and content. I purchased a 'prayer diary' and
would write all my prayers in there. I would read them
aloud each night and feel each word in my heart. I grew
more and more determined and so too did my faith. My
state of mind was at its best and I felt confident.

Joe and I told my obstetrician that we would like to try
for another baby, so we began extensive testing. The results
showed no abnormality with my husband or me. Although
we lost Jacinta an hour after birth due to placental problems,
the chances of it happening again were very small.

The next year I was pregnant again. The pregnancy was
closely monitored and managed with regular blood tests
and ultrasounds. I was happy, excited, nervous and anxious
but this time I had faith, and lots of it!

At thirteen weeks gestation, I was scheduled for an
amniocentesis as a precaution, given my history of
miscarriages and a neonatal death. The results came back
clear. Early the next morning, I felt the amniotic fluid leak.
I contacted the surgery and told them that I had lost some
fluid; it was suggested that I make an emergency ultrasound
appointment. I was told that during the procedure, a
membrane was ruptured, that my baby would die and there
was nothing I could do to prevent it. I refused to believe
this and continued to pray, and kept positive and focused.

The next day, another ultrasound showed that the baby
had placed itself where the tear was and acted like a plug.
No more fluid was escaping. Bed rest and plenty of it was
on the agenda. The next week, an ultrasound showed that

my baby's growth was lagging a week behind. I was fourteen weeks pregnant, but my baby was the size of a thirteen-week baby. I tried not to panic. It was so hard.

As the weeks proceeded, the baby's growth was progressively lagging. At twenty-three weeks gestation, my baby's growth was that of a nineteen-week baby. I was so scared and I knew that I didn't want to go down the same path as I did with Jacinta. I couldn't bear to lose another child. My faith became stronger along with my hopes. I kept repeating to myself that I was taking this baby home.

If the baby was born at twenty-eight weeks, and weighed only 385 grams, it would not survive. I had faith and believed with all my heart that all was well. The signs were not good so I stayed in hospital for a week with plenty of bed rest.

I was lonely and scared. All I could do was rest in bed, so boredom set in very quickly. Each day I used the time to pray, visualise and write. Despite the medical reports, despite the doctors' prognosis, my heart and soul felt alive. I was going to take this baby home.

The following week the doctors told me my baby had to come out but would not survive. The weight of my baby was 410 grams in utero. After all the hugs and apologies from the medical staff, I looked at them and said, 'No! Have faith and never ever give up! My baby has a strong heartbeat, so hold back on your condolences until the last beat.'

I stuck to this way of thinking the whole way through. I had to. I prayed with all my heart. I asked my daughter Jacinta in Heaven to send me an angel. A happy healthy angel. I knew she wouldn't let me down.

That evening I was scheduled for a Caesarean. I left it in God's hands. I lay on the operating table with many doctors and nurses around me. I told my husband not to come in with me, as I didn't want him to go through the same trauma again. I was okay on my own because I had so much faith, knowing I wasn't on my own.

My baby girl was born. I cried and cried and had an amazing feeling that I was not alone. The feeling was indescribable. I looked over to the bed where they laid her and I saw her little foot move. I heard a kitten sound. That was her cry. The room was filled with tears and joy. Paris Therese, my daughter, was born at twenty-eight weeks gestation, weighing 410 grams, and didn't need to be ventilated. The look on my doctor's face was disbelief. They told me she was okay. What a miracle.

Paris remained in hospital for just over three months and continued to thrive. The hospital staff were so tremendous, especially her neonatal paediatrician, who, when I asked, 'Is there hope?', replied, 'There is always hope.' I needed to hear that from someone. Joe and I will never forget the support and the care the staff provided to Paris. She was tiny, but miraculously she survived without brain haemorrhaging, hearing or eyesight defects.

Paris is the second smallest surviving baby born in Australia to date. Today she is the most beautiful, joyful and strong little girl. I sit in her bedroom (the old meditation room) on the same big chair, holding my baby, looking back at the days when I would visualise this experience. It is now a reality. What a tremendous feeling.

The journey was a long one but each day I look at my two children and I am so grateful and blessed. Hope, faith and trust are the elements that helped me get through the pregnancy with a positive outcome. Believe and never give up.

Eileen's Story

Mike and I had been married nine years when we decided to start a family. I remember the day like it was yesterday. It was so exciting, so when I missed my period the following month I couldn't believe that it had happened so soon.

I went out during a work lunchbreak and bought a pregnancy kit and the result was positive. I decided to surprise Mike with the news that evening, so after work I went downtown and bought a pair of booties and a beautiful box to wrap them in. I called him and asked him if he wanted to go out that evening for dinner. I was sure it was written all over my face when he saw me, it was so hard to contain my excitement, but Mike was none the wiser. So after dinner I presented him with the box. I will never forget the expression on his face when he pulled out the pair of booties; he just said, 'I am going to be a Dad.' It was such a beautiful moment, one I will always remember.

The next few weeks passed with little or no morning sickness. When the time came for my first ultrasound, I was so excited. I remember lying on the table looking at the monitor and seeing Hannah Grace moving on the screen — nothing could prepare me for this moment in my life. I asked the lady who was doing the test if she could see if it was a boy or a girl, and she replied very abruptly that she hadn't been asked to find the sex of our baby.

Time seemed to pass very slowly and I asked the lady a little later if everything was all right. She said we would have to move to another room as her computer was playing up. When we changed rooms there was another lady waiting for us and she took over the examination. I remember lying there thinking, 'Please let everything be okay with my baby'. After the ultrasound I was told to contact my doctor the following day for the results. I remember thinking everything must be okay; they wouldn't have let me leave without telling me there was a problem.

The following day I had an appointment with my doctor, so I decided to go and pick up the results of the ultrasound myself as the clinic was next to my work. I walked back to the office with the envelope hot in my hands. I couldn't wait till that afternoon to see my doctor; I had to open it then. As I read the results everything seemed normal until I got to the last two lines which read: 'No normal intracranial contents identified, suggests anencephaly.'

I remember sitting in my office saying to myself that this had to be a mistake and that it couldn't be happening to us. I decided to call my doctor first and talk to her; I didn't want to upset Mike if this was a mistake, but she confirmed the ultrasound results were correct. I called Mike and told him the story and asked him to meet me at the doctor's surgery. The train journey to the surgery was endless; I couldn't stop myself from crying. I saw Mike sitting outside on the steps of the doctor's office. He looked up and I could see the pain in his eyes.

We sat in the doctor's office as she explained to us what anencephaly was. When babies with anencephaly are born, they usually die during birth because they have no covering over their head to protect them when they come through the birth canal, or they die soon after birth due to infection.

I remember sitting there listening to our doctor say to us that she would book us in for a termination the following week, and all that was going through my mind were the words: 'Without faith it's impossible to please God.' We were not going to do anything until we had talked together, and had some counsel from our pastors.

We had invited some friends over for dinner that evening, and by the time we got home from the doctor's surgery it was too late to cancel. We tried our best to keep it together, but couldn't wait for everyone to leave so we could talk through all that had happened that day. We were both very sad and confused. If what the doctor was saying was true, our baby would not live through the birth, and if it did, it would die soon after. Could we spend the next six months of the pregnancy knowing that we would have no baby at the end of all this?

The next day we called our pastors and told them the news and organised to meet with them that evening. We loved and respected these people; they were like family. I had known them since I had come to Australia nine years before. They had taken me under their wing, encouraged me to go to college, where I met Mike, and they married us twenty months later. They were there for us when I lost my mother eighteen months before; she had committed suicide in Ireland after a long battle with depression. I thought at the time that it would be the hardest thing that we would ever go through, but I was wrong.

So as we sat in their office that day they were as devastated as we were. They listened and talked with us and they prayed that God would give us wisdom and strength to make the right decision. Driving home in the car that day I had such a peace about the whole situation; there was no natural way of explaining it, I just knew that we would carry our baby to full term, and that we would have the necessary strength whatever the outcome.

The next few months were so difficult. I was still grieving the loss of my mother and my emotional state was very frail, but we had decided shortly after we found out about Hannah Grace to tell our close friends, so they could support us. We had never realised before my mother's death the power of great friendships. There were many days in the months that followed when we arrived home to flowers on the doorstep, a card in the mail or an encouraging book to lift our spirits — and there was always a listening ear.

At twenty-eight weeks we went for another ultrasound; we wanted to find out if we were having a boy or a girl as we wanted to make a special quilt for the hospital. We were so excited to hear it was a little girl but the condition was still the same. I remember coming home from the hospital that day being so disappointed that we hadn't received our miracle. This was a real turning point for me as I began to talk to my friends about our situation, allowing them to see that whatever the outcome, our faith was going to see us through.

At forty-one weeks I still hadn't gone into labour so our doctor decided to induce me. After thirty-six hours of labour Hannah Grace was born. She was so beautiful; born with a perfect little body. I knew as they laid her on my stomach that she had gone to Heaven. Later that evening our friends came to visit. There was a beautiful peace in the room as we shared our memories. It was a very special few days as we spent time with our baby girl.

Looking back now I don't completely understand what happened but I believe you should never let life hand you a sorrow without taking something good from it. I know this may be difficult for some to understand, but I have known God as a friend and comforter since I was seven years old and my faith has only increased during this time.

Two years after Hannah Grace was born, we now have a beautiful little girl called Emma Maya. She looks very like her big sister, and you know, I think that's very special.

Little Angels

How to support someone who's had a miscarriage or stillbirth

It's hard to know how to help someone who has lost a baby to miscarriage or a stillbirth. Although you can't make the pain go away, there are many ways that you can support the parents and help them deal with their grief.

- Be there for them. Many grieving parents retreat from the world for a while, so make an effort to keep calling, visiting and just letting them know that you are there if they need you.
- Acknowledge their loss. Even an early miscarriage can cause significant and lasting grief to a couple, and should not be ignored or minimised.
- Listen. They may need to talk about the loss of their baby; some parents even keep photographs of a stillborn baby that they like to show to their friends. Just talk when they need to talk.
- Avoid saying 'It was for the best', or 'You can always have another baby.' Many people use statements like this in an effort to be helpful, but this is not what grieving parents need to hear.
- Offer to help them commemorate their baby. Some parents choose to hold funeral or memorial services to give them closure, while others choose to fill a journal or special box with thoughts and mementos of their lost baby. Ask if you can help them with any preparations they need to make.

- ❖ Help out by offering to field calls or answer letters and cards until they feel up to dealing with them.
- ❖ Remember that grandparents and siblings will also be feeling the loss, so including them in your support is important.
- ❖ Bring in meals and offer to help with cleaning and laundry. See what you can do to be of practical assistance.
- ❖ Help them find pregnancy and neonatal loss support groups in their area, as it may be helpful to meet other parents who have been through what they are going through.

Father's Day 2004

Dearest Dad,

To the best Dad in the entire universe … I love you. Thank you for being such a wonderful father to me and to so many others. Thank you for committing your love to Mum and for honouring your commitment and being such a beautiful example of that love. Thank you for raising us to believe in ourselves and to believe that we can be and do anything we want to. Thank you for believing in others, not with blind trust but always believing the best of another. Thank you for your kind generosity which has always given without bounds. You've taught me to want to do the same just by watching and following you. Thank you for putting the entire world first, ahead of any dream or desire you might have in your own heart. Thank you for providing such a rich inheritance for all of us, for reminding us of the value of a family and how important home really is.

I will always remember your beautiful face, your radiant smile and your continuously outstretched arms and hands, and I will never, ever forget how special you have always made me feel … your little girl … Even at thirty-six, nearly thirty-seven years old, I still feel like it's never too late to dream and to make something worthwhile of my future.

Thank you for being the most wonderful Grandfather to my babies, and to my sister's baby … it's no wonder you are their favourite. Thank you for having faith to hold on to life in all its fullness. Your example of believing in miracles is overwhelming. I love you more than I can express on paper … so please forgive my attempt at writing some simple words to show my love for you and all that you are.

God bless you, Daddy. Your little girl always, Dianne.

EPILOGUE

Heaven

the final frontier

*'Like a mighty raging sea, all the Heavens cry out
the anthem of the free.'*

⟼ WILLIAM CUSHING ⟻
AMERICAN CLERGYMAN AND HYMN WRITER (1823–1902)

The Passion of the Christ

The Passion of the Christ is a graphic and detailed movie portrayal of the last twelve hours of the life of Jesus Christ. From the opening scene with Jesus praying in the Garden of Gethsemane to the final scene showing Jesus' death, I found myself in awe of the courage, dedication and love of this Man.

Flashbacks offer a glimpse of what His everyday life used to be like. We see Jesus with His mother and with His disciples, as well as scenes of when he taught the multitude. You easily fall in love with this Man's honesty and compassion.

When people watch a movie like *The Passion of the Christ*, it seems absolutely unthinkable that someone would actually go through so much suffering for them. There is an overwhelming sense that this Man Jesus is infinitely more personal and real than they'd ever imagined.

As the movie progresses, we can easily see that this is an innocent Man with an inconceivable capacity to love people. As the beatings, accusations and lies grow in intensity, we find the Eternity moment. Every human being has been created with a sense of right and wrong, good and bad. I believe there is a common sense of injustice as you watch the last twelve hours of Jesus' life. The questions that often arise after a death — 'Why?' 'Why did they have to die?' 'Why did they have to suffer?' 'It's not right!' 'It should have been me!' — all these questions, even for a brief moment, arise in the viewer.

This highlights the great truth that often comes to the surface after death: that from death comes life. This is obvious in this movie because Jesus actually does come to life again and brings true life to all humanity. Even when someone dear to you dies, you still realise this truth on another level. You realise the things that really matter in life. Everything else fades away for a short while and all you see is your family and friends and all of the many blessings that you've been given. You realise that you still have life and you actually do have something to contribute to this world. So through a great loss, you can also gain great hope for the future.

Eternity is the focus of this movie, which offers viewers hope and eternal life, if they just believe.

Heaven

'Earth has no sorrow that Heaven cannot heal.'

—◦ THOMAS MOORE ◦—
IRISH POET (1779–1852)

EVERYONE HAS A FAVOURITE PLACE that makes them feel they don't want to be anywhere else on earth. One of my favourite places on earth is Disneyland. On 17 July 1955 Walt Disney welcomed all people to this happy place, telling them that Disneyland was also their land. In this speech he talked about the past, present and future dreams that he wanted people to enjoy there.

Walt Disney dedicated Disneyland to the ideals, dreams and realities that created America, with the aim that it would be a source of real joy and inspiration to the world. He certainly succeeded! For many visitors, Walt Disney's wish that it would be the happiest place on earth comes true — there is so much to see and do and so many happy memories to make.

Several charities such as the Starlight Foundation and the Make a Wish Foundation grant wishes to children with life-threatening diseases. One of the most popular wishes is a trip to Disneyland. This fun-filled vacation may be the last experience that the family have together away from the hospital; it gives not only the child but the entire family a happy image to remember during the difficult time ahead. After the child is gone, it remains a cherished memory.

I for one love Disneyland because I can dream about it at any time, even when I'm stuck in traffic in Sydney. Happy memories can flood my heart in the midst of whatever I'm doing and I can somehow know that same 'happiest place on earth' experience even when I'm not physically there. For you, a special beach or park or a holiday destination may give you that kind of warm experience.

My son Beau based the picture at the end of this book on a pin he collected from Disneyland. In the sketch you can see Mickey Mouse looking at himself in the mirror, yet when drawing his reflection, he depicts not himself, but his creator, Walt Disney. This is a great metaphor for Heaven. Our reflection will be God's reflection and we will be one for all Eternity. When I asked Beau if he had noticed that before, he said, 'Yes, Mum — of course.' I had looked at this pin many times, as Beau often brings out his collection to play with, yet I had never noticed the powerful message of the picture. Eternity enables me to look in the mirror and see all that I am meant to be, not just who I am right now. I can look in the mirror and see the wonder of my Creator.

Disneyland may have been created to be the happiest place on earth, but Heaven is the happiest place for all Eternity. Heaven is many things to many people. How can one describe a place that we can only receive glimpses of now? It will be, I believe, a place full of our favourite things and more — much, much more. I expect a 'beyond' experience; that it will be 'above and beyond anything we could ever ask or imagine.' I know I will not be disappointed!

'Death puts life into perspective.'

— RALPH WALDO EMERSON —
AMERICAN WRITER (1803–1882)

Here's a picture. A lonely man walks into a crowded restaurant and is greeted by the host who asks, 'How many?' He answers, 'Table for one, please.' The host leads him to a table in the corner of the room and clears away the cutlery and glassware opposite him. There he sits, one man with one menu, one glass, one bottle — all to himself, not because he wants a little peace and quiet, but because she's gone and now he's all alone.

There will be no tables for one in Heaven ...

Heaven is a place of my own but not on my own. For many, this life may not hold great prospects of a place of your own. When my Dad was growing up, he and his ten brothers and sisters shared a crowded but loving small family home in Sydney's inner west. I often hear Dad telling my kids that they shouldn't complain about space because when he was a boy, he slept on an open veranda with one of his brothers and often one of his Dad's mates or even the town drunk too. I know that my Dad's mansion awaits him in Heaven. He hasn't even tried to attain one here on earth. That has never been of primary interest to him and my Mum. His permanent address — Eternity — is what he's really looking forward to.

Heaven holds so much.

* full of healing — no more pain, tears, disappointment
* eternal — never ever ends
* amazing — full of wonderful surprises
* varied — so many people from so many walks of life
* exciting — the adventure begins!
* near — not a million miles away; close your eyes and feel it close.

In their book entitled *Heaven*, WA Criswell and Paige Patterson speak about Heaven being the abode of God.

'In this fast advancing technological age where scepticism rules and everything has to be proven and explained by science or it is deemed not true, the value of a human soul being is lost. It has been concluded that we are nothing more than a certain species of animal that can think and develop technology. If that was the case, obviously we would have no significant meaning beyond this

present life. Life would have no meaning and we would simply exist and then cease to exist.'[12]

The belief that life exists beyond death can seem almost quaint to some, an idealistic view that brings comfort and reassurance. Many people have rejected the belief of a life beyond this life, entered after death. In embracing that thought, they lose a priceless element of truth, which represents the value and meaning of human life.

It is a well-known fact that most people are afraid of dying. Most studies show death as either the number one or number two fear that people have (just ahead of or sometimes a close second to public speaking!). The question is: why are we so afraid of death? Could it be that the real terror behind it is the fact that it is completely outside our experience or comprehension? It is the unknown.

A baby in the womb of its mother demonstrates this truth. For nine months it has lived, completely secure, warm and sheltered, having everything it needs. In a way, life in the womb is perfect. But the day comes when the baby is forced out of that safe haven and into a world full of noise and lights ... the unknown. No wonder the baby comes out screaming!

Although that experience is tumultuous, there's not one of us who would have preferred to live in the enclosed womb rather than the world we live in. In a womb one could never watch a sunset, feel the rain, laugh with family, love, dance or play.

Death could actually be more like birth than we imagine. Our uncertainty about death could be very similar to a baby's uncertainty about birth — alleviated if we knew what lay ahead. Death is unknown, so some people feel a terrifying uncertainty every time they think about it.

While there are a great number of people who do not believe in life after death, there are a great number of people who do. In most religions you find the belief in life after death in some form or another. To many, instead of death being *an* event in life, it's almost *the* event. There is life after death. Instead of it being the end of life, it's just the beginning.

Psychologist CG Jung suggested that a belief in immortality has therapeutic power because 'No-one can live in peace in a house that he knows is shortly to tumble about his ears.' Believing in and coming to terms with the reality of life after death in Eternity and seeing it as a positive experience is a powerful way that we can have confidence and peace of mind here on earth.

Author Rebecca Ruter Springer (1832–1904) wrote one of my favourite books, entitled *My Dream of Heaven*, originally called *Intra Muros*.[13] This book is an inspirational work expressing the essence of Heaven like nothing I have ever read before. She wrote it while ill and it's clear that she was taken somewhere in her imagination that reflects what I believe in my own heart to be true of Heaven. The story itself presents it as a vision. She herself said that it wasn't a literal or exact picture, but that she felt it had been given to her to present an idea of Heaven in a general way. She took the dream and turned it into a story that has comforted many in their grief since 1898 when it was first published.

Author David Winter writes:

'While it is true that we shall be individual persons in Heaven, Heaven itself is a fellowship or communion centred on God, not on our personal desires or preferences. And God is selfless, self-sacrificing love. That suggests that at the heart of Heaven is not the fulfilment of our own wishes but the perfect expression of the will of God, which is itself pure love. Our joy in Heaven, in other words, will not be a private, selfish one but a marvellous shared experience of love in its fullness.'[14]

So often we hear the word 'up' when talking about Heaven. We seem to have this idea that Heaven is somewhere up above us. This makes no sense to the scientist looking for a physical place in space or the universe, but Heaven by definition is a place beyond time or space.

The concept of 'up' meaning that Heaven is greatly superior to anything 'down' here on earth would be more correct. To think of Heaven as though it were simply another place, like Mars or the Milky Way, would be to diminish it.

Heaven is eternal. It is a place specially prepared for us. Not in the sense of space, in that it goes on forever and ever, but in the sense of time. Heaven is beyond time, therefore it is eternal. But the idea of living forever in an eternal place doesn't sound too appealing to some people. Some have said that they'd rather cease to exist than spend Eternity 'playing harps'. The idea of anything going on forever and ever does not seem remotely attractive to the human mind.

Professor GR Evans from the University of Cambridge says of this perception:

'To modern eyes Heaven seems beautiful but dull. This conception of sameness as tedious is· a relatively modern one. It depends on our idea of time. Boredom requires longish stretches of time to take hold. We should not think of Heaven as being in one place for endless 'time'. We should be envisaging a freedom from the confinement of time and space which will make it possible for us to be with all our friends at once and individually, to be enjoying an infinite variety of things as we choose, without delay or hurry, crowding or isolation. It is something new, a new quality of life.'[15]

Imagine with me for a moment. Imagine a place of:

- ❖ greater love
- ❖ quiet patience
- ❖ genuine kindness
- ❖ no suffering
- ❖ frequent forgiving
- ❖ absolute truth
- ❖ deeper understanding
- ❖ intense generosity
- ❖ no pride
- ❖ no humiliation
- ❖ no segregation
- ❖ no pain
- ❖ no more tears
- ❖ no tables for one.

This is a picture of Heaven on earth that will ultimately be fulfilled in Eternity. Regardless of how 'perfect' life feels for us here on earth, it is a mere shadow of what genuine perfection awaits us in Heaven.

Both the written word and people's experience have revealed that the final journey from here to Eternity, from this earth to Heaven, is more a matter of *being* there rather than *going* there. The journey is not a natural or physical one, but a spiritual one. This doesn't mean that it is less real. On the contrary, it is the ultimate and true reality. Physical existence is temporary and changing; spiritual existence is eternal and unchanging.

This could very well be the experience that many terminally ill patients have. Relatives and friends observe a new calmness and peace about them and make remarks about how brave they are being. They are being secretly supplied with spiritual strength, which is preparing them for the final journey.

Writer and broadcaster Malcolm Muggeridge wrote of how, in his old age, he would often awake in the night, feeling himself half out of his body, hovering between life and death and wondering whether he would return or move on into Eternity. He describes: 'Eternity rising in the distance, a great expanse of ineffable light — so placed, I hear Jesus' words ring triumphantly through the universe, spanning my two existences, the one in Time drawing to a close and the one in Eternity at its glorious beginning.'[16]

Heaven, the final frontier, is a place of great and certain peace and joy. Heaven is my home. It's a home prepared for you. Eternity is deep within the heart of every human being. Some of us know where we are going, and have a clear sense of why we are here, which Malcolm Muggeridge describes as 'a certainty surpassing all words and thoughts'. We know and look forward to Heaven. But what about those who still aren't sure? They feel the longing for *home* as well; they just don't know what it is or what to do with it. It has been said that a longing for God implies His existence just as hunger for food implies its existence.

Sometimes people look for other ways to fill the void that only Eternity can satisfy. By denying or ignoring the longings that are divinely placed within us, the part of our soul that aches for Eternity will never be satisfied. That dissatisfaction produces even more discomfort, more denial and more empty attempts to satisfy it. This searching is an endless cycle. True security, joy, peace and love will only be found where God is present. There is no substitute.

When I think of Heaven, I think of a place that will be populated with so many people that it will take us an Eternity to meet everyone there. So many beautiful souls who received the gift of Eternity in Heaven, many of whom were misjudged on this earth; who lived lives less than great on earth, amongst great legends who made their lives truly marked for Eternity. Heaven is humanity's great equaliser.

John Newton, who wrote the famous hymn 'Amazing Grace', once said, 'If ever I reach heaven I expect to find three wonders there: first, to meet some I had not thought to see there; second, to miss some I had expected to see there; and third — the greatest wonder of all — to find myself there.'

Eternal life in Heaven depends upon what decision we make about God's saving grace, not upon when we make that decision. It's never too late to receive eternal life, but we can only do so in this lifetime. We don't know the hour when our last breath will come. Choose eternal life today.

When we make that decision, we are doing so on behalf of all we are, not just our spirit. We are tripartite beings: body, soul and spirit. Our soul and spirit live on in Eternity after our physical body shuts down here on earth.

❖ The body

Our body ages and eventually wears out, or else it can become broken or diseased in some way that prevents it from continuing to operate. But the essential person remains constant and unchanging. Ask an older person if the gradual ageing of their bodies changes who they are inside. A Grandmother in her seventies may be lively and sprightly and declare that she feels as if she is only twenty years old in her 'inner person'.

❖ The soul

Obviously the longer we live the more opportunity we have to grow and become all that we have been created to be on the inside. We also have the opportunity to pick up heavy weights in our 'inner person' or soul. These weights can be things like hurts, resentments, guilt, disappointments or fears. All these things take their toll on the inner person or soul. But essentially we still are who we are despite the process of time or the current state of our physical appearance. The human soul has the ability to rise up above the limitations of our physical being and express the true triumph of the human spirit.

The human soul or the *essential person* is merely being carried around in an amazing but decaying temple called the body. It is our soul, our essential person, that never dies. It lives on forever.

Upon our arrival in Heaven we will have a sense of being whole — all that we could ever hope to be, our full potential realised.

'I believe, to be sure, that any man who reaches Heaven will find that what he abandoned (even in plucking out his right eye) has not been lost: that the kernel of what he was really seeking even in his most depraved wishes will be there, beyond expectation.'

—❧ C.S. LEWIS ❧—
THE GREAT DIVORCE

In the fifth century BC the Greek philosopher Plato told a story about people chained in a dark cave. All they could see from outside were the shadows on the cave wall. That was until one escaped from the cave. What he found outside the cave was truly amazing. He saw incredible light, colours, shapes and animals. Upon his return to the cave he told the others about the outside world but they could not understand him. The notion of another world beyond the cave was something they could not comprehend.

The beginning of Heaven is not at that hour when the eye grows dim and the sound of friendly voices become silent, but at that hour when God draws near and the eyes of spiritual understanding are opened. Heaven isn't far away in the clouds; Heaven is close by; Heaven is here.

❖ The spirit

Our spirit is able to enter the Heavenly realm, while our body remains on this earth, through a personal connection with God.

> *'Do not let your hearts be troubled.*
> *Trust in God; trust also in me.*
> *In my Father's house are many rooms;*
> *if it were not so, I would have told you.*
> *I am going there to prepare a place for you.*
> *And if I go and prepare a place for you,*
> *I will come back again and take you to be with me,*
> *that you also may be where I am.*
> *You know the way to the place where I am going.'*

—◦ JESUS ◦—
JOHN 14:1–4, THE BIBLE

The journey from here to Eternity has been paved for us. It's up to us to read the signs, follow the way and keep on going until we reach our final destination. Regardless of who we are, what we've done and even what we have and haven't believed our entire lives, Jesus is willing to walk us over the rainbow, from here to Eternity — that transition to life without your loved ones on earth, and your own ultimate journey from here to Eternity. See you in Heaven!

Heaven

⟿ MICKEY AND HIS CREATOR WALT, BY BEAU ⟿

Footprints in the Sand

'One night I dreamed I was walking along the beach with the Lord.

Many scenes from my life flashed across the sky.

In each scene I noticed footprints in the sand.

Sometimes there were two sets of footprints,

other times there was one set of footprints.

This bothered me because I noticed

that during the low periods of my life,

when I was suffering from anguish, sorrow or defeat,

I could see only one set of footprints.

So I said to the Lord,

"You promised me, Lord, that if I followed you,

you would walk with me always.

But I have noticed that during the most trying periods of my life

there has only been one set of footprints in the sand.

Why, when I needed you most, have you not been there for me?"

The Lord replied,

"The times when you have seen only one set of footprints in the sand

are when I carried you."'

—◦ MARY STEVENSON ◦—

Until We Meet Again

Dear loved ones, my family and friends,
I hope by now that some of the initial shock of my departure has begun to wear away and that the pleasant memories have started to unfold. My only sadness at contemplating this moment for you is that I know I shall go and leave much I hoped to do with you undone. I only ask one thing, no sad tears for me, please.

Every wonderful, delightful thrill, experience and emotion life has to offer has been mine. So, no sad tears for me, please.

Rather, recall me with a fond smile as the wife, mother, Grandmother and friend who shared your laughter, tears and dreams through the years.

Save your sadness and sorrow for those who leave before they find, see, feel, taste and discover the precious pleasures of this world. No sad tears for me, please.

I've lived a goodly span of years — and enjoyed them all. I've laughed a lot, cried a little, seen a thousand sunsets — played many games. So, no sad tears for me, please.

I've loved someone whose love was returned. I've cradled a baby in my arms and walked with the hands of young children in my own, then one day welcomed into my heart others: sons, daughters and grandchildren. What blessings each of you have been to me. No sad tears for me, please.

The memories of the years I turn over slowly, like the pages of a book. There were victories, and they gave life zest. There were defeats, and they made me stronger. Many of them were vicarious, through family endeavours, and we all grew. Perhaps the greatest adventure of all has been the spiritual search. I cherish the peace and joy I have found. So, no sad tears for me, please.

Life was good. Think of those happy times: Christmases, Easter, birthdays, holidays, and most of all, remember the thousands of times we were all together as a family. No sad tears for me, please.

No-one dies as long as there is one person left in the living world who remembers with fond recall, and shares a thought, though that person has gone ahead.

Some day you may be looking thoughtfully at the vast oceans of this world, assessing their beauty and changing moods and you may feel a sudden warm, soft breeze across your cheek. You will know that I am there.

Or you might be standing on a mountain top, looking across a sweep of wooded foothills and valleys, and if there is a sudden gentle stirring amongst the trees, feel I am sharing the moment with you.

On Christmas Eve, if there is a small star in the sky, look at it with love and let it come into your heart. So, no sad tears for me, please, and remember me.

A person really never dies while there are those on earth who loved that person. One is never gone as long as there are those who remember with fondness, and as long as memory evokes a wistful smile. All those who have loved, and who have been loved, have earned a piece of immortality. No sad tears for me, please.

When I am gone fear not to say my name
nor speak of me in hushed tones
as though it were a shame for one to die.
Let me figure in your daily talks.
Speak of my loves and hates,
of how I used to laugh and take a walk.
This way I will be forever in your memory.

END NOTES

1   Ted Menten, *Gentle Closings: How to Say Goodbye to Someone you Love*, Running Press Book Publishers, Pennsylvania, USA, 1991 (page 75).

2   Reproduced from Rob Gilbert, *More of ... The Best of Bits and Pieces*, The Economics Press, Fairfield, New Jersey, USA, 1997.

3   Raymond J Corsini, *Encyclopedia of Psychology*, 2nd Edition, Vol. 2, Wiley-Interscience Publications, Ontario, Canada, 1994.

4   Kevin Roberts, *Lovemarks: The Future Beyond Brands*, Murdoch Books, Sydney, 2004.

5   The Medicine Chest, 'Coping with Grief and Fear', *Healthy Child Care*, www.healthychild.net, June–July 2005.

6   Jeff Morrow, *Homosexual to Husband*, Jeff Morrow Ministries, Sydney, 2005.

7   David Pillemer, *Momentous Events, Vivid Memories*, Harvard University Press, Cambridge, Massachusetts, USA, 1998. Dan L Schacter, *Searching For Memory*, Basic Books, New York, USA, 1996.

8   Susan Nolen-Hoeksema, *Women Who Think Too Much: How to Break Free of Overthinking and Reclaim Your Life*, Henry Holt and Co, New York, USA, 2003.

9   Oriah Mountain Dreamer, *The Invitation*, HarperSanFrancisco, San Francisco, USA, 1999.

10   Darlene Zschech, *Extravagant Worship: The Power of Praise*, Bethany House Publishers, Bloomington, Minnesota, USA, 2001.

11   Rick Warren, *The Purpose Driven Life*, Zondervan, Grand Rapids, Michigan, USA, 2002.

12   WA Criswell and Paige Patterson, *Heaven*, Library of Congress, USA, 1991 (page 62).

13   Rebecca Ruter Springer, *My Dream of Heaven*, Harrison House, Tulsa, Oklahoma, USA, 2002.

14   David Winter, *Where Do We Go From Here? The Case for Life Beyond Death*, Hodder and Stoughton, London, UK, 1996.

15   Professor GR Evans, from a booklet published by Canterbury Press, London, UK.

16   Malcolm Muggeridge, *Jesus: The Man Who Lives*, HarperCollins Publishers, New York, USA, 1975.

FINDING HELP

Bereavement CARE Centre

14 Hollis Avenue
Eastwood NSW 2122
PO Box 327
Epping NSW 2121
Tel: 1300 654 556
Email: info@bereavementcare.com.au
Websites: www.bereavementcare.com.au;
www.childhoodgrief.org.au

Beyond Blue

National Depression Initiative
50 Burwood Road (PO Box 6100)
Hawthorn VIC 3122
Tel: 03 9810 6100
Website: www.beyondblue.org.au

Careforce Lifekeys

89 Monbulk Road
Mt Evelyn VIC 3796
Tel: 03 9736 2273
Fax: 03 9737 0781
Website: www.careforcelifekeys.org

Centre for Grief Education

Website: www.grief.org.au

The Christian Wholeness Centre

John Warlow, Psychiatrist and
Peter Stebbins, Clinical Psychologist
5/18 Mt Gravatt Capalaba Road
Upper Mt Gravatt QLD 4122
Shop 7, Clock Corner Shopping Centre
Beams Road, Carseldine QLD 4034 (Foundations)
Tel: 07 3343 1677 (Christian Wholeness Counselling Centre)
Tel: 07 3263 9132 (Foundations/Kids Foundations Counselling
Centre)

The Compassionate Friends

PO Box 3696
Oak Brook, Illinois, USA
Tel: 0011 1 630 990 0010
Fax: 0011 1 630 990 0246

GriefLink

Website: www.grieflink.asn.au

GriefNet Internet Community

Website: www.griefnet.org

GriefShare

Church Initiative
Wake Forest, North Carolina, USA
Websites: www.griefshare.org; www.churchinitiative.com

Hillsong Health and Counselling Centre

Suite 5, Mileto House

2–4 Old Castle Hill Road

Castle Hill NSW 2154

Tel: 02 9680 4700

Email: healthcentre@hillsong.com

Website: www.hillsong.com

HillsongLIFE

188 Young Street

Waterloo NSW 2017

Tel: 02 8853 5353

Website: www.hillsong.com/life

Kids Help Line

PO Box 376

Red Hill QLD 4059

Tel: 07 3369 1588

Hotline: 1800 55 1800

Email: admin@kidshelp.com.au

Website: www.kidshelp.com.au

Koorong Books

28 West Parade

West Ryde NSW 2114

Tel: 02 9857 4477

Website: www.koorong.com

Life Line

24-hour hotline: 131 114

Website: www.lifeline.org.au

Mercy Ministries Australia (for young women)

PO Box 1537

Castle Hill NSW 1765

Tel: 02 9659 4180

Toll free: 1800 011 537

Email: info@mercyministries.com.au

Website: www.mercyministries.com.au

Mission Australia

National Office

4–10 Campbell Street

Sydney NSW 2000

Tel: 02 9219 2000

24-hour hotline: 1300 886 999

Website: www.mission.com.au

National Association for Loss and Grief (NSW)

Welchman Street

Dubbo NSW 2830

Tel: 02 6882 9222

Email: info@nalag.org.au

Website: www.nalag.org.au

National Association for Loss and Grief (Vic)

Suite 4, Level 1

182 Victoria Parade

East Melbourne VIC 3002

Tel: 03 9650 3000

Email: info@nalagvic.org.au

Website: www.nalagvic.org.au

Salvation Army

Headquarters
140 Elizabeth Street
Sydney NSW 2000
24-hour hotline: 1300 36 36 22
Website: www.salvationarmy.org.au

Southern Highlands Bereavement Care Service

Bowral Hospital
Bowral NSW 2576
Tel: 02 4862 1701
Website: www.thesouthernhighlands.com.au

Teen Challenge (for young men)

40 Hector Street
Chester Hill NSW 2076
Tel: 02 9644 7737
Email: info@tcnsw.org
Website: www.tcnsw.org

RECOMMENDED READING

Aspects of Grief by Jane Littlewood
   Tavistock/Routledge, London, UK

The Bible (New Living Translation)
   Tyndale House Publishers, Carol Stream, Illinois, USA

Caring for People in Grief by PJ Le Peau
   InterVarsity Press, Downers Grove, Illinois, USA

Children and Grief: When a Parent Dies by J William Worden
   Guilford Press, London, UK

Coping With Grief by M McKissock
   ABC Enterprises, Sydney

Disappointed with God by Philip Yancey
   Zondervan, Grand Rapids, Michigan, USA

Disenfranchised Grief: Recognising Hidden Sorrow by Kenneth J. Doka (Ed.)
   Lexington Books, New York, USA

Good Grief by Granger E. Westberg
   Augsburg Fortress Publishers, Minneapolis, USA

Grief and Powerlessness: Helping People Regain Control of Their Lives by Ruth Bright
   Jessica Kingley Publishers, London, UK

Grief Counselling and Grief Therapy by J William Worden
Routledge, London, UK

A Grief Observed by C.S. Lewis
Faber & Faber, London, UK

Grief: The Toothache of the Soul by Kindah Greening
Healing Hurting Supplies, Burleigh, Queensland

GriefShare
Church Initiative, Wake Forest, North Carolina, USA

Helping Women Recover from Abortion by Nancy Michels
Bethany House Publishing, Minneapolis, USA

Homosexual to Husband by Jeff Morrow
Jeff Morrow Ministries, Sydney

I'll Hold You in Heaven by Jack Hayford
Regal Books, Ventura, California, USA

In My Own Way by M McKissock and D McKissock
The Bereavement Centre, Sydney

The Journey Home by Bill Bright
Thomas Nelson Publishers, Nashville, Tennessee, USA

Learning to Grieve by Geoffrey Glassock and Louise Rowling
Millenium Books, London, UK

Lessons of Loss: A Guide to Coping by Robert A Neimeyer
Australian Centre for Grief and Bereavement, Clayton,
Victoria

*Living Through Loss: A Training Guide for Those Supporting People
Facing Loss* by Fay W Jacobsen, M Kindlen and A
Shoemark
Jessica Kingsley Publishers, London, UK

Loss of a Baby: Understanding Maternal Grief by Margaret Nicol
    Bantam Books, Sydney

My Dream of Heaven by Rebecca Ruter Springer
    Harrison House, Tulsa, Oklahoma, USA

Recovering from the Losses of Life by H Norman Wright
    Revell Books, Grand Rapids, Michigan, USA

Stick a Geranium in Your Hat and Be Happy! by Barbara Johnson
    W Publishing Group, Nashville, Tennessee, USA

To Live Again by Catherine Marshall
    Collins Fontana Books, London, UK

When Grief Leaves the Dictionary and Comes to Your Home
    by Kindah Greening
    Healing Hurting Supplies, Burleigh, Queensland

Where is God When it Hurts? by Philip Yancey
    Zondervan, Grand Rapids, Michigan, USA

Where's the Miracle? by Steve Penny
    Kings Christian Church, Buderim, Queensland

Will the Pain Ever Go Away? by Alice L Lawson Cox
    Navpress, Colorado Springs, Colorado, USA

RECOMMENDED VIEWING

GriefShare video seminars
    Church Initiative, Wake Forest, North Carolina, USA

Inside Your Feelings: Children Dealing with Loss and Grief
    National Association for Loss and Grief (Vic),
    East Melbourne, Victoria

The Journey Continues: The Wisdom of Youth —
    Young People Dealing with Loss and Grief
    National Association for Loss and Grief (Vic),
    East Melbourne, Victoria

Speaking from Experience: Grief and Older People — Older People
    Living with Loss and Grief
    National Association for Loss and Grief (Vic),
    East Melbourne, Victoria

Speaking from Experience: Trauma, Loss and Grief —
    Victims of Crime
    National Association for Loss and Grief (Vic),
    East Melbourne, Victoria

PERMISSIONS

Page 46: material by Ted Menton from *Gentle Closings: How to Say Goodbye to Someone You Love* (1992) reproduced with the permission of Running Press Book Publishers.

Page 57: material by Father James Keller reproduced with the kind permission of The Christophers, New York.

Page 69: lyrics from 'My Hope' by Darlene Zschech reproduced with the permission of the author.

Pages 106 to 107: material from *Homosexual to Husband* by Jeff Morrow reproduced with the permission of the author.

Page 111: *Mere Christianity* by C.S. Lewis copyright © C.S. Lewis Pte. Ltd. 1942, 1943, 1944, 1952. Extract reprinted with permission.

Page 174: quote from *The Wizard of Oz* used courtesy of Warner Bros Entertainment Inc.

Page 183: material from *Family Politics* copyright © 1993 by Letty Cottin Pobregin reproduced with permission. Originally published by McGraw-Hill Book Company.

Pages 201 to 202: lyrics from 'Wrinkles' copyright © 1983 by John Williamson reproduced with the permission of Emusic Pty Ltd (administered for the world by Matthews Music Pty Ltd).

Page 203: material from *We Bereaved* by Helen Keller (1929) courtesy of the American Foundation for the Blind, Helen Keller Archives.

Pages 214–215: material from *The Seven Sins of Memory: How the Mind Forgets and Remembers* by Daniel Schacter. Copyright © 2001 by Daniel L. Schacter. Reprinted by permission of Houghton Mifflin Company. All rights reserved.

Pages 248 and 254: material from *Where's the Miracle?* by Steve Penny reproduced with the permission of the author.

Pages 271–272: 'The Invitation' from *The Invitation* by Oriah Mountain Dreamer. Copyright © 1999 by Oriah Mountain Dreamer. Reprinted by permission of HarperCollins Publishers.

Page 349: material from *Where Do We Go From Here?* by David Winter reproduced by permission of Hodder and Stoughton Limited.

Page 350: material by Professor GR Evans reproduced with the permission of the author.

Page 354: *The Great Divorce* by C.S. Lewis copyright © C.S. Lewis Pte. Ltd. 1946. Extract reprinted with permission.

Page 357: 'Footprints in the Sand' by Mary Stevenson copyright © 1984 Footprints in the Sand, Ltd. All rights reserved. Reproduced with permission.

Bible quotations:

Scriptures taken from *The Holy Bible, New International Version* ®, *NIV* ®. Copyright © 1973, 1978, 1984 by International Bible Society ®. Used by permission. All rights reserved worldwide.

The Message by Eugene H. Peterson, copyright © 1993, 1994, 1995, 1996, 2000, 2001, 2002. Used by permission of NavPress Publishing Group. All rights reserved.

Scripture taken from the New King James Version ®. Copyright © 1982 by Thomas Nelson, Inc. Used by permission. All rights reserved.